Brand Name Fat-Fighter's
C·O·O·K·B·O·O·K

**OVER 150 LOW-FAT AND FAT-FREE RECIPES FROM
BREAKFAST TO DESSERT USING BRAND NAME PRODUCTS**

Brand Name Fat-Fighter's
C·O·O·K·B·O·O·K

**OVER 150 LOW-FAT AND FAT-FREE RECIPES FROM
BREAKFAST TO DESSERT USING BRAND NAME PRODUCTS**

Sandra Woodruff, R.D.

Avery Publishing Group
Garden City Park, New York

The trademarked brand names used in this book should not, in any way, be considered an endorsement of this book, or, any of the recipes contained in this book, by the trademark holders. The Publisher and Author acknowledge that all of the recipes within this book have been created and kitchen-tested independently of any food manufacturers mentioned within this work.

Text Illustrator: John Wincek
Interior Color Photographs: John Strange
Cover Photograph: John Strange
Cover Design: William Gonzalez
Typesetting: Bonnie Freid
In-House Editor: Joanne Abrams

Props in photos 2, 3, 5, 8, and 12 courtesy of Studio E, Design and Antiques; Elena Jackson, proprietor; 1700 South Main Street; Mansfield, OH 44907; (419) 756-6364.

BETTY CROCKER and GOLD MEDAL are registered trademarks of General Mills, Inc.
HEALTHY CHOICE is a registered trademark of ConAgra, Inc.
HUNT'S, LA CHOY, PETER PAN, WESSON, ORVILLE REDENBACHER'S, and SMART POP are registered trademarks of Hunt-Wesson, Inc.
KRAFT FOODS, INC.—Used with permission.
MR. TURKEY is a registered trademark of BIL MAR Foods, Inc.
PAM® is a registered trademark of American Home Food Products, Inc.
RAGU is a registered trademark of Van Den Bergh Foods Company.
WEIGHT WATCHERS is the registered trademark of Weight Watchers International, Inc.

Cataloging-in-Publication Data

Woodruff, Sandra L.
    The brand name fat-fighter's cookbook: over 150 low-fat and
fat-free recipes from breakfast to dessert using brand name
products / Sandra Woodruff.
    p. cm.
    Includes index.
    ISBN 0-89529-687-X

    1. Low-fat diet—Recipes. I. Title.
TX739.W66 1995

641.5'68
QBI95-20481

Printed in the United States of America

10 9 8 7 6 5 4

Contents

This book is dedicated to my favorite taste testers, Wiley and C.D.

Acknowledgments

It has been a great pleasure to produce this book with the talented and dedicated professionals at Avery Publishing Group, who have so generously lent their support and creativity at every stage of production. Special thanks go to Rudy Shur and Ken Rajman for providing the opportunity to publish this book, and to my editor, Joanne Abrams, whose hard work, endless patience, and diligent attention to detail have added so much.

Thanks also go to my dear friends and family members for their enduring support and encouragement, and to my clients and coworkers, whose questions and ideas keep me learning and experimenting with new things. Last, but not least, I would like to thank my husband, Tom Maureau, for his long-term support and encouragement, and for always being there for me.

Preface

Making and eating great food is one of life's simplest yet greatest pleasures. And there is nothing wrong with enjoying good food—except that for too long, good has often meant greasy, salty, sugary, and overly processed. Butter, margarine, and oils have long been prominent ingredients in both home-cooked and store-bought foods. Excessive amounts of sugar and salt are frequently added to foods during processing. And whole grains have taken a back seat to nutrient-poor refined grains like white rice and white flour. The result? The typical American diet has become woefully out of balance, and has contributed to an epidemic of obesity, cancer, diabetes, and other diet-related diseases. In fact, after smoking, diet is the number-one killer of Americans.

The good news is that the nation's growing awareness of the link between diet and health has led people to explore better ways of cooking and eating. As a result, manufacturers have flooded the supermarkets with new low-fat and fat-free products, making it easier than ever to eat healthfully. Yet many people remain confused—confused about how to interpret the information on food labels, and how to use the vast array of new products. That is why this book was written. Designed to be a very different kind of cookbook, *The Brand Name Fat-Fighter's Cookbook* not only guides you through each section of the supermarket, showing you how to make wise selections, but also shows you how to use these products to create delicious, nutrient-rich, low- and no-fat dishes.

The Brand Name Fat-Fighter's Cookbook begins by explaining why you should fight fat, and how you can go about doing just that without sacrificing great taste. You will discover how implementing some very simple dietary guidelines can help you lose weight, lower blood cholesterol, and reduce your risk for diet-related diseases. The book then goes on to demystify even the most confusing of food labels so that you can quickly and easily choose foods that will help you meet your nutrition and weight-management goals.

And there's more. Throughout the book, Fat-Fighter's Guides present an aisle-by-aisle tour of the grocery store, giving specific brand name recommendations for foods from every area of the store, from the dairy case, to the meat counter, to the cereal aisle, to the ever-tempting cookie section. These recommendations for the best low-fat and fat-free products will help you get off to a quick start on the road to healthful eating.

In addition to this important information, each chapter focuses on a specific meal of the day or a specific type of dish made with the most healthful low-fat and fat-free brand name products. Looking for breakfast foods that are not only tempting enough to lure family members out of bed, but also nutritious enough to give them the energy they'll need until lunch time? Chapter 1, "Bountiful Breakfast Dishes," presents a wide selection of early morning treats, from English Muffin French Toast to Country Morning Omelette. Or perhaps you've been searching for a special luncheon dish that will delight your guests without wreaking havoc on your healthy lifestyle. "Light and Luscious Lunches" will lead the way with a fabulous selection of creamy quiches, hearty sandwiches, and other palate-pleasing creations. Still other chapters will show you how to create refreshing salads, like Caesar Garden Salad; warming soups, like Split Pea Soup With Ham; festive hot and cold hors d'oeuvres, like Chili-Cheese Potato Skins; wholesome vegetable side dishes, like Streusel Sweet Potatoes; meatless main dishes, like Black Bean Quesadillas; hot and hearty entrées, like Crusty Chicken Pot Pie; and simple yet savory pasta dishes, like Ragin' Cajun Pasta. And because for some of us, the meal just isn't complete until we've enjoyed a taste of something sweet, there's a mouth-watering selection of deceptively decadent desserts—cakes, cobblers, pies, cookies, and other delights designed to provide a glorious but guilt-free conclusion to your low-fat meal.

It is my hope that *The Brand Name Fat-Fighter's Cookbook* will prove to you that shopping for healthy foods need not be a chore, and that any meal can be delicious and satisfying without being rich and fattening. So eat well, and enjoy! As you will see, it is possible to do both—at every meal of the day, and on every day of the year.

Introduction

During the last few years, Americans have become aware of the relationship between diet and health as never before. Most especially, they have focused on the health benefits of reduced dietary fat. As a result, counting fat grams has become a national pastime, and manufacturers, in response, have produced a multitude of excellent new products. Certainly, eating healthfully has never been easier or more enjoyable. However, along with the wholesome low-fat products has come a flood of fat-free junk foods. As you will see, a diet that includes too much of the latter can contribute to the growing national waistline—as well as to poor health.

How can you tell the difference between wholesome low- and no-fat foods and fat-free junk foods, and choose only those products that will contribute to good health? This is what *The Brand Name Fat-Fighter's Cookbook* is all about. The first part of this section will explain just why your dietary fat should be reduced. Following this, you will learn how to budget your own daily fat intake, and how, by following a few simple guidelines, you can not only stick to your fat budget, but also improve the overall quality of your diet. Finally, you'll discover how to decipher even the most confusing of food labels, and zero in on the best products available. Throughout the rest of the book, you'll find specific recommendations of brand name products, and you'll learn how to use these foods to create sure-fire family favorites.

WHY FIGHT FAT?

There are plenty of good reasons to fight fat, but perhaps the most common one is the desire to lose weight. How does fighting fat help with weight loss? With more than twice the calories of carbohydrates or protein, fat is a concentrated source of calories. Compare the calorie count of a cup of butter or margarine (almost pure fat) with that of a cup of flour (almost pure carbohydrates). The butter has 1,600 calories, and the flour has 400 calories. It's easy to see where most of our calories come from.

Besides being high in calories, fat is also readily converted into body fat when eaten in excess. Carbohydrate-rich foods eaten in excess are also stored as body fat, but they must first be converted into fat—a process that burns up some of the carbohydrates. The bottom line is that a high-fat diet will cause 20 percent more weight gain than will a high-carbohydrate diet, even when the two diets contain the same number of calories. So a high-fat diet is a double-edged sword for the weight-conscious person. It is high in calories, and it is the kind of nutrient that is most readily stored as body fat.

But high-fat diets pose a threat to much more than our weight. When fatty diets lead to obesity, diseases like diabetes and high blood pressure can result. And specific types of fats present their own unique problems. For example, eating too much saturated fat—found in meat, butter, margarine, and other solid fats—raises blood cholesterol levels, setting the stage for heart disease. Polyunsaturated fat, once thought to be the solution to heart disease, can also be harmful when eaten in excess. A diet overly rich in certain vegetable oils—corn, sunflower, and safflower, and products made from these oils—can alter body chemistry to favor the development of blood clots, high blood pressure, and inflammatory diseases. Too much polyunsaturated fat can also promote free-radical damage to cells, contributing to heart disease and cancer.

Where do monounsaturated fats fit in? Monounsaturated fats—found in olive oil, canola oil, avocados, and nuts—have no known harmful effects other than being a concentrated source of calories, like all fats.

One other kind of fat needs to be considered—especially if you are concerned about heart disease. Trans-fatty acids, also called trans fats, are chemically altered fats that are produced by adding hydrogen to liquid vegetable oils. This process, called hydrogenation, transforms liquid vegetable oils into solid margarines and shortenings, giving these products a butter-like consistency. While hydrogenation improves the cooking and baking qualities of oils, and extends their shelf life as well, it also creates trans fats. And trans fats, it has been found, act much like saturated fats to raise levels of LDL, or "bad" cholesterol, and at the same time lower levels of HDL, or "good" cholesterol.

Considering the problems caused by excess fat, you may think it would be best to completely eliminate fat from your diet. But the fact is that we do need some dietary fat. For instance, linoleic acid, a polyunsaturated fat naturally abundant in nuts and seeds, is essential for life. The average adult needs a minimum of 3 to 6 grams of linoleic acid per day—the amount present in one to two teaspoonfuls of polyunsaturated vegetable oil, or one to two tablespoonfuls of nuts or seeds. Linolenic acid, a fat present mainly in fish and green plants, is also essential for good health. Some dietary fat is also needed to help us absorb fat-soluble nutrients like vitamin E.

Unfortunately, many people are getting too much of a good thing. The liberal use of mayonnaise, oily salad dressings, margarine, and cooking oils has created an unhealthy overdose of linoleic acid in the American diet. And, of course, most people also eat far too much saturated fat. How can we correct this? We can minimize the use of refined vegetable oils, margarines, shortenings, and table fats, and eat a diet rich in whole grains, vegetables, and fruits, with moderate amounts of nuts and seeds, fish, and lean meats, if desired.

HOW TO FIGHT FAT

Now that you understand some of the reasons you should get the fat out of your diet, it's time to do just that. In this section, you will discover how to develop your own personal fat budget. Then, with the help of some simple guidelines for good eating and some supermarket strategies, you will learn how to live within the bounds of your fat budget—and still enjoy great food.

Budgeting Your Fat

For most Americans, about 34 percent of the calories in their diet come from fat. However, currently it is recommended that fat calories constitute no more than 30 percent of the diet, and, in fact, 20 to 25 percent would be even better in most cases. So the amount of fat you should eat every day is based on the number of calories you need. Because people's calorie needs depend on their weight, age, gender, activity level, and metabolic rate, these needs vary greatly from person to person. Most adults, though, must consume 13 to 15 calories per pound each day to maintain their weight. Of course, some people need even fewer calories, while very physically active people need more.

Once you have determined your calorie requirements, you can estimate a fat budget for yourself. Suppose you are a moderately active person who weighs 150 pounds. You will probably need about 15 calories per pound to maintain your weight, or about 2,250 calories per day. To limit your fat intake to 20 percent of your calorie intake, you can eat no more than 450 calories derived from fat per day (2,250 x .20 = 450). To convert this to grams of fat, divide by 9, as one gram of fat has 9 calories. Therefore, you should limit yourself to 50 grams of fat per day (450 ÷ 9 = 50).

The following table shows two maximum daily fat-gram budgets—one based on 20 percent of calorie intake, and one based on 25 percent of calorie intake. If you are overweight, go by the weight you would like to be. This will allow you to gradually reach your goal weight. And keep in mind that although you have budgeted X amount of fat grams per day, you don't *have* to eat that amount of fat—you just have to avoid going over budget.

Recommended Daily Calorie and Fat Intakes

Weight (pounds)	Recommended Daily Calorie Intake (13–15 calories per pound)	Daily Fat-Gram Intake (20% of Calorie Intake)	Daily Fat-Gram Intake (25% of Calorie Intake)
100	1,300–1,500	29–33	36–42
110	1,430–1,650	32–37	40–46
120	1,560–1,800	34–40	43–50
130	1,690–1,950	38–43	47–54
140	1,820–2,100	40–46	51–58
150	1,950–2,250	43–50	54–62
160	2,080–2,400	46–53	58–67
170	2,210–2,550	49–57	61–71
180	2,340–2,700	52–60	65–75
190	2,470–2,850	55–63	69–79
200	2,600–3,000	58–66	72–83

Remember that Calories Count Too

As you know by now, weight loss is the number-one reason that most people are trying to reduce their fat intake. And over the past decade, Americans have been able to reduce their fat consumption from 40 percent of calories to about 34 percent of calories. Yet during this same time, the rate of obesity has actually increased. One out of three Americans is now considered obese, compared with one out of four in 1980. How can this be? It's simple. People tend to forget that calories count too. The fact is that people now eat more calories than they did a decade ago—and exercise less.

In a way, the fat-free food frenzy has contributed to the expanding national waistline by creating a false sense of security. Many people mistakenly think that if a food is low in fat or fat-free, they can consume unlimited quantities of it. They may start their day with a jumbo fat-free muffin, keep a jar of jelly beans on their desk to nibble on throughout the day, snack on low-fat cookies at break time, and eat a bowl of fat-free ice cream—topped with fat-free chocolate syrup—for an evening snack. Although all of these foods are better choices than their full-fat counterparts, they are loaded with sugar and provide few or no nutrients. Moreover, some of these items have just as many calories as the full-fat versions. The truth is that any foods eaten in excess of calories burned in a day will be converted to body fat. And this is just as true of fat-free foods as it is of high-fat foods.

Does this mean that you should forget about using fat-free foods to lose weight? Not by any means. Chosen wisely, these foods can help you reach and maintain a healthy body weight. Setting up a fat budget is the best place to start, since a low-fat diet is generally low in calories too—unless you eat too many fat-free junk foods. If you then stay within the bounds of your fat budget and choose mostly nutrient-rich foods, you should be able to reach your weight-management goals. But if you have trouble losing or maintaining your weight, you must consider whether you are staying within the bounds of your calorie budget, as well.

The Guidelines for Good Eating

Once you have arrived at daily calorie and fat budgets, you can begin pruning unwanted fat

Simple Steps to Successful Weight Loss

When most people begin a weight-loss diet, they do so with monumental effort. Often, they eat ridiculously small amounts of food—so little food, in fact, that they feel weak, hungry, and deprived. Many also spend long hours in the kitchen, chopping, measuring, and cooking special diet foods, only to find that after a few weeks, the diet is just too much work to continue. Whatever the reason for the failure, 95 percent of all dieters abandon their diets before reaching their goal weight, and quickly regain the lost weight—plus a few additional pounds.

What's a dieter to do? Relax. Forget about special weight-loss diets, stop being a slave to the scale, and, above all, be patient. Concentrate on developing healthier habits, and weight loss will follow. Weight that is lost gradually, as the result of modest lifestyle changes, is much more likely to stay off than is weight lost on a quick-fix diet. Here are some simple tips that will help you get started on the road to successful weight loss.

■ Choose low-fat, fiber-rich foods. Watching your fat grams will help keep calories under control. Eating plenty of fiber will help keep you feeling full and satisfied.

■ Do not overwhelm yourself with cooking, measuring, and weighing foods. Try one or two new low-fat recipes a week. When you find a recipe that works for you, make it a regular part of your diet. Continue experimenting with new recipes and new foods at your own pace, phasing in the new and phasing out the old. Before you know it, you will have designed your own personal low-fat diet.

■ Eat when you are hungry, but learn the difference between hunger and other physical sensations. People often overeat because they confuse the feeling of hunger with that of thirst, fatigue, or stress. If you keep properly hydrated with six to eight glasses of water each day, get enough rest, and keep your stress under control, you will be less likely to overeat.

■ Eat slowly. As you eat, hormones and other chemicals are generated by your digestive system. These chemicals eventually make their way to the brain, which then lets you know that you have had enough to eat. Since it takes about twenty minutes for this to happen, people who eat quickly consume more food and more calories than they need before they begin to feel full.

■ Eat at least three meals a day, spacing them out evenly. Eating just one or two meals a day slows your metabolism, and increases the likelihood that your meals will be stored as body fat. Eating several meals throughout the day helps keep your metabolism going strong.

■ Don't forget to exercise. The two main predictors for weight-loss success are low-fat eating and exercise. By both decreasing your dietary fat and regularly exercising, you will maximize your chance for long-term success.

Small changes like the ones described above can make a big fat difference in your weight. For instance, by eliminating just 100 calories from your diet on a daily basis—the equivalent of one tablespoon of butter, mayonnaise, or other fat—you can lose ten pounds in a year. By eating a turkey sandwich for lunch instead of a deluxe cheeseburger, you can lose twenty pounds. Substitute water for those two daily high-sugar sodas, and lose thirty pounds.

Or walk five miles a week, and lose seven pounds. Changes like these, maintained for long periods of time, take weight off permanently. Need more help with your weight-loss program? A registered dietitian, nutritionist, or other qualified health professional can help you determine a healthy goal weight, and guide you in modifying your diet and lifestyle in a way that will allow you to reach your goal.

from your diet. This task is easier than it sounds—once you become acquainted with a few guidelines for good eating. The following are some simple but very effective strategies that will help you not only manage your weight, but also maximize your nutrients and promote optimum health.

❑ Choose Lean Meats and Poultry, and Limit Portions to Six Ounces or Less Per Day

Meats contribute more fat and cholesterol to the average diet than does any other food group. Does this mean that you are doomed to a diet of dried-out skinless chicken breasts? Absolutely not! In the Fat-Fighter's Guide to Meat, Poultry, and Seafood (page 140), you will discover how to select red meats, poultry, and even lunchmeats that have just a fraction of the fat found in their full-fat counterparts.

You may question why it's necessary to limit portion size to six ounces when so many lean meats are available. The fact is that even lean meats contain cholesterol. By keeping portions modest in size, you will ensure that your cholesterol intake remains below the recommended limit of 300 milligrams per day. This guideline will also help you leave room on your plate for the nutrient- and fiber-rich vegetables, grains, and fruits that should make up the biggest part of your diet.

❑ Substitute Legumes for Meat

The best way to keep meat portions modest in size is to substitute legumes—dried beans and peas—for meat as often as possible. Legumes are rich in protein and potassium, and provide many of the same nutrients found in meats. In addition, these tasty morsels contain little or no fat, are cholesterol-free, and are loaded with cholesterol-lowering soluble fiber. Moreover, beans help stabilize blood sugar levels and provide a feeling of fullness that helps prevent overeating. If this isn't reason enough to eat more legumes, consider that beans and peas are among the most economical foods you can buy. So substituting legumes for meat can have a big impact not only on your health, but also on your grocery bill. You don't know how to use legumes to make satisfying main dishes? Chapter 7 will show you how to make beans and peas a delicious part of your low-fat diet.

❑ Choose Nonfat and Low-Fat Dairy Products

Like meats, dairy products have long been a major source of fat and cholesterol in the average diet. Fortunately, this no longer has to be true. The Fat-Fighter's Guide to the Dairy Case (page 116) will introduce you to a delightful variety of nonfat and low-fat products that can beautifully replace full-fat cheeses, sour cream, and other popular foods. These new products not only will eliminate excess calories and artery-clogging saturated fat from your diet, but, by providing nutrients such as calcium and potassium, will help guard against osteoporosis, high blood pressure, and many other health problems.

❑ Limit Your Use of Table and Cooking Fats

Fats used for cooking and baking—like butter and margarine—and fats added at the table—oily salad dressings, mayonnaise, and butter, for instance—can really add up. In fact, in their full-fat versions, just one tablespoon of any of these products will add about 10 grams of fat to your meal. The good news is that for each of these foods, there is now a no- or low-fat alternative that can help you greatly reduce or eliminate the fats you use in cooking, in baking, and at the table. The Fat-Fighter's Guides on pages 52 and 188 will introduce you to many of these exciting new products, and recipes throughout the book will show you how to use them to create great-tasting dishes that your whole family will love.

❑ Limit Your Sodium Intake to 2,400 Milligrams Per Day

A limited sodium intake has many benefits, ranging from better-controlled blood pressure to stronger bones. But of all the guidelines for good eating, this one can be the most difficult to follow, since many low-fat and fat-free foods contain extra salt.

Fortunately, with a just a little effort, even this dietary goal can be met. The most effective sodium-control strategy is to avoid using salt for cooking and at the table. Believe it or not, just one teaspoon of salt contains 2,300 milligrams of sodium—almost your entire daily allowance—so it pays to put the salt shaker away. Another effective strategy is to limit your intake of high-sodium processed foods. Read labels, and choose the lower-sodium frozen meals, canned goods, broths, cheeses, and other products. Also, whenever you make a recipe that contains high-sodium cheeses, processed meats, or other salty ingredients, be sure not to add any extra salt. The recipes in this book will show you how to balance high-sodium products with low-sodium ingredients, herbs, and spices to make dishes that are low in sodium but high in flavor.

❑ Choose Whole Grains Over Refined Grains

Largely because of the widespread use of refined grains—white-flour products and white rice, for in-

stance—the average diet falls short of the 25 or more grams of dietary fiber recommended for daily consumption. Yet when changing your diet to promote good health, the importance of low-fat foods is rivaled only by the importance of fiber. Dietary fiber helps control blood cholesterol and blood sugar, and helps protect against colon cancer. Watching your weight? While a diet of refined, low-fiber foods will leave you feeling hungry, a high-fiber eating plan will keep you feeling full and satisfied. This is one of the reasons that several major weight-loss programs now emphasize the importance of low-fat, high-fiber eating.

But low fiber is just one of the problems posed by refined grains. The refining process strips grains of most of their nutrients. Whole grains, on the other hand, provide folate, vitamins B6 and E, chromium, magnesium, and a host of other disease-protective nutrients.

People who are not used to eating high-fiber foods should add these foods to their diets gradually. Why? Some people may experience bloating and gas when they begin a high-fiber regimen—although this usually passes in a few weeks as the body becomes accustomed to eating whole, natural foods. When following a high-fiber diet, it is also important to drink at least six to eight cups of water per day. Fiber needs to absorb water in order to move smoothly through the digestive system and exert its beneficial effects.

When made properly, breads, muffins, casseroles, breakfast foods, side dishes, soups, and even desserts can include wholesome whole grains. The inset on page 134 recommends a variety of versatile, fiber-rich grain products that can be found in your grocery store, while many tempting recipes show you how to use these and other foods to create hearty and wholesome dishes in your own kitchen.

❑ Eat At Least Five Servings of Fruits and Vegetables Every Day

Fruits and vegetables offer a bounty of nutrients,

fiber, and substances known as phytochemicals—all powerful preventive medicines against cancer, heart disease, and many other health problems. Since not all of the protective substances present in these foods have been identified, and some of them probably never will be, it is impossible to get all the benefits of fruits and vegetables from vitamin pills. So fruits and vegetables can and should be served in generous amounts at every meal.

Sadly, studies show that the average American eats only two to three servings of vegetables and fruits each day. Even worse, much of the time, these foods are laden with butter, margarine, cheese sauce, or other fats. But getting your five-a-day is not as hard as you may think. As the recipes in this book show, there are plenty of simple and delicious ways to serve these healthful foods without adding an unhealthy dose of fat. Also, you may not realize that a serving is really quite small. A medium-sized piece of fruit, a half cup of cooked or raw fruit or vegetables, a cup of leafy salad greens, a quarter cup of dried fruit, or three-fourths of a cup of fruit juice each constitute a serving. So if you include at least one cup of fruit or vegetables at each meal, you will be well on your way to five-a-day.

Finally, remember that five servings are the *minimum* recommended amount. To maximize your health, aim for seven to nine servings.

❑ Eat Sugar Only in Moderation

When people start reducing their fat intake, often, without really thinking about it, they greatly increase their sugar intake. This is easy to understand. Stroll down the aisles of your local grocery store, and you will see a mind-boggling array of fat-free cookies, brownies, ice creams, and other goodies. While these products may contain little or no fat, they usually contain as much sugar as their high-fat counterparts—and sometimes more!

What health threats are posed by sugar? First and foremost, sugar contains no nutrients, and, when eaten in excess, can actually deplete your body's stores of chromium, the B vitamins, and other vitamins and minerals. Second, it has been found that high-sugar diets are often deficient in nutritious foods. Finally, sugary foods are usually loaded with calories, making them a real menace if you're watching your weight.

The good news is that, in moderation, sugar can be enjoyed without harm to your health. What's a moderate amount? No more than 10 percent of your daily intake of calories should come from sugar. For a person who needs 2,000 calories a day to maintain his or her weight, this amounts to an upper limit of 50 grams or 12.5 teaspoons (about a quarter cup) of sugar a day. Naturally, a diet that is lower in sugar is even better.

While the guidelines for good eating are few in number, they can make a big difference both in your diet and in the way you look and feel. And you'll find that the recipes and Fat-Fighter's Guides throughout this book make it as easy as pie—low-fat pie, of course!—to follow these guidelines and build a healthful, enjoyable diet.

Reading a Food Label

Almost all food products today must, by law, provide certain nutrition facts on their labels. The only foods that do not have to list this information are foods sold in bulk; foods produced by small businesses; foods created to meet the needs of certain medical conditions; spices and other foods that contain insignificant amounts of nutrients; and fresh meats, seafood, and poultry. Some companies, however, voluntarily provide nutrition data on even these products.

While the new Nutrition Facts food labels were designed to give you the information you need to make wise food choices, in truth, many people are still baffled by much of the data presented on these labels. Below, you will learn to interpret each component of the Nutrition Facts label, and you will see how to easily apply this information to meet your personal nutrition goals. (For a quick overview of the Nutrition Facts label, see the figure on page 9.)

Components of the Nutrition Facts Label

Serving Size. It is crucial to understand what the manufacturer calls a serving, and to see how this compares with what *you* call a serving. This information should, of course, be kept in mind when evaluating the remaining nutrition data. Why? Although a sodium or fat count may seem fine when, for instance, only a quarter of the package is considered, if your idea of a portion is *half* of the package, the sodium and fat values may prove to be unhealthfully high.

Calories Per Serving. If you have not already done so, use the table on page 3 to determine your daily calorie budget. Then, keeping the manufacturer's definition of a serving in mind, see how the product fits into your calorie budget.

Total Fat Per Serving. To understand this information, you first must determine your daily fat-gram budget. (Again, see the table on page 3.) Then, again keeping in mind the manufacturer's serving size, evaluate how this food fits into your fat budget.

% Daily Value. In the case of certain dietary components—total fat, for instance—the amount is expressed not only in grams or milligrams, but also as a percentage of the Daily Value, a recommended daily amount based on a diet of 2,000 calories. When reading these Daily Value figures, keep in mind that if your calorie budget is more or less than 2,000 calories a day, these percentages will not hold true for you. Just as important, remember that the Daily Value for fat assumes that your fat budget is *30 percent* of your total calories. If you prefer a more prudent 20- or 25-percent fat budget, the Daily Value figure may lead you to overestimate your fat allowance.

Calories From Fat. Besides listing the calories and total fat grams in one serving of a product, the Nutrition Facts label tells you how many of the calories in a serving of the product come from fat. This figure is derived by multiplying the total fat grams by 9. (Each gram of fat provides 9 calories.)

While some people use the calories-from-fat information to calculate the percentage of calories that come from fat, remember that it is not necessary for *every* food in your diet to derive only 20 or 25 percent of its total calories from fat. If you stick to your fat budget and just count total fat grams, your diet will balance out. This means that even a food like peanut butter—which gets a whopping 76 percent of its calories from fat!—has a place in a healthy diet as long as you compensate by eating lower-fat foods throughout the day.

Saturated Fat. Besides listing the total fat grams per serving, the Nutrition Facts label tells you how much of the total fat is saturated fat. This is worth looking at because saturated fat is the kind that raises blood cholesterol levels and promotes heart disease. Saturated fat should constitute no more than one third of your total fat intake. So if your fat budget allows, say, 45 grams of fat per day, no more than 15 grams of this fat should be saturated. Of course, less saturated fat would be even better.

Bear in mind that trans fats, which are found in margarines and other solid shortening, raise cholesterol levels just as much as saturated fats do. These fats, however, are not listed separately on the food label. Instead, they are included in the figure for total fat. This means that if a food contains partially hydrogenated vegetable oil, the label underestimates the cholesterol-raising potential of the food.

Cholesterol. The recommended daily limit for this substance, which is found only in animal products, is 300 milligrams per day. By keeping your eye out for high cholesterol counts, you should be able to stay well within your budget.

Sodium. The recommended daily limit for sodium is 2,400 milligrams per day. Since so many

Serving Size. Similar foods (like cereals, cookies, etc.) have similar serving sizes. Be sure to compare the manufacturer's serving size with what you call a serving.

Total Fat. Compare the fat grams per serving to your personal fat budget to see how the food fits into your diet.

Saturated Fat. This should constitute no more than $\frac{1}{3}$ of your total fat budget. Realize that artery-clogging trans fats are not included in this number, but are part of the total fat figure.

Cholesterol. Limit yourself to 300 milligrams per day.

Sodium. Limit yourself to 2,400 milligrams a day.

Protein. Aim for .36 gram per pound of ideal body weight per day.

Nutrients. Expressed as a percentage of the Daily Value—a recommended daily amount based on a 2,000-calorie diet—this may not reflect your personal requirements.

Nutrition Facts

Serving Size ½ cup (114g)
Servings Per Container 4

Amount Per Serving

Calories 90 — Calories from Fat 30

	% Daily Value*
Total Fat 3g	5%
Saturated fat 0g	0%
Cholesterol 0mg	0%
Sodium 300mg	13%
Total Carbohydrate 13g	4%
Dietary Fiber 3g	12%
Sugars 3g	
Protein 3g	

Vitamin A 80% • Vitamin C 60% • Calcium 4% • Iron 4%

*Percent Daily Values are based on a 2,000 calorie diet. Your Daily Values may be higher or lower depending on your calorie needs:

Nutrient		2,000 Calories	2,500 Calories
Total fat	Less than	65g	80g
Sat Fat	Less than	20g	25g
Cholesterol	Less than	300mg	300mg
Sodium	Less than	2,400mg	2,400mg
Total Carbohydrate		300g	375g
Fiber		25g	30g

Calories per gram:
Fat 9 • Carbohydrates 4 • Protein 4

Calories. Compare the calories per serving to your personal calorie budget to see how the food fits into your diet.

Calories From Fat. This figure tells you how many of the calories in the product are contributed by fat. Your diet should get no more than 20% to 25% of its calories from fat. If you stick to your fat budget, this will automatically fall into place.

Dietary Fiber. Aim for at least 25 grams per day.

Sugar. Limit yourself to 50 grams of refined sugar per day. Realize that this number doesn't discriminate between natural, higher-nutrient fruit and milk sugars, and nutrient-poor refined sugars.

Daily Values Percentages and Footnotes. Both the Daily Value footnotes provided at the bottom of the label and the % Daily Value data found higher on the label assume a diet of either 2,000 or 2,500 calories. Also, the Daily Value for fat assumes you want to limit fat to 30% of calorie intake. If you're aiming for fewer calories or less fat, this information will overestimate your needs.

The Nutrition Facts Label at a Glance

processed foods are high in salt, it makes sense to check food labels for sodium counts and to avoid any foods with excessively high values.

Dietary Fiber. Fiber, a type of carbohydrate found only in grains, fruits, and vegetables, is listed under the "Total Carbohydrate" section of the Nutrition Facts label. Aim for at least 25 grams of fiber per day, and choose your products accordingly.

Sugars. Like fiber, sugars are found under "Total Carbohydrate." Because no more than 10 percent of your calories should come from refined sugar, you should probably limit yourself to no more than 50 grams per day. Keep in mind, though, that the figure given for sugar includes both refined sweeteners and the sugar that occurs naturally in fruits and milk. Because the sugar in fruit and milk comes packaged with nutrients and fiber, it should not be lumped in with refined sweeteners. Remember this when evaluating products like breakfast cereals and yogurt, which may derive some or much of their sugar from fruit and other wholesome ingredients.

Protein. Unlike most of the other nutrients, protein is not expressed as a percentage of the Daily Value. How do you know if you are getting enough of this nutrient? Most people need about 0.36 gram of protein per pound of ideal body weight. So if your ideal weight is 150 pounds, you will need about 54 grams of protein per day (150 x .36 = 54). Keep in mind that most Americans already get far more protein than they need, and that too much protein can contribute to kidney disease, osteoporosis, and other disorders. By following the strategies outlined in the guidelines for good eating, you will get all the protein your body needs for good health, but not more than your body can handle.

Nutrients. The Nutrition Facts label provides information on the vitamin A, vitamin C, calcium, and iron contents of a food. These values are expressed as a percentage of Daily Values, the recommended daily amount based on a 2,000-calorie diet. As the label warns, your needs may be higher or lower for certain nutrients.

Ingredients. This portion of the label—which is not a part of the Nutrition Facts section—lists the ingredients in a product in order of quantity (by weight). Those ingredients listed first are present in the greatest amount. So if sugar, white flour, or fat is the number-one ingredient, you'll know that the food does not merit a prominent place in your diet.

What You See Is What You Get— Most of the Time

On the new food labels, terms once used inconsistently, and often misleadingly, now must be applied uniformly to ensure that they mean the same thing on all products. Following are definitions of the most commonly used terms, as well as some cautions that will help you steer clear of common pitfalls.

Free. The product contains virtually none of a particular nutrient. (Beware, though: Just because a food is fat-free does not mean it is calorie-free, sugar-free, or sodium-free. Always read the entire label to see how other nutrients stack up.) The following specific terms are used:

Calorie Free. The product has less than 5 calories per serving.

Cholesterol Free. The product has less than 2 milligrams of cholesterol and no more than 2 grams of saturated fat per serving.

Fat Free. The product has less than 0.5 gram of fat per serving. (Beware: Fat-free does not necessarily mean low-calorie.)

Sodium Free. The product has less than 5 milligrams of sodium per serving.

Sugar Free. The product has less than 0.5 gram of sugar per serving. (Beware: Many sugar-free foods contain extra fat.)

Low. The product is low enough in a particular nutrient to allow frequent use with little danger of exceeding the recommended Daily Value. (Again, read the entire label whenever foods are labelled "low." Just because a food is low in sodium, for instance, does not mean it is low in calories, sugar, or fat.) Here are the specific terms you'll find on food labels:

Low Calorie. The product has no more than 40 calories per serving.

Low Fat. The product has no more than 3 grams of fat per serving. (Beware: Low-fat does not necessarily mean low-calorie.) There are exceptions to this rule. Frozen entrées, for instance, are allowed to have 3 grams of fat for every 3.5 ounces. So if an entrée weighs 10 ounces, it can contain up to 8.5 grams of fat and still be called low-fat. Another exception to the rule is 2-percent low-fat milk. Although one cup contains 5 grams of fat, this product can still be called low-fat.

Low Saturated Fat. The product has no more than 1 gram of saturated fat per serving, and no more than 15 percent of calories from saturated fat. In addition, no more than 1 percent of its total fat can be a trans fat. The exceptions to this rule include frozen entrées and meals, which can contain up to 1 gram of saturated fat for every 3.5 ounces.

Low Cholesterol. The product has no more than 20 milligrams of cholesterol and 2 grams of saturated fat per serving.

Low Sodium. The product has no more than 140 milligrams of sodium per serving.

Light (or Lite). This term could mean several different things. The light product could have a third less calories than the higher-calorie version, or it could contain no more than half the fat of the higher-fat version. (The label will specify which is true.)

"Light" can also refer to a product that has, at most, half the sodium of its higher-sodium counterpart. If this is the case, the product must say "light in sodium." However, if the light-in-sodium food is also a low-fat or low-calorie food, it can just be called "light."

The word "light" can also appear on products like brown sugar, corn syrup, and molasses to describe the product's color.

Reduced or Less. The product has at least 25 percent less of a nutrient such as fat, sodium, sugar, or calories than does the original version of the product.

Percent Fat Free. This term, which can be used only on foods that are low-fat or fat-free, refers to the percentage of a food by weight that is free of fat. For example, if 100 grams (about 3.5 ounces) of a particular brand of turkey bologna contain 3 grams of fat, the product can bear a label stating that it is 97 percent fat-free.

A word of warning is in order. Some people get "percent fat-free" confused with "percent of calories from fat." These are not the same thing. For instance, if a brand of 95-percent fat-free turkey bologna contains 80 calories and 2.5 grams of fat per serving, it gets 28 percent of its calories from fat—even though it is 95 percent fat-free by weight. How can this be? A good portion of the weight of bologna is made up of water. In fact, manufacturer's sometimes add water to products to reduce the percentage of fat per serving! Of course, water contains no calories, so that when looking at only the calorie-providing portion of the bologna, you find that fat provides well over 5 percent of the product's calories.

Don't get caught up comparing these two figures, or you might never get out of the grocery store. As long as you stay within your fat gram budget for the day, calories from fat and percentage of calories from fat will fall into place.

Lean. Found on packaged seafood and cooked meat and poultry products, this term indicates that the product has less than 10 grams of total fat, less than 4 grams of saturated fat, and less than 95 milligrams of cholesterol per serving.

Extra Lean. Also found on packaged seafood and cooked meat and poultry products, this indicates that the product has less than 5 grams of total fat, less than 2 grams of saturated fat, and less than 95 milligrams of cholesterol per serving.

Reduced Cholesterol. The product has at least 25 percent less cholesterol than the higher-cholesterol version, and no more than 2 grams of saturated fat per serving.

Good Source. The product provides 10 to 19 percent of the Daily Value for a particular nutrient.

High, Rich In, or Excellent Source. The product contains at least 20 percent of the Daily Value for that nutrient.

More. The product provides at least 10 percent more of a desirable nutrient than does a similar product.

Very Low Sodium. The product contains no more than 35 milligrams of sodium per serving.

Reduced Sodium. The product has at least 25 percent less sodium per serving than does the higher-sodium version.

High Fiber. The product provides at least 5 grams of fiber per serving.

Good Source of Fiber. The product provides 2.5 to 4.9 grams of fiber per serving.

Fat-Fighting Supermarket Strategies

If you feel that the new Nutrition Facts label provides more information than you need—or *want*—to know, take heart. You don't have to memorize the definitions of countless terms or understand Daily Values to shop smart. As long as you know your own personal fat and calorie budgets, and keep in mind the budgets for cholesterol, sodium, sugar, and fiber, you are ready to do some healthy grocery shopping. And this book will make your trips to the market easier than ever before with its Fat-Fighter's Guides, which provide an aisle-by-aisle tour of the supermarket. For every department, from the dairy case, to the baked goods, to the snack aisle, you will find recommendations for specific brand name products, as well as fat-fighting strategies that will help you zero in on those foods that will best meet your dietary and culinary needs. As you start using the suggested products and become familiar with their labels, you will become a whiz at picking out the best of the new foods as they enter the market.

Fat-Fighting Recipes

Of course, no matter how healthful a product may be, it won't reduce the fat in your diet unless you can successfully use it to prepare the dishes you serve to your family. That's why the recipes in *The Brand Name Fat-Fighter's Cookbook* show you how to use the best low-fat and nonfat brand name ingredients to make dishes that are low in fat, but high in taste and satisfaction. And these recipes do more than just eliminate or reduce fat. By using fiber-rich whole grains and whole grain flours, as well as plenty of vegetables and fruits, they help you follow all of the guidelines for good eating presented earlier. Whenever possible, natural sweeteners like fruits and juices are included to reduce the need for added sugar. And the skillful use of herbs, spices, and seasonings helps the sodium count remain low. So while keeping fat and calories under control, these recipes ensure the highest nutritional value, too.

Keep in mind that the use of brand name products in the recipes that follow is meant to illustrate the vast array of low- and no-fat products now available, and to show how these ingredients can be used to make a wide range of dishes. Once you have used a variety of products, you will develop your own personal brand name preferences. At that point, you should feel free to substitute your favorite nonfat cheeses, egg substitutes, and other products for those specified in the recipes. Many of the Fat-Fighter's Guides and boxed insets located throughout the book provide information on using specific kinds of low- and no-fat ingredients. This information will help you make successful substitutions so that you get the best possible results each and every time you cook or bake.

About the Nutritional Analysis

The Food Processor II (ESHA Research) computer nutrition analysis system, along with product information from manufacturers, was used to calculate the nutritional information for the recipes in this book. While branded ingredients are included in my recipes, I have taken responsibility for testing and providing accurate nutritional analyses of these recipes. Nutrients are always listed per one piece, one muffin, one slice of bread, one cookie, one serving, etc.

As you scan the recipes, you will notice that some of them give you options regarding the ingredients. For instance, you might be able to choose between raisins and nuts in a muffin recipe, or between whole wheat and sourdough bread in a sandwich recipe. Similarly, sometimes an ingredient is listed as being optional. These alternatives will help you create dishes that suit your tastes. Just keep in mind that the nutritional analysis is based on the first ingredient listed, and does not include optional ingredients.

Included in each nutritional analysis is an estimate of the calories and fat grams you save by using low- and no-fat products. This analysis is based on a comparison of the low-fat recipe with a standard recipe that uses full-fat cheeses; full-fat mayonnaise, sour cream, butter, and margarine; regular shortening-laden pie crusts; and other high-fat ingredients. This comparison becomes even more meaningful when you realize that for every 100 calories you trim from your diet on a daily basis, you can lose ten pounds in a year!

When examining your savings in calories and fat, you will want to avoid a very common pitfall. Earlier, we discussed how each gram of fat contains 9 calories. Because of this, when a recipe saves, say, 5 grams of fat, it might seem reasonable to assume that it has to save at least 45 calories (9 x 5 = 45). Keep in mind, though, that when fat is removed from a recipe, another ingredient—a lower-fat one—may be added to make the recipe work. For instance, when butter is eliminated from a cake, a fat substitute such as applesauce may be used instead. Therefore, this shortcut method of estimating calorie savings can be deceiving.

As you will see, watching your fat does not have to mean dieting, deprivation, or long hours spent deciphering food labels. This book is filled with fat-fighting shopping strategies, easy-to-follow recipes, and innovative ideas for using readily available brand name products to get the fat out of your own favorite dishes—and get more fiber and nutrients in. I wish you the best of luck and health with all of your fat-free cooking adventures!

1. Bountiful Breakfast Dishes

It's true—breakfast really is the most important meal of the day. Why, then, do so many people skip their morning meal? Many people are concerned about their weight, and find breakfast an easy place to cut calories. Others feel that they simply can't eat breakfast *and* get to work on time.

There are plenty of excellent reasons to enjoy a good breakfast, though, and this is especially true for people who are watching their weight. Why? Upon waking, your metabolism is operating at its lowest rate. By eating soon after you rise, you will give your metabolism the jump start it needs to burn more calories all day long. On the other hand, if you skip breakfast, you may actually keep your metabolism at a rate that's 3 to 4 percent below normal. Believe it or not, a metabolic slump like this can cause a weight gain of five to six pounds a year!

What other benefits does breakfast provide? People who enjoy a morning meal, as well as several meals throughout the day, tend to have lower blood cholesterol levels and more stable blood sugar levels than do people who skip breakfast and eat larger meals later in the day. And, of course, breakfast offers a great opportunity to get a head start on important nutrients like fiber and calcium, and on your five-a-day of vitamin-rich fruits.

Fortunately for fat-fighters, there are fat-free and low-fat alternatives to just about any breakfast food that comes to mind, from eggs to bacon to cheese. The recipes in this chapter use these and other wholesome ingredients to create savory omelettes; bubbling casseroles; crisp whole grain waffles; satisfying muffins and quick breads; and other tantalizing fare—dishes delicious enough to lure every member of your family to the breakfast table, and lean enough to take an honored place in a low-fat lifestyle.

To help you make the best food choices, three terrific Fat-Fighter's Guides have been included in this chapter. The guide on page 16 lists some of the most nutritious breakfast cereals available at your grocery store. The second guide steers you to the lowest-fat, highest-nutrient pancake mixes (page 21). And the third explains how to choose and use today's egg substitutes, so that you can make slimmed-down omelettes, breakfast casseroles, and many other dishes (page 28). Additionally, the Fat-Fighter's Guide on page 140 provides great tips on buying lower-fat ham, bacon, and sausage, and the guide on page 116 introduces a host of delicious low-fat and fat-free dairy products.

So heat up the griddle, and get ready for some eye-opening recipe ideas. Once you learn the secrets of low-fat cooking, you may never skip breakfast again.

FAT-FIGHTER'S GUIDE TO
Breakfast Cereals

Breakfast just doesn't get any easier than a bowl of cereal. And if you choose the right cereal, breakfast can be easy *and* nutritious. Fiber, complex carbohydrates, and B vitamins are just a few of the nutrients that a morning bowl of cereal can provide.

The first rule of buying cereal is this: Don't look down—to the lower shelves in the grocery store, that is. Quite often, the lower shelves, which are at a child's eye level, feature the sugary refined products that are meant to appeal to kids. The more nutritious choices tend to fill the store's upper shelves.

When selecting a cereal, keep in mind that most are quite low in fat. Old-fashioned granola is an exception to this rule, but these days, several brands of delicious low-fat and fat-free granolas are widely available. And don't automatically reject a cereal just because it contains a couple of grams of fat. The fact is that most whole grain cereals do contain a gram or two of fat per serving because whole grains include the wholesome *germ*—the inner portion of the grain that is an important source of essential fatty acids, vitamin E, and other nutrients. While some refined cereals may be lower in fat, nutritionally, they do not compare to whole grain products.

How can you tell which cereals are best? First, look at the ingredients list. A whole grain should be listed as the first—and, therefore, the main—ingredient. Whole grain cereals provide at least 4 grams of fiber per 2-ounce serving—unless, of course, they're puffed, like whole grain puffed wheat. Cereals that contain added bran provide even more fiber.

Next, look at the Nutrition Facts label to see how much sugar your cereal contains. Just 4 grams of sugar is the equivalent of 1 teaspoon of sugar, so that a cereal with 12 grams per serving

provides 3 teaspoons of sugar. The picture is not as clear, though, when cereals contain added fruit, because the label groups the fruit's sugar with the cereal's added refined sugar. Compare the amount of sugar in your cereal with a prudent daily limit of 50 grams (about 12½ teaspoons), and you will see how your cereal fits into your diet.

As already mentioned, whole grain cereals naturally contain a gram or two of fat per serving. Similarly, cereals that contain nuts get some fat from the nuts. But the oil in nuts, like that in whole grains, provides essential nutrients along with the fat. What you want to avoid is a cereal with *added* fat—like partially hydrogenated vegetable oil. As a general rule, try to keep the fat count per serving down to 2 grams.

RATING THE CEREALS

The very best cereal choices are those that are 100 percent whole grain, and contain no added sugar, salt, or fat. These include Nabisco Shredded Wheat, plain oatmeal or oat bran, Ralston hot cereal, Wheatena, and Quaker Multigrain Oatmeal. Other good cereal choices are whole grain products with low to moderate amounts of sugar. Among these are the Health Valley cereals; the Arrowhead Mills cereals; Kellogg's All-Bran; Nabisco 100% Bran; Post Grape-Nuts and Natural Bran Flakes; Quaker Oat Life and Oat Squares; Ralston Wheat Chex; and General Mills Cheerios, Fiber One, Total, and Wheaties.

When scanning your supermarket's shelves, don't overlook store brands. Compare the Nutrition Facts labels and ingredients lists, and you will see that many store brands are practically identical to national brands, but are a better value.

Banana Buttermilk Pancakes

1. Combine the flour, sugar, and baking soda in a medium-sized bowl, and stir to mix well. Add the buttermilk and egg substitute, and stir to mix well. Fold in the bananas and wheat germ.

2. Coat a griddle or large skillet with nonstick cooking spray, and preheat over medium heat until a drop of water sizzles when it hits the heated surface. (If using an electric griddle, heat the griddle according to the manufacturer's directions.)

3. For each pancake, pour $\frac{1}{4}$ cup of batter onto the griddle, and spread into a 4-inch circle. Cook for 1 minute and 30 seconds, or until the top is bubbly and the edges are dry. Turn and cook for an additional minute, or until the second side is golden brown. As the pancakes are done, transfer them to a serving plate and keep warm in a preheated oven.

4. Serve hot, topped with honey or maple syrup.

Variation

To make Banana Buckwheat Pancakes, substitute $\frac{3}{4}$ cup of Arrowhead Mills buckwheat flour for $\frac{3}{4}$ cup of the whole wheat flour.

Yield: 15 pancakes

$1\frac{1}{2}$ cups Arrowhead Mills whole wheat pastry flour

1 tablespoon sugar

1 teaspoon baking soda

$1\frac{3}{4}$ cups nonfat buttermilk

$\frac{1}{4}$ cup Egg Beaters egg substitute

$1\frac{1}{2}$ cups sliced banana (about $1\frac{1}{2}$ medium)

$\frac{1}{4}$ cup Kretschmer honey crunch wheat germ

NUTRITIONAL FACTS (PER PANCAKE)	
Calories: 78	Fiber: 1.9 g
Chol: 1 mg	Protein: 3.6 g
Fat: 0.7 g	Sodium: 121 mg

You Save: Calories: 39 Fat: 4.2 g

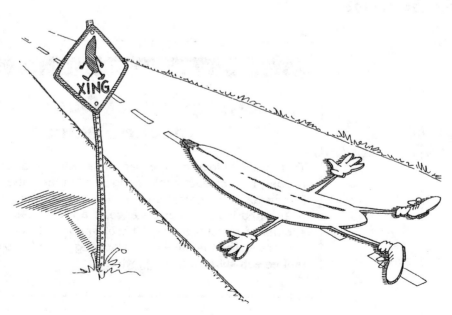

Blueberry-Cornmeal Cakes

Yield: 15 pancakes

¾ cup Arrowhead Mills whole wheat pastry flour

¾ cup Arrowhead Mills whole grain yellow cornmeal

1 tablespoon sugar

1 teaspoon baking soda

1¾ cups nonfat buttermilk

¼ cup Healthy Choice egg substitute

1½ cups fresh or frozen (unthawed) blueberries

NUTRITIONAL FACTS
(PER PANCAKE)

Calories: 67	Fiber: 1.6 g
Chol: 1 mg	Protein: 2.8 g
Fat: 0.6 g	Sodium: 124 mg

You Save: Calories: 34   Fat: 3.9 g

1.   Combine the flour, cornmeal, sugar, and baking soda in a medium-sized bowl, and stir to mix well. Add the buttermilk and egg substitute, and stir to mix well. Fold in the blueberries.

2.   Coat a griddle or large skillet with nonstick cooking spray, and preheat over medium heat until a drop of water sizzles when it hits the heated surface. (If using an electric griddle, heat the griddle according to the manufacturer's directions.)

3.   For each pancake, pour ¼ cup of batter onto the griddle, and spread into a 4-inch circle. Cook for 1 minute and 30 seconds, or until the top is bubbly and the edges are dry. Turn and cook for an additional minute, or until the second side is golden brown. As the pancakes are done, transfer them to a serving plate and keep warm in a preheated oven.

4.   Serve hot, topped with Fast and Easy Fruit Sauce (page 22), honey, or maple syrup.

FAT-FIGHTING TIP

Getting the Fat Out of Your Pancake Recipes

To make fabulous fat-free pancakes using your own favorite recipes, replace each tablespoon of oil in the batter with three-fourths as much nonfat buttermilk, nonfat yogurt, applesauce, or mashed banana. For instance, if a recipe calls for 2 tablespoons of oil, substitute 1½ tablespoons of your chosen fat substitute. Then replace each whole egg with 3 tablespoons of fat-free egg substitute or egg white.

New England Corncakes

1. Combine the flour, cornmeal, and baking soda in a medium-sized bowl, and stir to mix well. Add the buttermilk and egg substitute, and stir to mix well. Fold in the corn and the ham or bacon.

2. Coat a griddle or large skillet with nonstick cooking spray, and preheat over medium heat until a drop of water sizzles when it hits the heated surface. (If using an electric griddle, heat the griddle according to the manufacturer's directions.)

3. For each pancake, pour $\frac{1}{4}$ cup of batter onto the griddle, and spread into a 4-inch circle. Cook for 1 minute and 30 seconds, or until the top is bubbly and the edges are dry. Turn and cook for an additional minute, or until the second side is golden brown. As the pancakes are done, transfer them to a serving plate and keep warm in a preheated oven.

4. Serve hot, topped with maple syrup.

Yield: 16 pancakes

1 cup King Arthur white wheat flour

1 cup Arrowhead Mills whole grain yellow cornmeal

1 teaspoon baking soda

2 cups nonfat buttermilk

$\frac{1}{4}$ cup Egg Beaters egg substitute

1 cup frozen (thawed) whole kernel corn

$\frac{1}{2}$ cup finely chopped Butterball turkey ham, or 5 slices Butterball turkey bacon, cooked, drained, and crumbled

---

NUTRITIONAL FACTS
(PER PANCAKE)

Calories: 79	Fiber: 1.7 g
Chol: 3 mg	Protein: 4 g
Fat: 0.9 g	Sodium: 165 mg

You Save: Calories: 38 Fat: 3.9 g

Apple-Oatmeal Pancakes

Yield: 16 pancakes

1½ cups Quaker quick-cooking oats

2¼ cups nonfat buttermilk

½ cup Pillsbury's Best whole wheat flour

1 tablespoon sugar

1 teaspoon baking soda

¼ teaspoon ground cinnamon

½ cup Better'n Eggs egg substitute

2 cups chopped apples (about 2 medium)

NUTRITIONAL FACTS (PER PANCAKE)

Calories: 72	Fiber: 1.5 g
Chol: 1 mg	Protein: 3.6 g
Fat: 0.8 g	Sodium: 123 mg

You Save: Calories: 53 Fat: 4.1 g

1. Combine the oats and buttermilk in a large bowl. Stir to mix well, and set aside for 15 minutes.

2. Combine the flour, sugar, baking soda, and cinnamon in a small bowl. Stir to mix well, and set aside.

3. Add the egg substitute to the oat mixture, and stir to mix well. Add the flour mixture, and stir to mix well. Fold in the apples.

4. Coat a griddle or large skillet with nonstick cooking spray, and preheat over medium heat until a drop of water sizzles when it hits the heated surface. (If using an electric griddle, heat the griddle according to the manufacturer's directions.)

5. For each pancake, pour ¼ cup of batter onto the griddle, and spread into a 4-inch circle. Cook for 1 minute and 30 seconds, or until the top is bubbly and the edges are dry. Turn and cook for an additional minute, or until the second side is golden brown. As the pancakes are done, transfer them to a serving plate and keep warm in a preheated oven.

6. Serve hot, topped with Warm Strawberry Sauce (page 22), honey, or maple syrup.

FAT-FIGHTER'S GUIDE TO
Pancake Mixes

As the recipes in this chapter illustrate, pancakes are very simple to make from scratch. And when you make your own pancakes, you can include healthful whole grain flours, and leave out the oil.

How do pancake mixes compare with your homemade cakes? With a few exceptions, not very well. Most major brands of pancake and waffle mixes are made from refined flours, and so provide no fiber and few nutrients. Two exceptions are Hodgson Mill and Arrowhead Mills whole grain pancake mixes. Both manufacturers offer a variety of pancake mixes made with wholesome whole grain flours. Aunt Jemima Buckwheat pancake mix is also made with whole grain buckwheat flour. One

serving—four pancakes—supplies a respectable 4 grams of fiber. And if you leave out the oil and use an egg substitute or egg whites when mixing up the batter, your cakes will be practically fat-free. (The Fat-Fighting Tip on page 18 provides guidelines for replacing the oil in pancake recipes.)

Light and reduced-calorie pancake mixes also supply some fiber from added cellulose—a refined fiber used as a bulking agent in reduced-calorie baked goods. But since these products are still made mostly of white flour, nutritionally speaking, you will be better off with a whole grain product.

English Muffin French Toast

1. Combine the egg substitute, evaporated milk, orange rind, and vanilla extract in a shallow bowl, and stir to mix well. Dip each muffin half in the egg mixture for several seconds, turning to coat both sides thoroughly.

2. Coat a griddle or large skillet with nonstick cooking spray, and preheat over medium heat until a drop of water sizzles when it hits the heated surface. (If using an electric griddle, heat the griddle according to the manufacturer's directions.)

3. Arrange the English muffin slices on the griddle, and cook for 1½ to 2 minutes on each side, or until golden brown. As the slices are done, transfer them to a serving plate and keep warm in a preheated oven.

4. Serve hot, topped with Fast and Easy Fruit Sauce (page 22), Warm Strawberry Sauce (page 22), honey, or maple syrup.

Yield: *12 slices*

1½ cups Better'n Eggs egg substitute

¼ cup plus 2 tablespoons Pet evaporated skimmed milk

1 teaspoon dried grated orange rind

1 teaspoon vanilla extract

6 Thomas' Honey Wheat English muffins, split open

NUTRITIONAL FACTS
(PER SLICE)

Calories: 88	Fiber: 1.5 g
Chol: 0 mg	Protein: 5.8 g
Fat: 0.5 g	Sodium: 191 mg

You Save: Calories: 43 Fat: 4.9 g

Sweet Syrup Alternatives

Deliciously sweet syrups add that crowning touch to pancakes, waffles, and French toast. While all syrups are fat-free, they are generally almost pure sugar, and add up to 60 calories for each tablespoon used. Instead of the usual refined, sugary syrups, try either of the following fruit toppings over pancakes, waffles, and other breakfast treats. With less calories than even reduced-calorie syrups, these syrups are more natural, wholesome, and economical.

Fast and Easy Fruit Sauce

Yield: 2 cups

1 can (1 pound) Libby's Lite peaches or apricots, undrained

2–3 tablespoons sugar

1 teaspoon McCormick butter-flavored extract

1. Combine the peaches or apricots, including the juice, and the sugar in a blender, and process until smooth.

2. Pour the mixture into a 1-quart pot, place over medium heat, and cook until heated through. Remove the pot from the heat and stir in the butter-flavored extract.

3. Serve warm over pancakes, French toast, or waffles. Store any leftover sauce in the refrigerator for up to 1 week.

You Save: Cal: 203   Fat: 0 g

NUTRITIONAL FACTS (PER ¼-CUP SERVING)

Calories: 37	Fat: 0 g	Protein: 0.4 g
Cholesterol: 0 mg	Fiber: 0.8 g	Sodium: 2 mg

Warm Strawberry Sauce

Yield: 1½ cups

¼ cup sugar

1 tablespoon cornstarch

¾ cup After the Fall apple strawberry juice, or any strawberry juice blend

2 cups sliced fresh or frozen strawberries

1. Combine the sugar and cornstarch in a 1-quart saucepan, and slowly stir in the juice. Place over medium heat, and bring to a boil, stirring constantly.

2. Add the strawberries to the juice mixture, and bring to a second boil. Reduce the heat to low, and cook, stirring occasionally, for about 5 minutes, or until the fruit begins to break down and the mixture is thickened and bubbly.

3. Serve warm over pancakes, French toast, or waffles. Store any leftover sauce in the refrigerator for up to 1 week.

You Save: Cal: 171   Fat: 0 g

NUTRITIONAL FACTS (PER ¼-CUP SERVING)

Calories: 69	Fat: 0.2 g	Protein: 0.4 g
Cholesterol: 0 mg	Fiber: 0.9 g	Sodium: 2 mg

Three-Grain Waffles

Waffles are great for people with busy lifestyles, as they may be made in advance, placed in plastic zip-type bags, and frozen until needed. At breakfast time, heat the frozen waffles in a toaster, and serve.

1. Coat a waffle iron with nonstick cooking spray, and preheat according to the manufacturer's directions.

2. Combine the flour, oats, cornmeal, sugar, baking powder, and baking soda in a large bowl, and stir to mix well. Set aside.

3. Place the egg whites in the bowl of an electric mixer, and beat on high until soft peaks form. Set aside.

4. Add the buttermilk to the flour mixture, and stir to mix well. Gently fold in the egg whites.

5. Spoon $1\frac{1}{4}$ cups of batter (or the amount stated by the manufacturer) onto the prepared waffle iron. Bake for 5 to 7 minutes, or until the iron has stopped steaming and the waffle is crisp and brown.

6. Serve hot, topped with Fast and Easy Fruit Sauce (page 22), Warm Strawberry Sauce (page 22), honey, or maple syrup.

Yield: *12 waffles*

1 cup Arrowhead Mills whole wheat pastry flour

$\frac{1}{2}$ cup Minute Brand quick-cooking oats

$\frac{1}{2}$ cup Hodgson Mill whole grain yellow cornmeal

1 tablespoon sugar

2 teaspoons baking powder

$\frac{3}{4}$ teaspoon baking soda

4 egg whites

$1\frac{1}{2}$ cups nonfat buttermilk

NUTRITIONAL FACTS
(PER WAFFLE)

Calories: 82	Fiber: 1.9 g
Chol: 1 mg	Protein: 3.3 g
Fat: 0.8 g	Sodium: 174 mg

You Save: Calories: 53 Fat: 6.3 g

Potato Frittata

Yield: *4 servings*

¹⁄₃ cup chopped green bell pepper

¹⁄₃ cup chopped onion

1 teaspoon crushed fresh garlic

2 cups sliced cooked potatoes
(about 2 medium)

1 teaspoon dried Italian seasoning

¹⁄₈ teaspoon ground black pepper

2 cups Egg Beaters egg substitute

1 tablespoon plus 1 teaspoon
Kraft Free nonfat grated
Parmesan topping

³⁄₄ cup Sargento Light fancy
shredded natural mozzarella
cheese

NUTRITIONAL FACTS
(PER SERVING)

Calories: 212	Fiber: 2.4 g
Chol: 9 mg	Protein: 20 g
Fat: 2.1 g	Sodium: 316 mg

You Save: Cal: 183 Fat: 20.1 g

1. Coat a 10-inch oven-proof skillet with nonstick cooking spray, and preheat over medium heat. Add the peppers, onions, and garlic, and stir-fry for about 2 minutes, or just until the vegetables are crisp-tender.

2. Add the potatoes, Italian seasoning, and pepper to the skillet, and stir to mix well. Spread the mixture out to form an even layer over the bottom of the skillet.

3. Reduce the heat to low, and pour the egg substitute over the potato mixture. Cook for 10 to 12 minutes without stirring, or until the eggs are almost set.

4. Sprinkle first the Parmesan and then the mozzarella over the top of the frittata, and place the skillet under a preheated broiler. Broil for about 3 minutes, or until the eggs are completely set, the cheese is melted, and the top is nicely browned.

5. Cut the frittata into wedges, and serve hot.

Southern Breakfast Bake

1. Place the water in a 1½-quart pot, and bring to a boil over high heat. Reduce the heat to low, and whisk in the grits. Cook and stir for 2 minutes, or until the mixture is very thick.

2. Remove the pot from the heat, and slowly whisk in the evaporated milk. Whisk in the egg substitute, mustard, and Tabasco sauce. Stir in the ham, cheese, and scallions.

3. Coat a 9-inch deep dish pie pan with nonstick cooking spray, and pour the egg mixture into the pan. Bake uncovered at 375°F for 40 to 45 minutes, or until a sharp knife inserted in the center of the dish comes out clean.

4. Remove the dish from the oven, and let sit for 10 minutes before cutting into wedges and serving.

Yield: 6 servings

½ cup water

⅓ cup quick-cooking yellow grits

1 can (12 ounces) Pet evaporated skimmed milk

¾ cup Healthy Choice egg substitute

1 teaspoon dry mustard

½ teaspoon Tabasco pepper sauce

1 cup diced Hormel Light & Lean ham (about 5 ounces)

1 cup Kraft Healthy Favorites fat-free shredded Cheddar cheese

2 tablespoons finely chopped scallions

NUTRITIONAL FACTS (PER SERVING)		
Calories: 155	Fat: 1 g	Protein: 20 g
Cholesterol: 18 mg	Fiber: 1 g	Sodium: 506 mg

You Save: Calories: 145 Fat: 21 g

Turkey Breakfast Sausage

1. Combine all ingredients in a medium-sized bowl, and mix well. Cover and refrigerate for several hours to blend the flavors.

2. Shape the mixture into 6 (3-inch) patties. Coat a large skillet with nonstick cooking spray, and preheat over medium-low heat. Arrange the patties in the skillet, and cook for 4 minutes on each side, or until browned and no longer pink inside. Serve hot.

Yield: 6 servings

1 pound Butterball Extra Lean ground turkey or another brand of extra lean ground turkey

1 packet (about 1 teaspoon) Goya ham-flavored concentrate granules

2 teaspoons dried sage

½ teaspoon dried thyme

¼ teaspoon ground black pepper

⅛ teaspoon cayenne pepper (optional)

NUTRITIONAL FACTS (PER PATTY)		
Calories: 88	Fat: 2 g	Protein: 17 g
Cholesterol: 47 mg	Fiber: 0 g	Sodium: 257 mg

You Save: Calories: 166 Fat: 19.1 g

Breakfast Burritos

Yield: *4 servings*

¼ cup finely chopped onion

½ cup diced Hormel Curemaster 96% fat-free ham (about 2½ ounces)

3 tablespoons drained canned chopped green chilies

1¼ cups Egg Beaters egg substitute

4 Buena Vida fat-free flour tortillas (8-inch rounds) or other fat-free tortillas

¼ cup plus 2 tablespoons Healthy Choice fancy shredded fat-free Cheddar cheese

¼ cup picante sauce (optional)

NUTRITIONAL FACTS
(PER SERVING)

Calories: 186	Fiber: 1.3 g
Chol: 10 mg	Protein: 15.8 g
Fat: 0.7 g	Sodium: 735 mg

You Save: Calories: 187 Fat: 22 g

1. Coat a large nonstick skillet with nonstick cooking spray, and heat over medium heat. Add the onions, and cook, stirring constantly, for about 2 minutes, or until crisp-tender. Add the ham and chilies, and stir to mix well.

2. Pour the egg substitute over the onion mixture, and reduce the heat to medium-low. Cook without stirring for about 5 minutes, or until the eggs are almost set. Stirring gently to scramble, continue to cook for another minute or 2, or until the eggs are cooked but not dry.

3. While the eggs are cooking, warm the tortillas by wrapping them securely in aluminum foil and placing them in a 350°F oven for 10 minutes. (Or follow the manufacturer's directions for heating.)

4. Arrange the warm tortillas on a flat surface. Place a quarter of the egg mixture along the right side of each tortilla, stopping 1½ inches from the bottom. Top the eggs with 1½ tablespoons of the cheese and, if desired, 1 tablespoon of the picante sauce.

5. Fold the bottom edge of each tortilla up about 1 inch. (This fold will prevent the filling from falling out.) Then, beginning at the right edge, roll each tortilla up jelly-roll style. Serve hot.

Making Breakfast Burritos

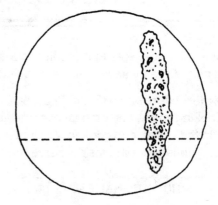

a. Arrange the filling along the right side of the tortilla.

Country Morning Omelette

1. Coat an 8-inch nonstick skillet with nonstick cooking spray, and heat over medium-low heat. Add the egg substitute, and cook without stirring for about 2 minutes, or until the eggs are set around the edges.

2. Use a spatula to lift the edges of the omelette, and allow the uncooked egg to flow below the cooked portion. Cook for another minute or 2, or until the eggs are almost set.

3. Arrange first the cheese, and then the sausage and vegetables over half of the omelette. Fold the other half over the filling, and cook for another minute or 2, or until the cheese is melted and the eggs are completely set.

4. Slide the omelette onto a plate, sprinkle with the paprika, and serve hot.

Yield: 1 serving

¾ cup Egg Beaters egg substitute

3 tablespoons Healthy Choice fancy shredded fat-free Cheddar cheese

2 tablespoons diced Healthy Choice smoked turkey sausage

1 tablespoon chopped tomato

1 tablespoon chopped green bell pepper

1 tablespoon chopped onion

Ground paprika

NUTRITIONAL FACTS (PER SERVING)

Calories: 150	Fat: 0.3 g	Protein: 27 g
Cholesterol: 10 mg	Fiber: 0.5 g	Sodium: 593 mg

You Save: Calories: 303   Fat: 33.3 g

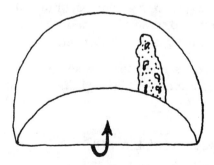

b. Fold the bottom edge of the tortilla up.

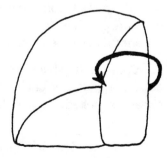

c. Fold the right side over the filling.

d. Continue folding to form a roll.

FAT-FIGHTER'S GUIDE TO
Eggs and Egg Substitutes

Everyone who cooks knows the value of eggs. Eggs are star ingredients in quiches, custards, French toast, casseroles, and countless other foods. Of course, eggs are also loaded with fat and cholesterol. The good news is that with the development of fat-free egg substitutes, you can now enjoy these and other egg dishes without the fat or cholesterol. Just how great are your savings in cholesterol and fat when whole eggs are replaced with a substitute? One large egg contains 80 calories, 5 grams of fat, and 210 milligrams of cholesterol. The equivalent amount of egg white or fat-free egg substitute—3 tablespoons—contains 20 to 30 calories, no fat, and no cholesterol. The benefits of these substitute ingredients are clear.

Many people simply substitute egg whites for whole eggs. While this is often a good option, in some cases, egg substitutes are preferred over egg whites. For instance, egg substitute is the best choice when making quiches and puddings. In addition, because they have been pasteurized (heat treated), egg substitutes are safe to use uncooked in eggnogs and salad dressings. On the other hand, when recipes require whipped egg whites, egg substitutes do not work.

Ham and Egg Scramble

Yield: *4 servings*

⅔ cup diced Hormel Curemaster 96% fat-free ham (about 3 ounces)

2 cups Better'n Eggs egg substitute

¼ cup plus 2 tablespoons Sargento Light fancy shredded natural Cheddar cheese

1. Coat a 10-inch nonstick skillet with nonstick cooking spray, and preheat over medium-high heat. Add the ham to the skillet, and cook for 1 to 2 minutes, or until nicely browned.

2. Reduce the heat to medium-low, and pour the egg substitute over the ham. Cook without stirring for 3 to 4 minutes, or until the eggs are partially set. Stirring gently to scramble, continue to cook for another minute or 2, or until the eggs are almost set.

3. Sprinkle the cheese over the eggs, and cook and stir gently for another minute, or until the eggs are cooked but not dry, and the cheese is melted. Serve hot.

NUTRITIONAL FACTS (PER SERVING)		
Calories: 106	Fat: 2.4 g	Protein: 18.5 g
Cholesterol: 14 mg	Fiber: 0 g	Sodium: 510 mg

You Save: Calories: 294 Fat: 27.6 g

When selecting an egg substitute, look for fat-free or very low-fat brands like Egg Beaters, Better'n Eggs, Scramblers, or Healthy Choice. Many stores also have their own brand of fat-free egg substitute. Some brands contain vegetable oil, and so have almost as much fat as the eggs you are replacing. Always check the label for fat content, and buy only those brands with no more than 1 gram of fat per egg equivalent.

When replacing egg whites with egg substitute, or whole eggs with egg whites or egg substitute, use the following guidelines:

1 large egg = $1\frac{1}{2}$ large egg whites	
1 large egg = 3 tablespoons egg substitute	
1 large egg white = 2 tablespoons egg substitute	

Spinnaker Omelette

1. Coat an 8-inch nonstick skillet with nonstick cooking spray, and heat over medium-low heat. Add the egg substitute, and cook without stirring for about 2 minutes, or until the eggs are set around the edges.

2. Use a spatula to lift the edges of the omelette, and allow the uncooked egg to flow below the cooked portion. Cook for another minute or 2, or until the eggs are almost set.

3. Arrange first the cheese, and then the crab meat and scallions over half of the omelette. Fold the other half over the filling, and cook for another minute or 2, or until the cheese is melted and the eggs are completely set.

4. Slide the omelette onto a plate, sprinkle with the paprika, and serve hot.

Yield: *1 serving*

$\frac{3}{4}$ cup Egg Beaters egg substitute

1 slice (1 ounce) Sargento Light Swiss cheese

$\frac{1}{4}$ cup (about $1\frac{1}{2}$ ounces) cooked lump crab meat

1 tablespoon thinly sliced scallions

Paprika

NUTRITIONAL FACTS
(PER SERVING)

Calories: 206	Fiber: 0.2 g
Chol: 38 mg	Protein: 33.8 g
Fat: 4.4 g	Sodium: 241 mg

You Save: Calories: 241 Fat: 25.8 g

Cocoa Banana Bread

Yield: *16 slices*

1²⁄₃ cups Arrowhead Mills whole wheat pastry flour

¹⁄₃ cup Hershey's Dutch Processed European Style cocoa powder

¹⁄₂ cup sugar

1 teaspoon baking powder

1 teaspoon baking soda

1¹⁄₂ cups mashed very ripe bananas (about 3 large)

¹⁄₃ cup WonderSlim fat substitute* or Prune Purée (page 190)

1 teaspoon vanilla extract

¹⁄₃ cup chopped walnuts

*WonderSlim, a nutritious fat substitute, can be found in health foods stores.

1. Combine the flour, cocoa, sugar, baking powder, and baking soda in a large bowl, and stir to mix well. Add the banana, the WonderSlim or Prune Purée, and the vanilla extract, and stir just until the dry ingredients are moistened. Fold in the walnuts.

2. Coat an 8-x-4-inch loaf pan with nonstick cooking spray, and spread the mixture evenly in the pan. Bake at 350°F for about 50 minutes, or just until a wooden toothpick inserted in the center of the loaf comes out clean.

3. Remove the bread from the oven, and let sit for 10 minutes. Invert the loaf onto a wire rack, turn right side up, and cool before slicing.

NUTRITIONAL FACTS (PER SLICE)

Calories: 109	Fat: 2.1 g	Protein: 2.9 g
Cholesterol: 0 mg	Fiber: 2.8 g	Sodium: 104 mg

You Save: Calories: 82   Fat: 8 g

FAT-FIGHTING TIP

Getting the Fat Out of Your Muffin and Quick Bread Recipes

To make your favorite muffin and quick bread recipes fat-free:

• If your recipe calls for oil, replace all or part of the oil with three-fourths as much applesauce, mashed banana, puréed fruit, Prune Purée (page 190), or WonderSlim fat substitute. If the recipe uses butter, margarine, or another solid shortening, replace all or part of it with half as much fat substitute. Mix up the batter. If it seems too dry, add a little more fat substitute. (Some recipes need a one-for-one substitution.)

• Replace each whole egg with 3 tablespoons of egg white or fat-free egg substitute.

• Bake fat-free muffins and quick breads at 350°F, and check for doneness a few minutes before the end of the usual baking time. Be careful not to overbake your fat-free treats, or they will become too dry.

Cinnamon Bran Muffins

1. Combine the cereal and milk in a medium-sized bowl. Stir to mix well, and set aside for 15 minutes.

2. Combine the flour, sugar, baking powder, and cinnamon in a large bowl, and stir to mix well.

3. Add the apple butter and egg substitute to the cereal mixture, and stir to mix well. Add the cereal mixture to the flour mixture, and stir just until the dry ingredients are moistened. Fold in the raisins and, if desired, the walnuts.

4. Coat muffin cups with nonstick cooking spray, and fill three-fourths full with the batter. Bake at 350°F for 17 minutes, or just until a wooden toothpick inserted in the center of a muffin comes out clean.

5. Remove the muffin tins from the oven, and allow them to sit for 5 minutes before removing the muffins. Serve warm or at room temperature.

Yield: 12 muffins

2 cups Kellogg's All-Bran Extra Fiber cereal

1½ cups skim milk

1¼ cups Gold Medal unbleached flour

¼ cup sugar

1 tablespoon plus 1 teaspoon baking powder

1½ teaspoons ground cinnamon

¼ cup apple butter

¼ cup Healthy Choice egg substitute

½ cup dark raisins

¼ cup chopped walnuts (optional)

NUTRITIONAL FACTS (PER MUFFIN)		
Calories: 126	Fat: 0.6 g	Protein: 4.4 g
Cholesterol: 0 mg	Fiber: 5.7 g	Sodium: 196 mg

You Save: Calories: 66 Fat: 6.7 g

Applesauce Oat Bran Muffins

Yield: *12 muffins*

1 cup Hodgson Mill oat bran or other coarsely ground oat bran*

¾ cup plus 2 tablespoons nonfat buttermilk

1⅓ cups Arrowhead Mills whole wheat pastry flour

¼ cup plus 2 tablespoons sugar

2 teaspoons baking powder

½ teaspoon baking soda

½ cup Musselman's Lite applesauce

¼ cup Better'n Eggs egg substitute

½ cup dried cherries, blueberries, cranberries, or dark raisins

¼ cup chopped pecans or almonds (optional)

*If you substitute a finer, softer brand of oat bran—such as Quaker or Mother's—for the Hodgson Mill oat bran, do not presoak the oat bran in the buttermilk. Instead, just add the oat bran to the dry ingredients, and add the buttermilk to the liquid ingredients. Check the muffins for doneness after about 15 minutes.

1.   Combine the oat bran and buttermilk in a small bowl. Stir to mix well, and set aside for 10 minutes.

2.   Combine the flour, sugar, baking powder, and baking soda in a large bowl, and stir to mix well.

3.   Add the buttermilk mixture, applesauce, and egg substitute to the flour mixture, and stir just until the dry ingredients are moistened. Fold in the fruit and, if desired, the nuts.

4.   Coat muffin cups with nonstick cooking spray, and fill three-fourths full with the batter. Bake at 350°F for 16 minutes, or just until a wooden toothpick inserted in the center of a muffin comes out clean.

5.   Remove the muffin tins from the oven, and allow them to sit for 5 minutes before removing the muffins. Serve warm or at room temperature.

NUTRITIONAL FACTS (PER MUFFIN)

Calories: 131	Fat: 1.4 g	Protein: 5.1 g
Cholesterol: 0 mg	Fiber: 5.4 g	Sodium: 139 mg

You Save: Calories: 67   Fat: 7.2 g

Apricot-Oat Scones

1. Combine the flour, oats, sugar, baking powder, and baking soda in a medium-sized bowl, and stir to mix well. Using a pastry cutter or 2 knives, cut in the butter until the mixture resembles coarse crumbs. Stir in 3 tablespoons of the egg substitute and just enough of the buttermilk to form a stiff dough. Stir in the apricots or raisins.

2. Form the dough into a ball, and turn onto a lightly floured surface. With floured hands, pat the dough into a 7-inch circle.

3. Coat a baking sheet with nonstick cooking spray. Place the dough on the sheet, and use a sharp floured knife to cut it into 12 wedges. Pull the wedges out slightly to leave a $\frac{1}{4}$-inch space between them. Brush the tops lightly with the remaining table-spoon of egg substitute.

4. Bake at 375°F for 16 to 18 minutes, or until lightly browned. Transfer to a serving plate, and serve hot.

Yield: 12 servings

1$\frac{2}{3}$ cups Pillsbury's Best unbleached flour

1 cup Quaker quick-cooking oats

2 tablespoons sugar

1 tablespoon baking powder

$\frac{1}{4}$ teaspoon baking soda

3 tablespoons Land O Lakes light butter, cut into pieces

$\frac{1}{4}$ cup Scramblers egg substitute, divided

$\frac{1}{2}$ cup nonfat buttermilk

$\frac{1}{4}$ cup plus 2 tablespoons chopped dried apricots or golden raisins

NUTRITIONAL FACTS (PER SCONE)

Calories: 123	Fat: 2 g	Protein: 3.7 g
Cholesterol: 5 mg	Fiber: 1.6 g	Sodium: 132 mg

You Save: Calories: 60 Fat: 6.9 g

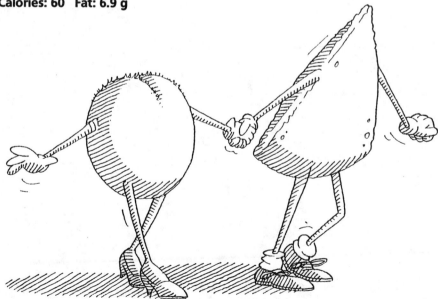

2. Light and Luscious Lunches

Mention lunch, and most people immediately think of the sandwich. Versatile, portable, and fast and easy to make and eat, this is perhaps the most popular weekday lunch choice of both active children and on-the-go adults. On weekends, when a more leisurely meal is possible, another popular midday choice is the creamy quiche. Paired with a green salad or a cup of soup, the sandwich and quiche seem like perfect light lunch entrées.

But are these dishes *really* light? If you think about what goes into some of your lunch-time favorites, you will realize that all is not what it seems. Everyone knows that a deli-style Reuben sandwich is loaded with fat and calories, but even a seemingly innocent chicken salad sandwich can contain over 40 grams of fat and 600 calories. Is a veggie-and-cheese sandwich any better? Not if it's made with several ounces of high-fat Swiss or Cheddar. And the quiche? Between the shortening in the crust, the cheese, the eggs, and the cream, that "light" wedge of quiche can supply you with an entire day's worth of fat and *two* days' worth of cholesterol!

If you now fear that you must forever abandon your favorite lunch foods, take heart. A whole world of light and luscious lunch dishes awaits you. New low- and no-fat ingredients—from ultra-lean meat, to nonfat cheese, to reduced-fat sandwich spreads, to nonfat egg substitutes—provide dozens of lunch-time possibilities. Add a few low-fat cooking tricks, and you'll find that even the Monte Cristo Sandwich can take its place on a low-fat lunch menu.

This chapter offers a selection of hearty sandwiches that are special enough to serve to guests, yet low enough in fat and calories to be enjoyed every day. Also included is a variety of tempting quiches. With their easy-to-make crusts and their savory fillings of nonfat cheese and eggs, fresh vegetables, and other wholesome ingredients, you'll find these healthful pies deceptively rich and creamy.

To help you choose the best breads for your sandwiches, a Fat-Fighter's Guide (page 36) tells you which brands are not only low in fat, but also high in fiber and other nutrients. Other guides will fill you in on lean lunchmeats (page 140), low-fat cheeses (page 116), and reduced-fat sandwich spreads (page 52).

As you glance through the recipes in this chapter, keep in mind that these are just a few of the lunch-time dishes that you can whip up for family and friends. Use your new fat-fighting ingredients to give your favorite sandwich a slimming makeover. Or build your lunch around one of the satisfying salads presented in Chapter 3, or one of the hearty low-fat soups provided in Chapter 4. Then enjoy a meal that is high in nutrients, packed with flavor, and truly light and healthful.

FAT-FIGHTER'S GUIDE TO

Breads

Bread really is the staff of life. If you don't believe it, just consider the Food Guide Pyramid created by the U.S. Department of Agriculture. Bread and other grain products form the base of this guide to dietary choices, with six to eleven servings of these products recommended daily. Can you possibly eat this much bread without gaining weight? Most definitely. Contrary to popular belief, bread is not fattening. A one-ounce slice of sandwich bread, pita bread, French bread, sourdough bread, English muffin, or bagel contains about 80 calories and only 1 gram of fat. Croissants, biscuits, and most muffins and quick breads, however, can contain 5 or more grams of fat for the same size serving.

While most sandwich loaves and other breads are low in fat, these products do vary in other respects. Let's take a look at some of the factors you'll want to consider when buying bread for your family.

WHITE VERSUS WHOLE WHEAT

Whole wheat bread, which is made with the entire wheat kernel, is far better than white bread. Why? Whole wheat bread's superior fiber count is one reason. Breads made from 100-percent whole wheat flour—or other whole grains like oats, rye, and barley—provide 4 to 5 grams of fiber for each two-slice serving, while the same-size serving of white bread contains only a gram. Whole grain breads also provide a wealth of nutrients that refined white breads do not. Vitamins E and B6, folate, copper, zinc, iron, chromium, manganese, and magnesium are just a few of the nutrients you'll get every time you eat a slice of your favorite whole grain loaf.

How do you know if a bread is whole grain? Look at the ingredients list. Whole wheat flour or another whole grain should be the first ingredient

listed. Be aware that some breads, although bearing names like "natural wheat" and "honey wheat," contain little whole wheat flour. Instead, they are made with "wheat flour" or "unbleached wheat flour"—both of which refer to refined white flour.

LIGHT VERSUS REGULAR BREAD

In "light" breads, indigestible plant fibers replace part of the flour. Because these fibers cannot be digested, breads made with these ingredients have half the calories of regular breads.

How does light bread compare with 100-percent whole grain bread? Most light breads contain as much or more fiber than whole grain breads do. However, most are also made with refined wheat flour, and so do not provide the same nutrients as 100-percent whole grain bread. If you prefer light bread, you will get the most nutritional value by choosing a brand that lists whole wheat flour as the first ingredient.

SODIUM

Over the course of a day, bread can contribute a surprising amount of sodium to your diet, with most breads providing 130 to 175 milligrams of sodium per slice. And pumpernickel, rye bread, biscuits, and quick breads tend to contain *twice* as much sodium as whole wheat and white breads. To keep your sodium intake under control, look for breads that contain no more than 150 milligrams per slice.

SOME BREADS TO PUT IN YOUR BASKET

Since most breads are very low in fat, it is impossible to list all of the many brands from which you can choose. However, a few brands are noteworthy for their excellent nutritional value.

Top: Applesauce Oat Bran Muffins (page 32), Center: English Muffin French Toast (page 21), With Warm Strawberry Sauce (page 22), Bottom: Country Morning Omelette (page 27)

Top: Shrimp and Asparagus Quiche (page 46), Center: Italian Meatball Sub (page 38),
Bottom: Monte Cristo Sandwich (page 40)

As already discussed, because whole grain breads provide the most fiber and nutritional value, they should be selected for regular use. Among the best choices are Arnold Bran'nola Dark Wheat, Arnold Stoneground 100% Whole Wheat, Arnold Honey Wheatberry, Country Hearth 100% Whole Wheat, Nature's Own 100% Whole Wheat, Oroweat Light 100% Whole Wheat, Pepperidge Farm 100% Stoneground Whole Wheat, Pepperidge Farm Natural Whole Grain Crunchy Grains, and most brands labelled "100% Whole Wheat." In addition, Matthew's and Brownberry each offer a fine selection of preservative-free whole grain breads. When available, you might also try your local bakery's whole wheat loaves. Because these products are made daily, they, too, tend to be free of preservatives.

Oatmeal, rye, pumpernickel, and mixed grain breads are also acceptable choices, since they contain at least some whole grain flour. But realize that these breads tend to contain more refined wheat flour than whole grain flour. As previously mentioned, they also tend to be rather high in sodium. Two good products—ones that are relatively low in sodium—are Arnold Pumpernickel and Arnold Rye.

For a change of pace, you might try whole grain English Muffins such as Matthew's All Natural 100% Whole Wheat; whole grain bagels; and whole grain pita bread, such as Tofuyan Whole Wheat, Tofuyan Oat Bran, Sahara Whole Wheat, and Sahara Oat Bran. French bread, sourdough bread, and similar specialty breads are other low-fat options, though they do not provide the fiber and nutrients that whole grain breads do.

Curried Turkey Salad Sandwiches

1. Combine the turkey, apple, celery, and raisins in a medium-sized bowl, and toss to mix well. Combine the sour cream, mayonnaise, curry powder or paste, and pepper in a small bowl, and stir to mix well. Add the sour cream mixture to the turkey mixture, and toss to mix well. Cover the mixture, and chill for at least 2 hours.

2. To assemble the sandwiches, place 1 lettuce leaf in each pita pocket half. Fill the pocket with ½ cup of the turkey mixture, and some of the sprouts. Serve immediately.

Yield: *6 servings*

2 cups diced cooked turkey breast (about 10 ounces)

1 cup chopped tart apple (about 1 medium)

½ cup thinly sliced celery

¼ cup golden raisins

⅓ cup Sealtest Free nonfat sour cream

⅓ cup Kraft Free mayonnaise

¾ teaspoon curry powder or curry paste (or more to taste)

⅛ teaspoon ground white pepper

6 lettuce leaves

3 Tofuyan whole wheat pita pockets, 2 ounces each, cut in half

1⅛ cups alfalfa sprouts

NUTRITIONAL FACTS (PER SERVING)

Calories: 195	Fat: 1.1 g	Protein: 18.3 g
Cholesterol: 40 mg	Fiber: 3.1 g	Sodium: 307 mg

You Save: Calories: 92 Fat: 12.3 g

Italian Meatball Subs

Yield: *5 servings*

1 pound 95% lean ground beef

1 cup soft Italian bread crumbs

¼ cup Scramblers egg substitute

¼ cup finely chopped onion

1 teaspoon dried Italian seasoning

¼ teaspoon ground black pepper

1¼ cups Ragu Light pasta sauce, any variety

1 medium green bell pepper, cut into thin strips

1 medium onion, cut into thin wedges

5 submarine-sandwich rolls, each 6 inches long, or 5 pieces Italian bread, each 6 inches long

½ cup plus 2 tablespoons Healthy Choice fancy shredded fat-free mozzarella cheese

1. Combine the ground beef, bread crumbs, egg substitute, onion, Italian seasoning, and pepper in a large bowl, and mix thoroughly. Coat a baking sheet with nonstick cooking spray. Shape the meatball mixture into 15 (1¾-inch) balls, and arrange on the baking sheet.

2. Bake the meatballs at 350°F for about 23 minutes, or until the meat is no longer pink inside. Remove the meatballs from the oven, and cover to keep warm.

3. Place the pasta sauce in a small saucepan, and simmer over medium heat just until hot.

4. Coat a large nonstick skillet with nonstick cooking spray, and preheat over medium-high heat. Add the peppers and onions, and stir-fry for about 4 minutes, or until the vegetables are just tender. Add a little water if the skillet becomes too dry.

5. To assemble the subs, slice the rolls or Italian bread in half lengthwise, being careful to avoid cutting all the way through. Lay the rolls open on a flat surface, and arrange 3 meatballs in each one. Top with ¼ cup of the peppers and onions, ¼ cup of the sauce, and 2 tablespoons of the cheese. Serve hot.

NUTRITIONAL FACTS (PER SERVING)		
Calories: 394	Fat: 6.5 g	Protein: 31.2 g
Cholesterol: 64 mg	Fiber: 5 g	Sodium: 810 mg

You Save: Calories: 243 Fat: 28.1 g

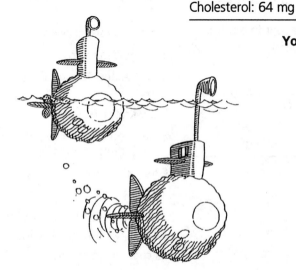

Fabulous French Dips

1. To make the broth, combine all of the broth ingredients in a 1-quart pot, and bring to a boil over high heat. Reduce the heat to low, cover, and simmer for 15 minutes, or until the flavors are well blended.

2. While the broth is simmering, coat a medium-sized nonstick skillet with nonstick cooking spray, and preheat over medium heat. Add the mushrooms and onions, and sauté for 5 minutes, or until the vegetables are tender. Add a little water or dry sherry if the skillet gets too dry.

3. To assemble the sandwiches, slice the French bread in half lengthwise, and lay the pieces open on a flat surface. Arrange 3 ounces of beef on the bottom half of each piece. Top with some of the sautéed mushrooms and onions and 1 ounce of the cheese. Replace the tops of the sandwiches, and cut each one in half.

4. Arrange the sandwiches on a microwave-safe platter. Cover with a paper towel, and microwave at high power for 2 minutes, or until the cheese is melted. (If using a conventional oven, wrap each sandwich in aluminum foil and bake at 400°F for 10 minutes, or until the cheese is melted.) Place the sandwiches on serving plates, accompany each plate with a dish of the broth, and serve.

Yield: 6 servings

2 cups sliced fresh mushrooms

1 medium yellow onion, cut into thin wedges

6 pieces French bread, each 6 inches long

1 pound 2 ounces thinly sliced Boar's Head no salt added oven roasted top round or Healthy Choice roast beef

6 ounces block-style Polly-O Free natural nonfat mozzarella cheese or Alpine Lace reduced-fat provolone cheese, thinly sliced

BROTH

1 can (14½ ounces) Health Valley no salt added beef broth

½ teaspoon crushed fresh garlic

¼ teaspoon coarsely ground black pepper

1 bay leaf

¼ teaspoon dried marjoram

¼ teaspoon dried thyme

NUTRITIONAL FACTS (PER SERVING)

Calories: 365	Fat: 6.2 g	Protein: 40 g
Cholesterol: 50 mg	Fiber: 3.3 g	Sodium: 567 mg

You Save: Calories: 191   Fat: 18.9 g

Monte Cristo Sandwiches

Yield: *4 servings*

12 slices Cobblestone Mill sourdough or Brownberry natural wheat bread

2 tablespoons Dijon mustard

4 slices (1 ounce each) Boar's Head lower sodium turkey breast

8 thin slices ($\frac{1}{2}$ ounce each) Sargento Light Swiss cheese

4 slices (1 ounce each) Boar's Head lower sodium ham

$\frac{1}{2}$ cup Scramblers egg substitute

$\frac{1}{4}$ cup skim milk

Pinch ground nutmeg

NUTRITIONAL FACTS
(PER SERVING)

Calories: 373	Fiber: 3.2 g
Chol: 38 mg	Protein: 33 g
Fat: 6.7 g	Sodium: 834 mg

You Save: Calories: 315   Fat: 30.4 g

1. To assemble the sandwiches, arrange 3 pieces of the bread on a flat surface, and spread each with $\frac{1}{2}$ teaspoon of the mustard. Place 1 slice of turkey and 1 slice of cheese over the mustard on one bread slice. Top with a second bread slice, mustard side up, and lay 1 slice of ham and 1 slice of cheese on the second bread slice. Top with the remaining bread slice, mustard side down. Repeat this procedure with the remaining ingredients to make 4 sandwiches.

2. Combine the egg substitute, milk, and nutmeg in a shallow dish, and stir to mix well. Dip both sides of each sandwich into the egg mixture.

3. Coat a large griddle or nonstick skillet with nonstick cooking spray, and preheat over medium heat until a drop of water sizzles when it hits the heated surface. Arrange the sandwiches on the griddle, and cook for $1\frac{1}{2}$ to 2 minutes on each side, or until golden brown.

4. Coat a baking sheet with nonstick cooking spray, and transfer the sandwiches to the sheet. Bake at 450°F for 5 to 7 minutes, or until the sandwiches are heated through and the cheese is melted. Cut each sandwich in half diagonally, and serve hot.

Grilled Hummus Pitawiches

1. Combine all of the filling ingredients in the bowl of a food processor, and process until smooth. Set aside.

2. Using a sharp knife or scissors, cut each pita round about two-thirds of the way around the edges. Carefully open the pita bread round, and spread $\frac{1}{4}$ cup of the filling over the bottom layer. Arrange first 3 spinach leaves, then 3 slices of tomato, and finally $\frac{1}{4}$ cup of cheese over the filling.

3. Coat a large nonstick griddle or skillet with nonstick olive oil cooking spray, and preheat over medium heat. Lay the sandwiches on the griddle, and cook for about 2 minutes on each side, or until the bread is lightly toasted, the filling is hot, and the cheese is melted.

4. Cut each sandwich into 4 wedges, and serve hot.

Yield: *6 servings*

6 Sahara whole wheat or oat bran pita pockets (6-inch rounds)

18 fresh spinach leaves

3 medium plum tomatoes, thinly sliced

1½ cups Healthy Choice fancy shredded fat-free mozzarella cheese

FILLING

1 can (1 pound) Garcia's garbanzo beans, rinsed and drained

½ cup sliced scallions

¼ cup finely chopped fresh parsley

¼ cup Dannon nonfat plain yogurt

1 tablespoon sesame tahini (sesame seed paste)

1½ teaspoons crushed fresh garlic

¼ teaspoon ground black pepper

NUTRITIONAL FACTS (PER SERVING)

Calories: 293	Fat: 4 g	Protein: 18 g
Cholesterol: 1 mg	Fiber: 7.4 g	Sodium: 552 mg

You Save: Calories: 121 Fat: 14.6 g

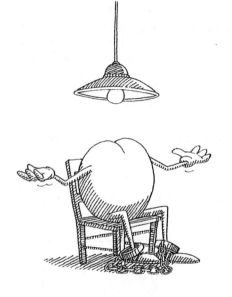

Crusty Calzones

Yield: *6 servings*

CRUST

1¾ cups bread flour

½ cup Quaker oat bran

2 tablespoons Weight Watchers grated nonfat Parmesan cheese

1½ teaspoons Fleischmann's Rapid Rise yeast

1 teaspoon sugar

¼ teaspoon salt

¾ cup plus 1 tablespoon water

FILLING

6 ounces Turkey Italian Sausage (page 182)

1 teaspoon crushed fresh garlic

1 small green bell pepper, cut into thin strips

1 small yellow onion, cut into thin wedges

4 ounces Polly-O Free natural nonfat mozzarella cheese, thinly sliced

DIPPING SAUCE

1¼ cups Enrico's all natural Italian style no salt added pasta sauce

---

NUTRITIONAL FACTS
(PER SERVING)

Calories: 254	Fiber: 3.8 g
Chol: 21 mg	Protein: 19 g
Fat: 2.3 g	Sodium: 382 mg

You Save: Calories: 182 Fat: 23.3 g

1. To make the crust, in a large bowl, combine 1 cup of the bread flour with all of the oat bran, Parmesan, yeast, sugar, and salt, and stir to mix well. Place the water in a small saucepan, and heat until very warm (125°F to 130°F). Add the water to the flour mixture, and stir for 1 minute. Stir in enough of the remaining flour, 2 tablespoons at a time, to form a stiff dough.

2. Sprinkle 2 tablespoons of the remaining flour over a flat surface, and turn the dough onto the surface. Knead the dough for 5 minutes, gradually adding enough of the remaining flour to form a smooth, satiny ball. Coat a large bowl with nonstick cooking spray, and place the dough in the bowl. Cover the bowl with a clean kitchen towel, and let rise in a warm place for about 35 minutes, or until doubled in size.

3. Coat a large nonstick skillet with nonstick cooking spray, and preheat over medium heat. Add the sausage, and cook, stirring to crumble, until the meat is no longer pink. (There will be no fat to drain off.) Transfer the sausage to a bowl, and set aside.

4. Place the same skillet over medium-high heat, and add the garlic, peppers, and onions. Stir-fry for about 3 minutes, or until the vegetables are crisp-tender. Remove the skillet from the heat, add the sausage, and toss to mix well. Set aside.

5. When the dough has risen, punch it down, divide it into 6 portions, and shape each portion into a ball. Using a rolling pin, roll each piece into a 6½-inch circle. Top the bottom half of each circle with ⅙ of the sausage mixture and ⅙ of the mozzarella, spreading the filling to within ½ inch of the edge. Brush a little water around the outer edges of each circle, fold the top half over the bottom half, and firmly press the edges together to seal.

6. Coat a baking sheet with nonstick cooking spray, and arrange the calzones on the sheet. Spray the tops of the calzones lightly with the cooking spray, and bake at 450°F for 10 minutes, or until lightly browned.

7. While the calzones are baking, place the pasta sauce in a small saucepan, and cook over medium heat until hot. Serve the hot calzones accompanied by a small dish of pasta sauce.

Time-Saving Tips

To make the dough for Crusty Calzones in a bread machine, place all of the dough ingredients, except for $\frac{1}{4}$ cup of the bread flour, in the machine's bread pan. (Do not heat the water.) Turn the machine to the "rise," "dough," "manual," or equivalent setting so that the machine will mix, knead, and let the dough rise once. Check the dough about 5 minutes after the machine has started. If it seems too sticky, add more of the remaining flour, a tablespoon at a time. When the dough is ready, remove it from the machine and proceed to shape, fill, and bake it as directed in the recipe.

As an alternative to making your crust from scratch, substitute 1 pound of Bridgeport Honey Wheat frozen bread dough for the home-made crust. (You'll find this product in the freezer section of the grocery store.) Simply thaw the dough, roll it out into circles, add the filling, and fold and bake as directed.

Tuna Cheddar Melts

1. Combine the tuna, celery, onion, mayonnaise, relish, and pepper in a small bowl, and stir to mix well. Set aside.

2. Toast the English muffins, and arrange on a baking sheet, split side up. Spread a fourth of the tuna mixture on each piece, and place under a preheated broiler for 2 to 3 minutes, or until the tuna mixture is hot. Top each sandwich with a fourth of the cheese, and broil for another minute or 2, or until the cheese is melted. Serve hot.

Yield: 4 servings

1 can (6 ounces) Chicken of the Sea low sodium chunk light tuna in spring water, drained

$\frac{1}{4}$ cup finely chopped celery

$\frac{1}{4}$ cup finely chopped onion

3 tablespoons Kraft Free mayonnaise

2 tablespoons sweet pickle relish

$\frac{1}{8}$ teaspoon ground black pepper

2 Matthew's all natural 100% whole wheat English muffins, split open

2 ounces Cracker Barrel $\frac{1}{3}$ Less Fat sharp Cheddar cheese, thinly sliced

NUTRITIONAL FACTS (PER SANDWICH)

Calories: 182	Fat: 3.9 g	Protein: 16.8 g
Cholesterol: 19 mg	Fiber: 3.4 g	Sodium: 399 mg

You Save: Calories: 119　Fat: 13.5 g

California Veggiewiches

Yield: *4 servings*

¼ cup Smart Beat nonfat mayonnaise

¼ cup Breakstone's Free nonfat sour cream

8 slices Arnold Honey Wheatberry bread, toasted if desired

8 thin slices tomato

24 fresh spinach leaves

½ cup coarsely shredded carrot

16 thin slices cucumber

4 ounces Lifetime fat-free process sharp Cheddar cheese, thinly sliced, or 4 slices (1 ounce each) Sargento Light Swiss cheese

8 thin rings green bell pepper

4 thin slices sweet onion, separated into rings

8 slices avocado, each ¼-inch thick

½ cup alfalfa or spicy sprouts

1. Combine the mayonnaise and sour cream in a small bowl, and stir to mix well.

2. Arrange the bread slices on a flat surface, and spread 1 tablespoon of the mayonnaise mixture on each slice of bread. On each of 4 of the slices, layer 2 tomato slices, 6 spinach leaves, 2 tablespoons of carrot, 4 cucumber slices, 1 ounce of cheese, 2 green pepper rings, and a fourth of the onion rings. Top with 2 slices of avocado and 2 tablespoons of sprouts.

3. Top each sandwich with another bread slice, and cut in half. Secure each half with a toothpick, and serve.

NUTRITIONAL FACTS (PER SERVING)

Calories: 316	Fat: 6.4 g	Protein: 16.4 g
Cholesterol: 5 mg	Fiber: 6.7 g	Sodium: 650 mg

You Save: Calories: 246 Fat: 27.5 g

Spinach and Bacon Quiche

1. Arrange the bacon slices in a large nonstick skillet, and cook for 2 minutes over medium heat. Turn and cook for 2 or 3 additional minutes, or until crisp and brown. Transfer the bacon to paper towels, and set aside to drain.

2. Place the same skillet over medium heat, and add the onion. Stir-fry for about 3 minutes, or until the onion is crisp-tender. Add a little water if the skillet becomes too dry. Add the spinach, and stir-fry for another minute or 2, or until the spinach is wilted. Remove the skillet from the heat, and set aside to cool slightly.

3. Combine the cheese, flour, and pepper in a large bowl, and toss to mix well. Add the egg substitute and evaporated milk, and stir to mix well. Stir in the spinach and onion. Crumble the bacon, and add to the egg mixture. Set aside.

4. Coat a 9-inch deep dish pie pan with nonstick cooking spray. Slice the unpeeled potatoes $\frac{1}{4}$-inch thick, and arrange the slices in a single layer over the bottom and sides of the pan to form a crust. Pour the egg mixture into the crust, and sprinkle with the Parmesan topping.

5. Bake uncovered at 375°F for 45 to 50 minutes, or until the top is golden brown and a sharp knife inserted in the center of the quiche comes out clean. Remove the dish from the oven, and let sit for 10 minutes before cutting into wedges and serving.

Yield: 6 servings

4 slices Butterball turkey bacon

$\frac{1}{2}$ cup chopped onion

2 cups (packed) chopped fresh spinach

1$\frac{1}{4}$ cups Polly-O Free natural shredded nonfat mozzarella cheese

1 tablespoon plus 1 teaspoon unbleached flour

$\frac{1}{8}$ teaspoon ground black pepper

1$\frac{1}{4}$ cups Better'n Eggs egg substitute

1 cup Carnation Lite evaporated skimmed milk

2 medium baking potatoes, scrubbed

1 tablespoon Kraft Free nonfat grated Parmesan topping

NUTRITIONAL FACTS (PER SERVING)

Calories: 173	Fat: 1.9 g	Protein: 18 g
Cholesterol: 11 mg	Fiber: 1.9 g	Sodium: 472 mg

You Save: Calories: 415 Fat: 43.1 g

Shrimp and Asparagus Quiche

Yield: *6 servings*

1 cup (about 5 ounces) diced cooked shrimp or crab meat

1 cup Healthy Choice fancy shredded fat-free mozzarella cheese, or shredded Jarlsberg Lite Swiss cheese

1 tablespoon unbleached flour

1 cup Egg Beaters egg substitute

1 cup Pet evaporated skimmed milk

1½ teaspoons Dijon mustard

12 fresh asparagus spears, each 4 inches long

1 tablespoon Weight Watchers grated nonfat Parmesan cheese

CRUST

1½ cups cooked brown rice

2 tablespoons Weight Watchers grated nonfat Parmesan cheese

1 tablespoon Egg Beaters egg substitute

1. To make the crust, combine the rice, Parmesan, and egg substitute in a medium-sized bowl, and stir to mix well. Coat a 9-inch deep dish pie pan with nonstick cooking spray, and place the mixture in the pan. Using the back of a spoon, pat the mixture over the bottom and sides of the pan, forming an even crust. Set aside.

2. In a large bowl, combine the shrimp or crab meat, mozzarella or Swiss cheese, and flour, and stir to mix well. Add the egg substitute, milk, and mustard, and stir to mix well. Pour the egg mixture into the crust.

3. Arrange the asparagus spears on top of the quiche like the spokes of a wheel, with the tips pointing outward. Sprinkle with the Parmesan.

4. Bake uncovered at 375°F for 50 minutes, or until the top is golden brown and a sharp knife inserted in the center of the quiche comes out clean. Remove the dish from the oven, and let sit for 10 minutes before cutting into wedges and serving.

NUTRITIONAL FACTS (PER SERVING)		
Calories: 188	Fat: 1.1 g	Protein: 23.5 g
Cholesterol: 60 mg	Fiber: 1.7 g	Sodium: 334 mg

You Save: Calories: 293 Fat: 35.5 g

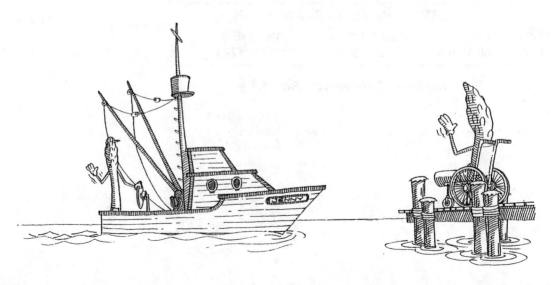

Chili-Cheese Quiche

1. To make the crust, combine the rice and egg substitute in a medium-sized bowl, and stir to mix well. Coat a 10-inch pie pan with nonstick cooking spray, and place the mixture in the pan. Using the back of a spoon, pat the mixture over the bottom and sides of the pan, forming an even crust. Set aside.

2. Cut the chilies open, lay them flat, and arrange half of them in a single layer over the rice crust. Sprinkle half of the cheese over the chilies. Arrange the remaining chilies over the cheese, and finish with a layer of the remaining cheese.

3. Combine the egg substitute, evaporated milk, flour, cumin, and pepper in a blender, and process until well mixed. Pour the egg mixture over the chili-cheese layers.

4. Bake uncovered at 375°F for 40 minutes, or until the top is golden brown and a sharp knife inserted in the center of the quiche comes out clean. Remove the dish from the oven, and let sit for 10 minutes before cutting into wedges and serving.

Yield: 6 servings

2 cans (4 ounces each) whole mild green chilies, drained

1 cup Sargento Light fancy shredded natural Cheddar cheese

1 cup Healthy Choice egg substitute

1 cup Pet evaporated skimmed milk

1 tablespoon unbleached flour

$\frac{1}{2}$ teaspoon ground cumin

$\frac{1}{8}$ teaspoon ground black pepper

CRUST

2 cups cooked brown rice

2 tablespoons Healthy Choice egg substitute

NUTRITIONAL FACTS (PER SERVING)

Calories: 186	Fat: 3.7 g	Protein: 15 g
Cholesterol: 8 mg	Fiber: 1.7 g	Sodium: 350 mg

You Save: Calories: 253 Fat: 31.7 g

FAT-FIGHTING TIP

Creamy Richness Without Cream

To make creamy quiches, casseroles, sauces, custards, puddings, and other dishes without the usual cream, simply replace this high-fat ingredient with an equal amount of evaporated skimmed milk. Or use 1 cup of regular skim milk plus $\frac{1}{3}$ cup of instant nonfat dry milk powder for each cup of cream. In many quiches and casseroles, you can also replace cream with nonfat or low-fat cottage cheese. For a firmer, richer texture, add a tablespoon of flour to the filling for each cup of cream substitute that you use.

Replacing just one cup of heavy cream with any of these healthful nonfat dairy products saves you over 600 calories and 88 grams of fat. As a bonus, the substitute ingredients add calcium and other essential nutrients to your dish.

Ham and Swiss Quiche

Yield: *6 servings*

1 cup shredded Jarlsberg Lite Swiss cheese

1 cup (about 5 ounces) diced Boar's Head lower sodium ham

3 tablespoons finely chopped onion

2 tablespoons finely chopped fresh parsley

1 tablespoon plus 1 teaspoon unbleached flour

⅛ teaspoon ground black pepper

Pinch ground nutmeg

1¼ cups Egg Beaters egg substitute

1 cup Sealtest Free nonfat cottage cheese

1 tablespoon Kraft Free nonfat grated Parmesan topping

CRUST

1½ cups cooked brown rice

2 tablespoons Kraft Free nonfat grated Parmesan topping

1 tablespoon Egg Beaters egg substitute

1. To make the crust, combine the rice, Parmesan topping, and egg substitute in a medium-sized bowl, and stir to mix well. Coat a 9-inch deep dish pie pan with nonstick cooking spray, and place the mixture in the pan. Using the back of a large spoon, pat the mixture over the bottom and sides of the pan, forming an even crust. Set aside.

2. In a large bowl, combine the Swiss cheese, ham, onion, parsley, flour, pepper, and nutmeg, and toss to mix well. Add the egg substitute and cottage cheese, and stir to mix well. Pour the egg mixture into the crust, and sprinkle with the Parmesan topping.

3. Bake uncovered at 375°F for 45 minutes, or until the top is golden brown and a sharp knife inserted in the center of the quiche comes out clean. Remove the dish from the oven, and let sit for 10 minutes before cutting into wedges and serving.

NUTRITIONAL FACTS (PER SERVING)

Calories: 187	Fat: 3.3 g	Protein: 22 g
Cholesterol: 23 mg	Fiber: 1.1 g	Sodium: 336 mg

You Save: Calories: 318   Fat: 34.6 g

Zucchini-Wild Rice Quiche

1. Coat a large nonstick skillet with nonstick cooking spray, and preheat over medium heat. Add the zucchini, red pepper, garlic, Italian seasoning, and black pepper. Cover, and, stirring occasionally, cook for about 5 minutes, or until the vegetables are crisp-tender. Add a little water if the skillet gets too dry. Remove the skillet from the heat, let the vegetables cool slightly, and drain off any liquid. Set aside.

2. To make the crust, combine the rice, Parmesan topping, and egg substitute in a medium-sized bowl, and stir to mix well. Coat a 9-inch deep dish pie pan with nonstick cooking spray, and place the mixture in the pan. Using the back of a spoon, pat the mixture over the bottom and sides of the pan, forming an even crust.

3. Add the mozzarella to the zucchini mixture, and toss to mix well. Spread the mixture evenly over the crust.

4. Combine the egg substitute, evaporated milk, and flour in a blender, and process until well mixed. Pour the egg mixture over the vegetables, and sprinkle with the Parmesan topping.

5. Bake uncovered at 375°F for 45 minutes, or until the top is golden brown and a sharp knife inserted in the center of the quiche comes out clean. Remove the dish from the oven, and let sit for 10 minutes before cutting into wedges and serving.

Yield: 6 servings

2 cups zucchini sliced ¼-inch thick (about 2 medium)

⅓ cup chopped red bell pepper

1 teaspoon crushed fresh garlic

1 teaspoon dried Italian seasoning

⅛ teaspoon ground black pepper

1 cup Polly-O Free natural shredded nonfat mozzarella cheese

1 cup Egg Beaters egg substitute

1 cup Carnation Lite evaporated skimmed milk

2 tablespoons unbleached flour

1 tablespoon Kraft Free nonfat grated Parmesan topping

CRUST

1½ cups cooked wild rice

2 tablespoons Kraft Free nonfat grated Parmesan topping

1 tablespoon Egg Beaters egg substitute

NUTRITIONAL FACTS (PER SERVING)

Calories: 149	Fat: 0.3 g	Protein: 17 g
Cholesterol: 7 mg	Fiber: 1.2 g	Sodium: 271 mg

You Save: Calories: 283 Fat: 35.4 g

Sicilian Mushroom and Onion Quiche

Yield: *6 servings*

1¾ cups sliced fresh mushrooms

1 medium yellow onion, sliced
into thin wedges

1 tablespoon water or chicken
broth

1 cup Sargento Light fancy
shredded natural mozzarella
cheese

1 tablespoon unbleached flour

¼ cup sliced black olives

1 cup Better'n Eggs egg substitute

1 cup Pet evaporated skimmed
milk

1 tablespoon Kraft Free nonfat
grated Parmesan topping

CRUST

1½ cups cooked orzo pasta
(about ½ cup dry)

2 tablespoons Kraft Free nonfat
grated Parmesan topping

1 tablespoon Better'n Eggs egg
substitute

1. Place the mushrooms, onion, and water or broth in a 1-quart pot. Cover the pot, and cook over medium heat, stirring occasionally, for about 5 minutes, or until the vegetables are tender. Remove the pot from the heat, drain off any excess liquid, and set aside to cool slightly.

2. To make the crust, combine the orzo, Parmesan topping, and egg substitute in a medium-sized bowl, and stir to mix well. Coat a 9-inch deep dish pie pan with nonstick cooking spray, and place the mixture in the pan. Using the back of a spoon, pat the mixture over the bottom and sides of the pan, forming an even crust. Set aside.

3. In a large bowl, combine the mozzarella and flour, and toss to mix well. Add the olives and the mushroom mixture, and toss to mix well. Add the egg substitute and evaporated milk, and stir to mix well. Spread the mixture evenly in the crust, and sprinkle with the Parmesan topping.

4. Bake uncovered at 375°F for 45 minutes, or until the top is golden brown and a sharp knife inserted in the center of the quiche comes out clean. Remove the dish from the oven, and let sit for 10 minutes before cutting into wedges and serving.

NUTRITIONAL FACTS (PER SERVING)

Calories: 193	Fat: 3 g	Protein: 17 g
Cholesterol: 10 mg	Fiber: 1.3 g	Sodium: 342 mg

You Save: Calories: 342 Fat: 38 g

3. Salads for All Seasons

Salads are among the most versatile of dishes. Depending on their ingredients, they can be light or substantial; sweet or savory; a protein-packed entrée, or a refreshing side dish. Because most salads can be made ahead of time, they are great for entertaining. And because they are portable, they are as much at home at picnics and pot-luck suppers as they are on your own dining room table.

If you're a fight-fighter, though, beware. Despite the salad's reputation for being a "diet food," many have no place in a low-fat menu. Take your typical chef's salad, for instance. A pile of greens topped with strips of full-fat cheese and meat, a hard-boiled egg, and 2 tablespoons of regular salad dressing can deliver as much as 650 calories and 50 grams of fat—and that's if you stop at just 2 tablespoons of dressing! And just a half-cup of a mayonnaise-dressed cole slaw, potato salad, or macaroni salad can provide 10 grams of fat.

Made properly, though, salads are just what the doctor ordered. Ingredients like nonfat and reduced-fat mayonnaise, oil-free salad dressings, nonfat sour cream, nonfat and reduced-fat cheeses, and ultra-lean lunchmeats make it possible to create a dazzling array of salads with little or no fat, and with much fewer calories than tradi-

tional versions. The recipes in this chapter combine these ingredients with crisp vegetables, ripe fruits, satisfying pastas, and nutritious whole grains to create a variety of fresh salads that will help you get your five-a-day of fruits and veggies in the most healthful and enjoyable way possible. Need a dressing to complement your low-fat salad? This chapter also presents a selection of healthful homemade dressings that won't blow either your fat or your sodium budget.

To help you make all the right choices when shopping for salad ingredients, this chapter presents a helpful Fat-Fighter's Guide to low- and no-fat dressings, mayonnaise, and condiments (page 52). Additionally, the guide on page 100 steers you toward the freshest, ripest produce available; the guide on page 140 provides great tips on buying lower-fat meats; and the guide on page 116 makes it a snap to choose low-fat cheeses and other dairy products.

So whether you're looking for a lighter way of dressing your tossed green salad, a creamy macaroni salad, or a temptingly sweet fruit salad, you need look no further. You'll find that any salad can be delicious, satisfying, and healthy once you know the secrets of low-fat cooking.

FAT-FIGHTER'S GUIDE TO
Mayonnaise, Salad Dressings, and Condiments

Ingredients like mayonnaise, salad dressings, ketchup and mustard, and other condiments play a multitude of culinary roles, from dressing and binding salad ingredients, to moistening sandwich fillings, to adding zip to vegetable casseroles. And these days, there are just as many low-fat and no-fat options as there are oily, fatty ones. Let's take a look at some of the many products that can help you fight fat as you boost flavor.

MAYONNAISE

Nonfat mayonnaise is highly recommended over regular mayonnaise, which provides 10 grams of fat per tablespoon. How can mayonnaise be made without all that oil? Manufacturers use more water and vegetable thickeners. Some widely available nonfat brands are Kraft Free, Miracle Whip Free, Smart Beat, and Weight Watchers Fat Free. In the low-fat category, you will find Hellmann's (Best Foods) Low Fat, with only 1 gram of fat per tablespoon, and Weight Watchers Light, with 2 grams of fat. A variety of reduced-fat brands are also available, with half to two thirds less fat and calories than regular mayonnaise. Look for brands like Hellmann's Light, Kraft Light, Miracle Whip Light, and Blue Plate Light.

SALAD DRESSINGS

Now made in a wide variety of flavors, fat-free dressings contain either no oil or so little oil that they have less than 0.5 gram of fat per tablespoon. Compare the no- and low-fat products to their full-fat counterparts, which provide 6 to 9 grams of fat per tablespoon, and your savings are clear. Use these dressings instead of oil-based brands to dress your favorite salads or as a delicious basting sauce for grilled foods. Look for nonfat brands like Good Seasons Fat Free, Hidden Valley Ranch Fat Free, Knott's Berry Farm Low Fat, Kraft Free, Marie's Fat Free, Pritikin, Marzetti's Fat Free, Seven Seas Free, Walden Farms Fat Free, and Wishbone Fat Free. Beware though—many fat-free dressings are quite high in sodium, so compare brands and flavors, and choose those that are on the lower end of the sodium range. Another option is to dress your salads only with flavored vinegars. Try raspberry, rice, balsamic, herb, and red wine vinegars. And keep in mind that most vinegars are salt-free as well as fat-free.

CONDIMENTS

Condiments like mustard, ketchup, barbecue sauce, horseradish, soy sauce, Worcestershire sauce, and pepper sauce can really perk up an otherwise-bland dish. And, generally speaking, these ingredients are fat-free. The bad news is that many are quite high in sodium.

In some cases, you will be able to find a lower-sodium version of your sauce. For instance, no-salt-added ketchups include Del Monte No Salt Added and Hunt's No Salt Added, while reduced-sodium products include Healthy Choice and Heinz Light Harvest. Low-sodium soy sauces include Kikkoman Lite, La Choy Lite, and Eden Reduced Sodium. When such alternatives are not available, limit the sodium content of your dish by avoiding the use of other salty ingredients.

Caesar Garden Salad

1. To make the croutons, combine the Butter Buds liquid or broth, Parmesan topping, garlic, and oregano in a small dish, and stir to mix well. Rub the mixture over the inside of a medium-sized bowl. Place the bread cubes in the bowl, and toss gently to coat the cubes with the garlic mixture.

2. Coat a baking sheet with nonstick cooking spray, and arrange the cubes in a single layer on the sheet. Bake at 350°F for 16 minutes, or until the croutons are lightly browned and crisp.

3. Turn the oven off, and let the croutons cool in the oven with the door ajar for 30 minutes. Store in an airtight container until ready to use.

4. Combine the lettuce, cucumber, and tomatoes in a large salad bowl, and toss to mix well.

5. To make the dressing, combine all of the dressing ingredients in a blender, and process for about 1 minute, or until smooth. Pour the dressing over the salad, and toss to mix well. Add the croutons and Parmesan topping, and toss once more. Serve immediately.

NUTRITIONAL FACTS (PER 2-CUP SERVING)

Calories: 126	Fat: 3.5 g	Protein: 8 g
Cholesterol: 11 mg	Fiber: 2.2 g	Sodium: 194 mg

You Save: Calories: 121 Fat: 15.9 g

Time-Saving Tip

Substitute 2 cups of ready-made croutons, such as Toastettes fat-free classic caesar croutons, for the homemade garlic croutons.

Yield: 6 servings

9 cups torn romaine lettuce

1 medium cucumber, peeled, halved, and sliced

9 cherry tomatoes, halved

¼ cup Kraft Free nonfat grated Parmesan topping

GARLIC CROUTONS

1 tablespoon Butter Buds liquid or chicken broth

1 tablespoon Kraft Free nonfat grated Parmesan topping

2 teaspoons crushed fresh garlic

¼ teaspoon dried oregano

2½ cups French bread cubes

DRESSING

½ cup Kraft Free nonfat grated Parmesan topping

¼ cup Healthy Choice egg substitute

1 tablespoon plus 1 teaspoon Da Vinci extra virgin olive oil

3 tablespoons white wine vinegar

1 tablespoon white wine Worcestershire sauce

2 tablespoons lemon juice

1 teaspoon crushed fresh garlic

Sesame Shrimp and Noodle Salad

Yield: *6 servings*

8 ounces Creamette fettuccine pasta

2 cups cooked shrimp (about 10 oz.)

1 medium red bell pepper, cut into thin strips

1 medium cucumber, peeled, seeded, and diced

4 scallions, thinly sliced

DRESSING

⅓ cup Kimono seasoned rice vinegar

2 tablespoons Eden reduced-sodium soy sauce

1 tablespoon sesame oil

1 teaspoon crushed fresh garlic

¼ teaspoon ground white pepper

¼ teaspoon ground ginger

For variety, substitute thin strips of cooked chicken breast for the shrimp.

1. Cook the fettuccine al dente according to package directions. Drain, rinse with cool water, and drain again.

2. Place the fettuccine in a large bowl. Add the shrimp and vegetables, and toss to mix.

3. Combine the dressing ingredients in a small bowl, and stir to mix well. Pour the dressing over the pasta mixture, and toss to mix well.

4. Cover the salad, and chill for several hours before serving.

NUTRITIONAL FACTS (PER 1⅓-CUP SERVING)

Calories: 219	Fat: 3.4 g	Protein: 15 g
Cholesterol: 92 mg	Fiber: 1.4 g	Sodium: 321 mg

You Save: Calories: 100   Fat: 11.4 g

FAT-FIGHTING TIP

Getting the Oil Out of Your Oil and Vinegar Dressings

Vinegar and oil dressings are often thought of as being the most "heart healthy" of dressings. While these dressings are low in saturated fat, they are quite high in total fat. In fact, most vinegar and oil dressings contain two parts oil to one part vinegar, which means that each tablespoon of dressing contains over 8 grams of fat!

The good news is that you can dramatically reduce the fat in these dressings and still enjoy a delicious, well-dressed salad. One way is to reverse the standard proportions of oil to vinegar by using two parts vinegar to one part oil. Or replace part of the oil with fruit juice, tomato juice, or lemon juice to add extra zip. To add even more flavor, increase the seasonings by 25 percent. Dressings made with less oil, more vinegar, and a generous sprinkling of herbs and spices are so flavorful that you can often *halve* the amount used to dress your salad.

Oriental Asparagus Salad

1. Rinse the asparagus under cool running water, and snap off the tough stem ends. Cut the spears into 1-inch pieces. Fill a 2-quart pot half-full with water, and bring to a boil over high heat. Add the aspargaus to the boiling water, and boil for about 30 seconds, or just until the asparagus pieces turn bright green and are crisp-tender.

2. Drain the asparagus, and plunge them into a large bowl of ice water to stop the cooking process. Drain once more, and transfer to a shallow dish.

3. Add the peppers and water chestnuts to the asparagus, and toss to mix.

4. Combine the dressing ingredients in a small bowl, and stir to mix well. Pour the dressing over the vegetable mixture, and toss to mix well.

5. Cover the salad, and chill for 8 hours or overnight, stirring every few hours, before serving.

Yield: *8 servings*

1¼ pounds fresh asparagus spears

1 medium red bell pepper, cut into matchstick-sized pieces

1 can La Choy sliced water chestnuts, drained

DRESSING

¼ cup Marukai seasoned rice vinegar

1 tablespoon La Choy Lite soy sauce

2 teaspoons sesame oil

½ teaspoon crushed fresh garlic

⅛ teaspoon ground ginger

NUTRITIONAL FACTS (PER ¾-CUP SERVING)

Calories: 42	Fat: 1.3 g	Protein: 1.8 g
Cholesterol: 0 mg	Fiber: 2 g	Sodium: 150 mg

You Save: Calories: 51 Fat: 5.7 g

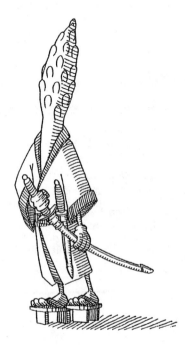

The Well-Dressed Salad

These days, there are nearly as many low-fat and nonfat dressings available as there are high-fat dressings. Still, many commercial brands contain far too much sodium—sometimes as much as 200 milligrams per tablespoon. Use a couple of tablespoons of one of these dressings on your salad, and you will really cut into your daily sodium budget. Make your own dressing, though, and the result will be low in sodium, low in fat, and high in the fresh-made flavor that only homemade dressings have. Here are some quick and easy ideas.

Creamy Mustard Dressing

Yield: 1½ cups

½ cup Hellmann's low-fat mayonnaise

½ cup Sealtest Free nonfat sour cream

¼ cup prepared mustard (yellow, Dijon, or spicy)

2–3 tablespoons honey

2 tablespoons skim milk

1. Combine the mayonnaise, sour cream, mustard, and honey in a small bowl, and stir to mix well. Add the milk, and stir to mix well.

2. Transfer the dressing to a covered container, and chill for several hours before serving.

NUTRITIONAL FACTS (PER TABLESPOON)

Calories: 20	Fat: 0.4 g	Protein: 0.4 g
Cholesterol: 0 mg	Fiber: 0 g	Sodium: 82 mg

You Save: Calories: 48 Fat: 6.8 g

Tex-Mex Salad Dressing

Yield: 1⅛ cups

⅓ cup Breakstone's Free nonfat sour cream

⅓ cup Smart Beat nonfat mayonnaise

½ cup Old El Paso thick and chunky salsa

1. Combine the sour cream and mayonnaise in a small bowl, and stir to mix well. Stir in the salsa.

2. Transfer the dressing to a covered container, and chill for several hours before serving.

NUTRITIONAL FACTS (PER TABLESPOON)

Calories: 10	Fat: 0 g	Protein: 0.1 g
Cholesterol: 0 mg	Fiber: 0 g	Sodium: 68 mg

You Save: Calories: 40 Fat: 5.1 g

Thick and Creamy Thousand Island Dressing

1. Combine the mayonnaise and sour cream in a small bowl, and stir to mix well. Add the chili sauce and relish, and stir to mix well.

2. Transfer the dressing to a covered container, and chill for several hours before serving.

Yield: 1²/₃ cups

¾ cup Weight Watchers fat-free mayonnaise

½ cup Land O Lakes no-fat sour cream

¼ cup chili sauce

2 tablespoons sweet pickle relish

NUTRITIONAL FACTS (PER TABLESPOON)

Calories: 13	Fat: 0.1 g	Protein: 0.2 g
Cholesterol: 0 mg	Fiber: 0 g	Sodium: 96 mg

You Save: Calories: 52 Fat: 6.4 g

Tangy Tomato Dressing

1. Combine all of the ingredients in a blender, and process for 1 minute, or until the mixture is smooth and well mixed.

2. Transfer the dressing to a covered container, and chill for several hours before serving.

Yield: 2 cups

1 can (10¾ ounces) Campbell's Healthy Request condensed tomato soup, undiluted

¼ cup plus 3 tablespoons white wine vinegar

2 tablespoons honey

2 tablespoons Pompeian extra virgin olive oil (optional)

2 teaspoons ground paprika

1 teaspoon dry mustard

¼ teaspoon ground black pepper

½ cup chopped onion

3 cloves garlic

1 tablespoon finely chopped fresh thyme, or 1 teaspoon dried

NUTRITIONAL FACTS (PER TABLESPOON)

Calories: 12	Fat: 0.1 g	Protein: 0.2 g
Cholesterol: 0 mg	Fiber: 0.1 g	Sodium: 35 mg

You Save: Calories: 55 Fat: 6.3 g

Creamy Coleslaw

Yield: *8 servings*

6 cups coarsely shredded cabbage

1 cup shredded carrot

1 medium green bell pepper, cut into very thin strips

DRESSING

¾ cup Hellmann's low-fat mayonnaise

3 tablespoons distilled white vinegar

2 tablespoons sugar

1 tablespoon Dijon mustard

¼ teaspoon celery seed

⅛ teaspoon ground white pepper

1. Combine the cabbage, carrots, and peppers in a large bowl, and toss to mix well.

2. Combine the dressing ingredients in a small bowl, and stir to mix well. Pour the dressing over the cabbage mixture, and toss to mix well.

3. Cover the salad, and chill for 8 hours or overnight before serving.

NUTRITIONAL FACTS (PER ⅔-CUP SERVING)

Calories: 56	Fat: 1.4 g	Protein: 0.8 g
Cholesterol: 0 mg	Fiber: 1.2 g	Sodium: 199 mg

You Save: Calories: 89 Fat: 12 g

Old-Fashioned Macaroni Salad

Yield: *8 servings*

8 oz. Creamette elbow macaroni

¼ cup sliced black olives

¼ cup thinly sliced celery

¼ cup finely chopped red bell pepper or shredded carrot

¼ cup chopped onion

1 tablespoon minced fresh chives or dill, or 1 teaspoon dried

DRESSING

½ cup Kraft Free mayonnaise

¼ cup Land O Lakes no-fat sour cream

1 tablespoon spicy mustard

⅛ teaspoon ground black pepper

1. Cook the macaroni al dente according to package directions. Drain, rinse with cool water, and drain again.

2. Place the macaroni in a large bowl. Add the olives, celery, peppers or carrots, onion, and chives or dill, and toss to mix.

3. Combine the dressing ingredients in a small bowl, and stir to mix well. Pour the dressing over the macaroni mixture, and toss to mix well.

4. Cover the salad, and chill for several hours before serving.

NUTRITIONAL FACTS (PER ⅔-CUP SERVING)

Calories: 130	Fat: 0.8 g	Protein: 4.1 g
Cholesterol: 0 mg	Fiber: 1 g	Sodium: 177 mg

You Save: Calories: 131 Fat: 16.5 g

Zesty German Potato Salad

1. Combine $\frac{1}{4}$ cup of the broth with the flour, mustard, and pepper in a small jar with a tight-fitting lid. Shake until smooth, and set aside.

2. Halve the unpeeled potatoes lengthwise, and then slice $\frac{1}{4}$-inch thick. Measure the potatoes. There should be 5 cups. (Adjust the amount if necessary.)

3. Place the potatoes in a 4-quart pot, and barely cover with water. Add the salt, and bring the potatoes to a boil over high heat. Reduce the heat to medium, and boil for 8 to 10 minutes, or until tender. Drain the potatoes, and return them to the pot. Set aside.

4. While the potatoes are cooking, place the bacon in a large skillet, and cook over medium heat for about 2 minutes on each side, or until crisp and brown. Remove the bacon, drain on paper towels, crumble, and set aside.

5. Add the celery and onion to the skillet, and stir-fry for about 2 minutes, or until crisp-tender. Add the vinegar, sugar, and remaining 2 tablespoons of chicken broth to the skillet, and bring to a boil, stirring frequently to dissolve the sugar. Reduce the heat to low.

6. Shake the flour mixture, and add it to the skillet. Cook, stirring constantly, until the mixture starts to boil and thickens slightly.

7. Add the potatoes to the skillet, and toss gently to coat with the dressing. Remove the skillet from the heat, and toss in the bacon and parsley. Serve warm or at room temperature.

Yield: 8 servings

$\frac{1}{4}$ cup plus 2 tablespoons Swanson Natural Goodness chicken broth, divided

1 tablespoon plus 1 teaspoon unbleached flour

$\frac{3}{4}$ teaspoon dry mustard

$\frac{1}{8}$ teaspoon ground black pepper

1 $\frac{1}{4}$ pounds potatoes, scrubbed

$\frac{1}{4}$ teaspoon salt

4 slices Louis Rich turkey bacon

$\frac{1}{2}$ cup sliced celery

$\frac{1}{2}$ cup chopped onion

$\frac{1}{3}$ cup apple cider vinegar

2 tablespoons sugar

1 tablespoon minced fresh parsley

NUTRITIONAL FACTS
(PER $\frac{2}{3}$-CUP SERVING)

Calories: 116	Fiber: 2 g
Chol: 5 mg	Protein: 3 g
Fat: 1.4 g	Sodium: 218 mg

You Save: Calories: 70 Fat: 8 g

Pasta Salad Niçoise

Yield: *5 servings*

8 ounces Ronzoni mostaccioli rigati, or another tube-shaped pasta

1½ cups young tender fresh green beans

1 can (9 ounces) StarKist solid white tuna in spring water, drained

¾ cup chopped frozen (thawed) or canned (drained) artichoke hearts

¾ cup matchstick-sized pieces of red bell pepper

½ cup diced red onion

⅓ cup sliced black olives

2 tablespoons finely chopped fresh lemon thyme, or 2 teaspoons dried thyme

DRESSING

½ cup Hidden Valley Ranch fat-free Italian Parmesan salad dressing

1 tablespoon Dijon mustard

¾ teaspoon crushed fresh garlic

1. Cook the pasta until almost al dente according to package directions. Two minutes before the pasta is done, add the green beans, and cook until the beans are crisp-tender and the pasta is al dente. Drain well, rinse with cool water, and drain again. Return the pasta and green beans to the pot.

2. Add the tuna, artichoke hearts, red pepper, onion, olives, and thyme to the pasta mixture, and toss gently to mix well.

3. Combine the dressing ingredients in a small bowl, and stir to mix well. Pour the dressing over the pasta mixture, and toss gently to mix.

4. Transfer the salad to a covered container, and chill for at least 2 hours before serving.

NUTRITIONAL FACTS (PER 1¾-CUP SERVING)

Calories: 284	Fat: 2.5 g	Protein: 19.6 g
Cholesterol: 14 mg	Fiber: 4.5 g	Sodium: 543 mg

You Save: Calories: 149   Fat: 16.9 g

Tuscan Lentil Salad

1. Place the lentils and the water in a 1½-quart pot, and bring to a boil over high heat. Reduce the heat to low, cover, and simmer for 20 to 25 minutes, or until the lentils are tender. Remove the pot from the heat, and set aside to cool to room temperature.

2. While the lentils are cooking, place the whole red pepper on a small baking sheet, and position the sheet about 2 inches below a preheated broiler. Broil the pepper for 15 to 20 minutes, turning every 3 to 5 minutes, or until the skin is blistered and charred. Transfer the pepper to a bowl, cover the bowl with a lid or plastic wrap, and let stand until cool enough to handle. Peel the charred skin off the pepper (it will slip off easily), cut off the top, and remove and discard the seeds. Dice the remaining pepper, and set aside.

3. Drain any excess water from the cooled lentils, and place them in a large bowl. Add the corn, artichoke hearts, onion, and red pepper, and toss to mix.

4. Combine the dressing ingredients in a small bowl, and stir to mix well. Pour the dressing over the lentil mixture, and toss to mix well.

5. Cover the salad, and chill for several hours or overnight before serving.

Yield: 8 servings

¾ cup dried brown lentils, cleaned (page 130)

2 cups water

1 large red bell pepper

2 cups frozen (thawed) whole kernel corn

1 cup chopped frozen (thawed) or canned (drained) artichoke hearts

¼ cup chopped onion

DRESSING

⅓ cup Kraft Free or Marie's Zesty Fat Free red wine vinegar salad dressing

2 teaspoons Dijon mustard

1 teaspoon dried oregano

NUTRITIONAL FACTS (PER ¾-CUP SERVING)

Calories: 114	Fat: 0.4 g	Protein: 7.1 g
Cholesterol: 0 mg	Fiber: 4.5 g	Sodium: 111 mg

You Save: Calories: 72   Fat: 8.9 g

Seashell Seafood Salad

Yield: *6 servings*

12 oz. Mueller's seashell pasta or De Bole's whole wheat seashell pasta

2 cups (about 10 oz.) cooked lump crab meat, lobster, or shrimp

1 cup frozen (thawed) green peas

½ cup chopped red bell pepper

⅓ cup chopped onion

DRESSING

⅔ cup Kraft Free mayonnaise

⅓ cup Breakstone's Free nonfat sour cream

1 tablespoon plus 1 teaspoon lemon juice

1 tablespoon minced fresh dill

1. Cook the pasta al dente according to package directions. Drain, rinse with cool water, and drain again.

2. Place the pasta in a large bowl. Add the seafood and vegetables, and toss to mix.

3. Combine the dressing ingredients in a small bowl, and stir to mix well. Pour the dressing over the pasta mixture, and toss to mix well.

4. Cover the salad, and chill for several hours before serving.

NUTRITIONAL FACTS (PER 1½-CUP SERVING)		
Calories: 310	Fat: 1.5 g	Protein: 17 g
Cholesterol: 30 mg	Fiber: 2.8 g	Sodium: 382 mg

You Save: Calories: 198   Fat: 24.8 g

Spruced-Up Spinach Salad

Yield: *6 servings*

9 cups fresh spinach leaves

2 cups sliced fresh mushrooms

1 small red bell pepper, sliced into thin strips

3 thin slices sweet onion, separated into rings

¾ cup Healthy Choice fancy shredded fat-free Cheddar cheese

6 slices Butterball turkey bacon, cooked, drained, and crumbled

¾ cup Tangy Tomato Dressing (page 57)

1. Arrange the spinach in a large salad bowl. Top with the mushrooms, peppers, onions, cheese, and bacon.

2. Serve immediately on individual serving plates, topping each serving with a few spoonsfuls of Tangy Tomato Dressing.

NUTRITIONAL FACTS (PER 2-CUP SERVING)		
Calories: 102	Fat: 3.1 g	Protein: 9.7 g
Cholesterol: 12 mg	Fiber: 2.9 g	Sodium: 405 mg

You Save: Calories: 154   Fat: 17.9 g

Pacific Chicken Salad

1. Combine the rice, chicken or turkey, pineapple, water chestnuts, and celery in a large bowl, and toss to mix well.

2. Combine the dressing ingredients in a small bowl, and stir to mix well. Pour the dressing over the rice mixture, and toss to mix.

3. Cover the salad, and chill for several hours before serving.

NUTRITIONAL FACTS (PER 1⅓-CUP SERVING)

Calories: 239	Fat: 1.9 g	Protein: 17.4 g
Cholesterol: 36 mg	Fiber: 3.5 g	Sodium: 213 mg

You Save: Calories: 152 Fat: 18.4 g

Yield: 6 servings

3 cups cooked Mahatma brown rice

2 cups diced cooked chicken or turkey breast (about 10 ounces)

2 cups diced fresh pineapple, or 1 can (20 ounces) Dole unsweetened pineapple chunks, drained

1 can (8 ounces) La Choy sliced water chestnuts, drained

¾ cup celery cut into matchstick-sized pieces

DRESSING

½ cup Kraft Free mayonnaise

2 tablespoons mango chutney

1 teaspoon curry powder

¼ teaspoon ground white pepper

¼ teaspoon ground ginger

Terrific Taco Salad

Yield: *6 servings*

6 Buena Vida fat-free flour or
   corn tortillas or other fat-free
   tortillas (8-inch rounds)

9 cups shredded romaine lettuce

TACO FILLING

1 pound 95% lean ground beef

1/3 cup chopped onion

1 tablespoon chili powder

1/2 cup Louise's salsa

GARNISH

2 medium tomatoes, diced

1 cup Kraft Free fat-free shredded
   Cheddar cheese

3/4 cup Sealtest Free nonfat sour
   cream

NUTRITIONAL FACTS
(PER SERVING)

Calories: 306   Fiber: 3.3 g
Chol: 57 mg   Protein: 28 g
Fat: 4.3 g   Sodium: 623 mg

You Save: Calories: 388 Fat: 49 g

1. To make the shells, brush both sides of each flour tortilla with water. (If using corn tortillas, immerse each tortilla in very warm water for about 3 seconds to soften.)

2. Invert six 6-ounce custard cups on a large baking sheet, and coat the bottom of each cup with nonstick cooking spray. Place each tortilla over a cup, allowing the sides of the tortilla to drape down over the sides of the inverted cup. (Note that the tortilla will not drape enough to touch the sides of the cup, but will bend just enough to form a basket for the salad.) Bake at 350°F for 10 to 12 minutes, or until the tortillas are crisp and the edges are lightly browned.

3. Remove the pan from the oven, and let the shells cool to room temperature. Remove the shells from the custard cups, and transfer each one to an individual serving plate.

4. To make the taco filling, coat a large nonstick skillet with nonstick cooking spray, and preheat over medium-high heat. Add the ground beef, and cook, stirring to crumble, until the meat is no longer pink.

5. Add the onion, chili powder, and salsa to the beef, and stir to mix well. Reduce the heat to low, cover the skillet, and cook for 5 minutes, or until the onions are tender and the flavors are blended. Remove the skillet from the heat.

6. To assemble the salads, arrange 1½ cups of the lettuce over the bottom of each tortilla shell, and top with a sixth of the meat mixture. Garnish with the tomatoes, cheese, and sour cream, and serve immediately, accompanying the salad with Tex-Mex Salad Dressing (page 56) if desired.

Fiesta Layered Salad

1. Combine the sour cream and mayonnaise in a small bowl. Stir to mix well, and set aside.

2. Place the lettuce in a 3-quart glass serving bowl. Arrange the kidney beans in a layer over the lettuce, followed by layers of cheese, green pepper, onions, tomatoes, and avocados. Spread the sour cream mixture over the avocado layer, and garnish with a sprinkling of cheese and olives.

3. Serve immediately, or cover the salad and chill for up to 3 hours. To serve, dip a serving spoon down through all of the layers so that each serving includes some of each ingredient.

NUTRITIONAL FACTS (PER 1½-CUP SERVING)		
Calories: 166	Fat: 3.5 g	Protein: 11 g
Cholesterol: 4 mg	Fiber: 5.2 g	Sodium: 413 mg

You Save: Calories: 101 Fat: 11.7 g

Yield: *8 servings*

¾ cup Sealtest Free nonfat sour cream

¾ cup Kraft Free mayonnaise

8 cups torn romaine lettuce

1 can (1 pound) Joan of Arc red kidney beans, rinsed and drained

1 cup Healthy Choice fancy shredded fat-free Cheddar cheese

1 cup chopped green bell pepper

½ medium sweet onion, thinly sliced

1 cup diced plum tomato

1 cup diced avocado

GARNISH

¼ cup Healthy Choice fancy shredded fat-free Cheddar cheese

¼ cup sliced black olives

Refreshing Fruit Salad

Yield: 10 servings

2 cups sliced bananas (about 2 large)

2 cups diced fresh pineapple (about ½ large)

2 cups sliced fresh strawberries

3 kiwis, peeled and cut into chunks

DRESSING

1 block (8 ounces) Philadelphia Free nonfat cream cheese, softened to room temperature

3 tablespoons honey

3 tablespoons skim milk

1 tablespoon poppy seeds

1. To make the dressing, place the cream cheese and honey in the bowl of an electric mixer, and beat until smooth. Beat in the milk, and stir in the poppy seeds. Set aside.

2. Combine the fruits in a large bowl, and toss to mix well. To assemble the salads, place ¾ cup of fruit in each of 10 serving bowls, and top with 2 tablespoons of the dressing. Serve immediately.

NUTRITIONAL FACTS (PER ¾-CUP SERVING)

Calories: 112	Fat: 0.9 g	Protein: 4.2 g
Cholesterol: 1 mg	Fiber: 2.3 g	Sodium: 112 mg

You Save: Calories: 60 Fat: 8.1 g

Blueberry-Banana Salad

Yield: 6 servings

2 cups sliced bananas (about 2 large)

1 cup fresh blueberries

½ cup miniature marshmallows

2 tablespoons shredded sweetened coconut

½ cup Land O Lakes no-fat sour cream

1 can (10 ounces) mandarin oranges, well drained

1. In a medium-sized bowl, combine the bananas, blueberries, marshmallows, and coconut, tossing to mix. Add the sour cream to the fruit mixture, and toss to mix. Add the oranges, and toss gently.

2. Cover the salad, and chill for 1 to 3 hours before serving.

NUTRITIONAL FACTS (PER ¾-CUP SERVING)

Calories: 116	Fat: 0.9 g	Protein: 1.7 g
Cholesterol: 1 mg	Fiber: 1.9 g	Sodium: 33 mg

You Save: Calories: 30 Fat: 4.5 g

Shamrock Fruit Salad

1. Drain the pineapple, pouring the juice into a 1-cup measure. Add enough water to bring the volume up to ¾ cup. Set aside.

2. Place the gelatin in a large heat-proof bowl, and add the boiling water. Stir until the gelatin is dissolved. Add ½ cup of the reserved pineapple juice, and stir to mix well. Place the bowl in the refrigerator, and chill for about 30 minutes, or until the gelatin is the consistency of raw egg whites.

3. While the gelatin is chilling, place the cream cheese in a medium-sized bowl, and beat with an electric mixer until smooth. Beat in the remaining ¼ cup of pineapple juice, and set aside.

4. When the gelatin reaches the proper consistency, beat with an electric mixer for about 1 minute, or until foamy. Add the cream cheese mixture, and beat until smooth. Gently fold in first the Cool Whip, and then the drained pineapple, mandarin oranges, and, if desired, the pecans.

5. Pour the mixture into an 8-inch square pan, and chill for 8 hours, or until firm. Cut into squares to serve.

Yield: *9 servings*

2 cans (8 ounces each) Dole unsweetened crushed pineapple in juice, undrained

1 package (4-serving size) Jell-O sugar-free or regular lime gelatin

½ cup boiling water

1 block (8 ounces) Healthy Choice fat-free cream cheese, softened

1 cup Cool Whip Lite

1 can (10 ounces) mandarin oranges, well drained

⅓ cup chopped pecans (optional)

NUTRITIONAL FACTS (PER ¾-CUP SERVING)

Calories: 73	Fiber: 0.5 g
Chol: 2 mg	Protein: 3.9 g
Fat: 0.9 g	Sodium: 126 mg

You Save: Calories: 145 Fat: 17.9 g

FAT-FIGHTING TIP

Creamy Lightness With Less Whipped Cream

Most creamy gelatin salads and mousses get their lightness—and much of their fat—from whipped cream. But you can have the same light and creamy texture with far less fat if you whip the gelatin, as is done in Shamrock Fruit Salad. Whipping gelatin incorporates air into the mixture, making it light and fluffy, and reducing the need for ingredients like fatty whipped cream. For gelatin salads, whip for just a minute or 2, or until foamy. For light-as-air mousses, whip for about 4 minutes, or until the gelatin has the consistency of soft whipped cream. Then, to eliminate even more fat, replace the whipped cream with one-half to two-thirds as much light whipped topping.

4. Sensational Soups

Hearty and satisfying, soup is one of the original comfort foods. And few foods can match the versatility of soup. Although often thought of as a seasonal dish, soup is perfect year round, whether served as a first course, paired with a salad at lunch time, or presented as a main dish.

Unfortunately, while some soups have always been low in fat, many popular varieties—New England Clam Chowder, for instance—are usually loaded with fat. Yet another problem is that canned soups, while convenient and tasty, often have staggering sodium counts. In some cases, a single bowlful can provide more than 1,000 milligrams of sodium! The good news is that once you learn a few salt- and fat-fighting strategies, and become familiar with the many healthful products now available, you can make hearty homemade soups with little or no fat, and with a lot less salt than that found in most store-bought brews.

The recipes in this chapter start out with wholesome ingredients like beans, vegetables, grains, and pasta. Then fat is kept to a minimum by substituting ultra-lean meats for fatty hams, sausages, and other meats. The oil normally used for sautéing vegetables is also eliminated or greatly reduced, and when a creamy consistency is desired, no- and low-fat dairy products, as well as puréed vegetables, are used in lieu of full-fat cheeses and heavy cream. Finally, salt is kept to a minimum through a wise use of spices and a careful selection of low-salt products.

Will your low-salt, low-fat soups taste flat? Absolutely not! Vegetables like celery, onion, and mushrooms; herbs like sage, thyme, and cumin; a clove or two of fresh garlic; a pinch of pepper; a splash of lemon juice; and other flavorful ingredients will make your soups so savory that no one will miss the salt and fat.

To help you choose the most healthful ingredients for your homemade soups, this chapter includes a terrific Fat-Fighter's Guide to canned foods (page 70), which steers you toward the best low-fat and low-salt canned vegetables available at your local supermarket, as well as to other canned goods that are great not just in soup making, but in many kinds of cooking. And for those days when cooking time is limited to the five minutes it takes to open a can and microwave its contents, the Fat-Fighter's Guide on page 82 clues you in to the most nutritious canned and dry soups. Additionally, the Fat-Fighter's Guide on page 140 provides great tips on buying lean meats that can add flavor to your soups without adding an unhealthy dose of fat.

Whether you are looking for a hearty bean soup, a golden chicken soup, or a creamy clam chowder, this chapter provides a recipe that will meet your needs with great taste *and* great nutrition. You'll even find tips for reducing the fat and salt in your own treasured recipes. So get out your kettle, and get ready to enjoy a sensational bowl of slimming, satisfying soup.

FAT-FIGHTER'S GUIDE TO
Canned Goods

No one can dispute the convenience of canned foods. It is true that canned foods tend to be very salty. In fact, a one-pound can of vegetables often contains up to a teaspoon of salt—nearly a full-day's allowance of sodium. But many manufacturers are now producing reduced-salt and unsalted products that work beautifully in a healthy low-fat, low-sodium diet.

How do canned foods compare with fresh nutritionally? In general, fresh and frozen foods retain more nutritional value than do canned foods. The reason? The heating process required for canning foods destroys some nutrients, including vitamin C and the B vitamin folate. In addition, minerals like potassium and the B vitamins leach into the canning liquid. If you pour off the canning liquid in an effort to reduce the salt, you will also lose some of these nutrients.

However, it may surprise you to learn that canned foods are sometimes *more* nutritious than fresh. How can this be? Properly canned foods are picked at their peak of ripeness and then quickly processed. Produce that is destined to be sold fresh, however, is often picked slightly underripe, transported across the country, and then left to sit in storage for as much as several days before being purchased. Once you get the food home, it may then sit in the refrigerator for several days more before you eat it. If this is the case, you could be better off with a canned product—although frozen produce would be an even better choice.

Which canned foods should you keep in stock? Unsalted canned tomato products—like Hunt's No Salt Added tomatoes, tomato sauce, and tomato paste; Eden crushed tomatoes and tomato sauce; Cento crushed tomatoes; and Del Monte No Salt Added stewed tomatoes—are excellent choices for your pantry. Progresso Recipe Ready crushed tomatoes with added purée is another handy ingredient that contains far less sodium than most brands of canned tomatoes. Use these products in your soups, chilies, pasta sauces, and countless other dishes.

Canned beans are another good item to have on hand. Full of fiber and nutrients, canned garbanzos, kidney beans, black beans, and the many other varieties now available make wonderful additions to soups, salads, and casseroles. If you drain and rinse the beans before adding them to your recipe, you will reduce the sodium by about 40 percent. Or try Eden canned beans, which are grown organically and processed without salt.

Another must for your low-fat pantry is evaporated skimmed milk, which is a wonderfully versatile ingredient that can be substituted for cream in many dishes. Try brands like Carnation Lite and Pet, which are both widely available. Fruits packed in juice, such as Libby's Lite and Del Monte Lite; unsweetened applesauce; and crushed pineapple in juice, are also good choices for snacking or for use in any number of recipes. Light (reduced-sugar) pie fillings—like Comstock Light and Lucky Leaf Lite—are also nice to keep on hand. These products make a tasty topping for waffles or pancakes, and contain a lot less sugar than syrup. Other worthwhile pantry staples include water-packed canned tuna, chicken, and turkey. And of course, canned low-fat soups and pasta sauces (see the Fat-Fighter's Guides on pages 82 and 168) enable the fat-fighting cook to prepare tasty, nutritious meals in a matter of minutes.

Mama Mia Minestrone

1. Place the olive oil in a 4-quart pot, and preheat over medium-high heat. Add the garlic, onion, and celery, and stir-fry for about 3 minutes, or until the vegetables are crisp-tender.

2. Add the water or broth, undrained tomatoes, carrots, cabbage, Italian seasoning, bouillon granules, and pepper to the pot, and bring to a boil. Stir the mixture, reduce the heat to low, cover, and simmer for 12 minutes, or until the vegetables are barely tender.

3. Add the zucchini, macaroni, and beans to the pot, and bring to a boil over high heat. Reduce the heat to low, cover, and simmer for about 8 minutes, or until the macaroni is al dente. (Be careful not to overcook, as the pasta will continue to soften in the hot soup.)

4. Remove the pot from the heat, and stir in the parsley. Ladle the soup into individual serving bowls, and serve hot, topping each serving with a rounded teaspoon of the Parmesan topping.

NUTRITIONAL FACTS (PER 1-CUP SERVING)

Calories: 117	Fat: 1.9 g	Protein: 6.2 g
Cholesterol: 2 mg	Fiber: 4.4 g	Sodium: 273 mg

You Save: Calories: 49 Fat: 5.8 g

Yield: 10 servings

1 tablespoon Bella extra virgin olive oil

2 teaspoons crushed fresh garlic

1 medium Spanish onion, chopped

$\frac{1}{2}$ cup thinly sliced celery (include leaves)

4 cups water or Health Valley no salt added beef broth

1 can (14$\frac{1}{2}$ ounces) Hunt's no salt added tomatoes, crushed

2 medium carrots, peeled, halved lengthwise, and sliced $\frac{1}{4}$ inch thick

2 cups coarsely shredded cabbage

2$\frac{1}{2}$ teaspoons dried Italian seasoning

2$\frac{1}{2}$ teaspoons Maggi instant beef bouillon granules

$\frac{1}{4}$ teaspoon ground black pepper

2 medium zucchini, quartered lengthwise and sliced $\frac{1}{4}$ inch thick

4 ounces De Bole's whole wheat elbow macaroni

1 can (1 pound) La Russa cannellini or navy beans, rinsed and drained

3 tablespoons finely chopped fresh parsley

$\frac{1}{3}$ cup Kraft Free nonfat grated Parmesan topping

Savory Italian Sausage Soup

Yield: *11 servings*

¾ pound Turkey Italian Sausage (page 182)

1 can (14½ ounces) Hunt's no salt added tomatoes, crushed

1 can (1 pound) Eden garbanzo beans

2¼ cups water

2 cans (14½ ounces each) Swanson Natural Goodness chicken broth

1 medium onion, chopped

1 cup sliced fresh mushrooms

1 large carrot, peeled, halved lengthwise, and sliced

1 teaspoon dried oregano

1 teaspoon crushed fresh garlic

¼ teaspoon ground black pepper

1½ medium zucchini, halved lengthwise and sliced

6 ounces Pritikin tri-color rotini pasta

⅓ cup Kraft Free nonfat grated Parmesan topping (optional)

1. Coat a 4-quart pot with nonstick cooking spray, and preheat over medium heat. Add the sausage, and cook, stirring to crumble, until the meat is no longer pink inside. (There should be no fat to drain.)

2. Add the remaining ingredients except for the zucchini, pasta, and cheese topping to the pot, and bring to a boil over high heat. Reduce the heat to low, cover, and simmer for 20 minutes, or until the vegetables are tender.

3. Add the zucchini and pasta to the pot, and bring to a boil. Reduce the heat to low, cover, and simmer for 10 minutes, or until the pasta is tender. (Be careful not to overcook, as the pasta will continue to soften in the hot soup.)

4. Ladle the soup into individual serving bowls, and serve hot, topping each bowl with a rounded teaspoon of the Parmesan topping if desired.

NUTRITIONAL FACTS (PER 1-CUP SERVING)		
Calories: 139	Fat: 1.9 g	Protein: 12 g
Cholesterol: 19 mg	Fiber: 3.9 g	Sodium: 371 mg

You Save: Calories: 64 Fat: 7.1 g

Beef and Barley Soup

1. Coat a 2½-quart pot with nonstick cooking spray, and preheat over medium heat. Add the ground meat, and cook, stirring to crumble, until the meat is no longer pink.

2. Add the remaining ingredients except for the barley to the pot, and bring to boil over high heat. Reduce the heat to low, cover, and simmer for 20 minutes, or until the vegetables are tender.

3. Add the barley, and bring to boil over high heat. Reduce heat to low, cover, and simmer for 10 minutes, or until the barley is tender.

4. Ladle the soup into individual serving bowls, and serve hot.

Yield: *6 servings*

8 ounces coarsely ground top beef round

1 can (10½ ounces) Campbell's condensed beef broth

3 cups water

2 cups sliced fresh mushrooms

1 medium yellow onion, chopped

⅔ cup thinly sliced celery

½ teaspoon crushed dried thyme or marjoram

1 bay leaf

¼ teaspoon coarsely ground black pepper

¾ cup Mother's quick-cooking barley

NUTRITIONAL FACTS (PER 1-CUP SERVING)

Calories: 140	Fat: 2.4 g	Protein: 13 g
Cholesterol: 26 mg	Fiber: 2.7 g	Sodium: 440 mg

You Save: Calories: 47 Fat: 5.4 g

Lentil and Sausage Soup

1. Combine all of the ingredients except for the tomato paste in a 4-quart pot, and bring to a boil over high heat. Reduct the heat to low, cover, and simmer for 30 minutes, or until the lentils are soft.

2. Stir in the tomato paste, and simmer for 5 additional minutes. Ladle the soup into individual serving bowls, and serve hot.

Yield: *9 cups*

1½ cups dried brown lentils, cleaned (page 130)

8 oz. Healthy Choice smoked turkey sausage, sliced ¼ inch thick

1 cup sliced peeled carrots

1 cup diced unpeeled potatoes

1 medium yellow onion, chopped

6 cups water

1¼ teaspoons Maggi instant chicken bouillon granules

2 bay leaves

¼ teaspoon ground black pepper

2 tbsp. Contadina tomato paste

NUTRITIONAL FACTS (PER 1-CUP SERVING)

Calories: 163	Fat: 0.9 g	Protein: 13.4 g
Cholesterol: 11 mg	Fiber: 5.1 g	Sodium: 366 mg

You Save: Calories: 108 Fat: 11.4 g

Turkey Gumbo Soup

Yield: *9 cups*

1 medium yellow onion, chopped

1 medium green bell pepper, chopped

2 stalks celery, thinly sliced (include leaves)

1 can (14½ ounces) Hunt's no salt added tomatoes, crushed

1 cup diced Healthy Choice smoked turkey sausage (about 5 ounces)

4 cups Health Valley no salt added chicken broth or water

2 bay leaves

1½ teaspoons Cajun seasoning

2 cups diced cooked turkey or chicken breast (about 10 ounces)

2 cups fresh or frozen (unthawed) cut okra

1 cup Uncle Ben's instant brown rice

1. Combine the onion, green pepper, celery, tomatoes, sausage, broth, bay leaves, and Cajun seasoning in a 3-quart pot, and bring to a boil over high heat. Stir the mixture, reduce the heat to low, cover, and simmer for 20 minutes, or until the vegetables are tender.

2. Add the turkey or chicken, okra, and rice to the pot, and bring to a boil over high heat. Reduce the heat to low, cover, and simmer for about 10 minutes, or until the rice and okra are tender.

3. Ladle the soup into individual serving bowls, and serve hot.

NUTRITIONAL FACTS (PER 1-CUP SERVING)		
Calories: 142	Fat: 1.3 g	Protein: 14.4 g
Cholesterol: 34 mg	Fiber: 2.9 g	Sodium: 232 mg

You Save: Calories: 56   Fat: 7 g

Golden Chicken and Dumpling Soup

1. Combine the broth, water, sweet potatoes, onion, and pepper in a 3-quart pot, and bring to a boil over high heat. Reduce the heat to low, cover, and simmer for 15 minutes, or until the potatoes are tender.

2. Remove the pot from the heat. Using a slotted spoon, transfer the sweet potatoes and onions to a blender. Add $1\frac{1}{2}$ cups of the broth, and place the lid on the blender, leaving the top slightly ajar to allow steam to escape. Carefully process the mixture at low speed until smooth.

3. Return the blended mixture to the pot, and place over high heat. Add the carrots and celery, and bring the mixture to a boil. Reduce the heat to low, cover, and simmer for 6 to 8 minutes, or until the vegetables are barely tender. Stir in the chicken.

4. To make the dumplings, combine the flour and baking powder in a medium-sized bowl, and stir to mix well. Add enough of the buttermilk to form a moderately stiff batter, stirring just until the dry ingredients are moistened.

5. Drop rounded teaspoons of batter onto the simmering soup. Cover and simmer for 12 minutes, or until the dumplings are fluffy.

6. Ladle the soup into individual bowls, and serve hot.

Yield: 9 servings

2 cans (1 pound each) Campbell's Healthy Request chicken broth

1 cup water

1 pound sweet potatoes (about 2 medium), peeled and diced

1 medium onion, chopped

$\frac{1}{4}$ teaspoon ground white pepper

2 medium carrots, peeled, halved lengthwise, and sliced

1 stalk celery, thinly sliced (include leaves)

2 cups diced cooked chicken breast

DUMPLINGS

$1\frac{1}{4}$ cups Pillsbury's Best unbleached flour

$1\frac{1}{2}$ teaspoons baking powder

$\frac{3}{4}$ cup nonfat buttermilk

NUTRITIONAL FACTS (PER 1-CUP SERVING)

Calories: 163	Fat: 0.8 g	Protein: 10.6 g
Cholesterol: 15 mg	Fiber: 2.2 g	Sodium: 315 mg

You Save: Calories: 55 Fat: 5.6 g

FAT-FIGHTING TIP

Defatting Canned Broths

When using canned broths, keep in mind that most broths are quite low in fat, and that any fat present will have floated to the top. When you open the can, simply spoon out and discard the fat. Now you have a fat-free broth!

French Onion Soup

Yield: *4 servings*

1 large Spanish onion (about 1 pound)

2 tablespoons dry sherry

1 teaspoon Maggi instant beef bouillon granules

¼ teaspoon dried marjoram

⅛ teaspoon ground black pepper

2 cans (14¼ ounces each) Health Valley no salt added beef broth

4 slices (¾ inch thick each) French bread, lightly toasted

2 tablespoons Alpine Lace fat-free grated Parmesan cheese

¾ cup shredded Alpine Lace reduced-fat provolone cheese

1. Cut the onion in half, and slice each half into thin wedges.

2. Place the onion, sherry, bouillon granules, marjoram, and pepper in a 2-quart pot. Place the pot over medium heat, and stir-fry the mixture for 3 to 4 minutes, or until the onions are crisp-tender. Add a little more sherry if the pot becomes too dry.

3. Add the broth to the pot, and bring the mixture to a boil over high heat. Reduce the heat to low, and cover, leaving the lid slightly ajar. Simmer, stirring occasionally, for 30 minutes, or until the soup is reduced by about a quarter.

4. Divide the soup among four 12-ounce oven-proof bowls. Float a piece of French bread on top of each serving, and sprinkle the bread first with 1½ teaspoons of the Parmesan, and then with 3 tablespoons of the provolone.

5. Place the soup bowls under a preheated broiler for about 1 minute, or until the cheese is melted and nicely browned. Serve immediately.

NUTRITIONAL FACTS (PER SERVING)

Calories: 170	Fat: 4.4 g	Protein: 14 g
Cholesterol: 14 mg	Fiber: 2.1 g	Sodium: 463 mg

You Save: Calories: 90 Fat: 11 g

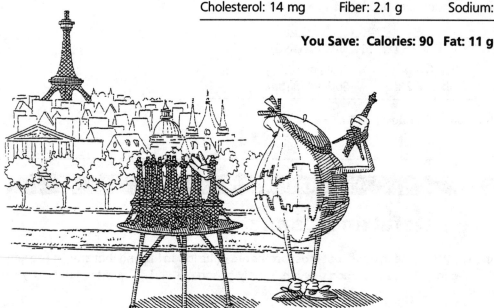

Creamy Carrot Soup

1. Combine the carrots, onion, potato, broth, marjoram, salt, and pepper in a 4-quart pot, and bring to a boil over high heat. Reduce the heat to low, cover, and simmer for 25 minutes, or until the carrots are soft.

2. Place 2½ cups of the soup—including both vegetables and broth—in a blender, and place the lid on the blender, leaving the top slightly ajar to allow steam to escape. Carefully blend the mixture at low speed until smooth. Repeat this procedure until all of the soup has been blended smooth.

3. Return all of the puréed soup to the pot, and place the pot over medium heat. Add the evaporated milk, and cook, stirring constantly, for several minutes, or until the mixture is heated through.

4. Ladle the soup into individual serving bowls, sprinkling each serving with a bit of fresh dill. Serve hot.

Yield: 6 servings

4 cups diced carrots

1 medium onion, chopped

1 large baking potato (about 8 ounces), peeled and diced

2 cans (14¼ ounces each) Health Valley no salt added chicken broth

½ teaspoon crushed dried marjoram

¼ teaspoon salt

⅛ teaspoon ground white pepper

1 can (12 ounces) Pet evaporated skimmed milk

Minced fresh dill (garnish)

NUTRITIONAL FACTS (PER 1-CUP SERVING)

Calories: 137	Fat: 0.5 g	Protein: 8.5 g
Cholesterol: 2 mg	Fiber: 3.4 g	Sodium: 211 mg

You Save: Calories: 152   Fat: 20.9 g

Broccoli-Cheddar Soup

Yield: *6 servings*

$^1/_3$ cup finely chopped onion

$^1/_2$ teaspoon dried thyme

$^1/_8$ teaspoon ground white pepper

1$^1/_4$ cups Health Valley no salt added chicken broth

3 cups skim milk, divided

$^1/_4$ cup Gold Medal unbleached flour

$^1/_2$ cup Carnation instant nonfat dry milk powder

1 package (10 ounces) frozen chopped broccoli, thawed and squeezed dry

1$^1/_4$ cups Sargento Light fancy shredded natural Cheddar cheese

1. Combine the onion, thyme, pepper, and broth in a 3-quart pot, and bring to a boil over high heat. Reduce the heat to low, cover, and simmer for about 5 minutes, or until the onion is tender.

2. Add 2$^1/_2$ cups of the milk to the pot. Increase the heat to medium and cook, stirring constantly, until the mixture begins to boil.

3. Combine the flour, the dry milk powder, and the remaining $^1/_2$ cup of milk in a jar with a tight-fitting lid, and shake until smooth. Add the flour mixture to the pot, and cook, stirring constantly, until the mixture begins to boil and thicken slightly.

4. Reduce the heat to medium-low. Add the broccoli and cheese to the pot, and cook, stirring constantly, for about 5 minutes, or until the cheese is melted and the soup is heated through.

5. Ladle the soup into individual serving bowls, and serve hot.

NUTRITIONAL FACTS (PER 1-CUP SERVING)

Calories: 164	Fat: 4.3 g	Protein: 16.8 g
Cholesterol: 13 mg	Fiber: 1.7 g	Sodium: 282 mg

You Save: Calories: 194   Fat: 25 g

FAT-FIGHTING TIP

Creamy Soups Without the Cream

Cream soups are among the most delicious—and most fattening—of all the soups. Just one cup of cream added to a soup provides over 800 calories and 80 grams of fat! Happily, fat-fighters can continue to enjoy smooth, creamy soups by replacing the cream with evaporated skimmed milk. Fat-free and rich in calcium, this product can be substituted on a one-for-one basis for the cream in any of your favorite soup recipes.

Here's another tip for adding creamy richness to low-fat soups. Purée some of the cooked vegetables and broth in your blender, and return the mixture to the pot to thicken the soup. Adding a potato to a cream soup that is to be puréed—as is done in the recipe for Creamy Carrot Soup (page 77)—will further enhance body and richness.

Chunky Clam Chowder

1. Drain the clams, reserving the juice, and set aside.

2. Combine the water, potatoes, celery, onion, savory, pepper, and ½ cup of the reserved clam juice in a 2½-quart pot, and bring to a boil over high heat. Reduce the heat to low, cover, and simmer for 5 to 7 minutes, or until the potatoes are almost tender.

3. Add the corn to the pot. Cover and simmer for 5 minutes, or until the potatoes and corn are tender. Add all of the skim milk and ½ cup of the evaporated milk to the pot. Cook, stirring constantly, for about 5 minutes, or until the mixture is heated through.

4. Place 1 cup of the soup—including both broth and vegetables—in a blender, and place the lid on the blender, leaving the top slightly ajar to allow steam to escape. Carefully blend the mixture at low speed until smooth. Return the blended mixture to the pot.

5. Add the clams to the pot. Combine the remaining ¼ cup of evaporated milk and the cornstarch in a small dish, and stir until the cornstarch is dissolved. Add the cornstarch mixture to the soup, and, stirring constantly, simmer the soup for 5 additional minutes, or until thickened and bubbly.

6. Ladle the soup into individual serving bowls, and serve hot.

Yield: 6 servings

2 cans (6½ ounces each) Gorton's chopped clams, undrained

½ cup water

2 cups diced peeled potatoes (about 1 pound)

⅓ cup thinly sliced celery

⅓ cup chopped onion

½ teaspoon dried savory

⅛ teaspoon ground white pepper

2 cups fresh or frozen (thawed) whole kernel corn

1 cup skim milk

¾ cup Carnation Lite evaporated skimmed milk, divided

1 tablespoon cornstarch

NUTRITIONAL FACTS (PER 1-CUP SERVING)		
Calories: 176	Fat: 0.8 g	Protein: 13.8 g
Cholesterol: 21 mg	Fiber: 2.2 g	Sodium: 144 mg

You Save: Calories: 122 Fat: 16.1 g

Lemony Lentil Soup

Yield: 5 servings

2 teaspoons Bella extra virgin olive oil

1 teaspoon crushed fresh garlic

1 medium yellow onion, chopped

1 stalk celery, thinly sliced (include leaves)

1 medium carrot, peeled, halved, and sliced

1 cup dried brown lentils, cleaned (page 130)

½ teaspoon dried thyme

¼ teaspoon coarsely ground black pepper

1 can (14½ ounces) Swanson Natural Goodness chicken broth

2½ cups water

2 tablespoons finely chopped fresh parsley

1 tablespoon lemon juice

1½ teaspoons freshly grated lemon rind

¼ cup plus 1 tablespoon Kraft Free nonfat grated Parmesan topping

1. Place the olive oil in a 2½-quart pot, and preheat over medium-high heat. Add the garlic, onion, and celery, and stir-fry for about 2 minutes, or until the vegetables are crisp-tender.

2. Add the carrots, lentils, thyme, pepper, broth, and water to the pot, and bring to a boil. Reduce the heat to low, cover, and simmer, stirring occasionally, for about 35 minutes, or until the lentils are soft and the liquid is thick.

3. Stir the parsley, lemon juice, and lemon rind into the soup. Cover, and simmer for another minute.

4. Remove the pot from the heat, and stir in the Parmesan topping. Ladle the soup into individual serving bowls, and serve hot.

NUTRITIONAL FACTS (PER 1-CUP SERVING)

Calories: 191	Fat: 2.2 g	Protein: 16 g
Cholesterol: 3 mg	Fiber: 6 g	Sodium: 457 mg

You Save: Calories: 38   Fat: 5.5 g

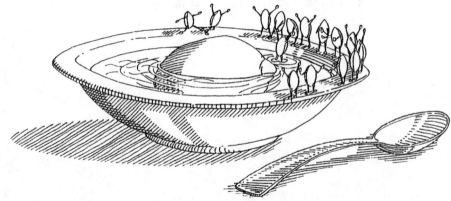

Bean and Bacon Soup

1. Coat a 3-quart pot with nonstick cooking spray, and preheat over medium-high heat. Add the Canadian bacon, and stir-fry for about 2 minutes, or until the meat is lightly browned.

2. Add all of the remaining ingredients to the pot, and bring to a boil over high heat. Reduce the heat to low, cover, and simmer, stirring occasionally, for about 1 hour and 30 minutes, or until the beans are soft and liquid is thick. Add a little more water during cooking if the soup begins to dry out.

3. Ladle the soup into individual serving bowls, and serve hot.

Yield: 8 cups

6 ounces diced Jones Lean Choice Canadian-style bacon

4 cups water

1 can (1 pound) Campbell's Healthy Request chicken broth

2 cups dried navy beans, cleaned and soaked (page 130)

1 cup chopped onion

³⁄₄ teaspoon dried sage

¹⁄₄ teaspoon ground black pepper

NUTRITIONAL FACTS (PER 1-CUP SERVING)

Calories: 191	Fat: 1.8 g	Protein: 15.8 g
Cholesterol: 12 mg	Fiber: 9 g	Sodium: 317 mg

You Save: Calories: 93 Fat: 9.2 g

Split Pea Soup With Ham

1. Combine all of the ingredients in a 3-quart pot, and bring to a boil over high heat. Reduce the heat to low, cover, and simmer, stirring occasionally, for about 45 minutes to 1 hour, or until the peas are soft and the liquid is thick.

2. Ladle the soup into individual serving bowls, and serve hot.

Yield: 6 cups

1¹⁄₂ cups split peas, cleaned (page 130)

1 can (14¹⁄₄ ounces) Health Valley no salt added chicken broth

2¹⁄₂ cups water

1 medium yellow onion, chopped

1 medium carrot, peeled, halved lengthwise, and sliced

1 stalk celery, thinly sliced (include leaves)

6 ounces diced Boar's Head Black Forest ham

1 bay leaf

¹⁄₄ teaspoon ground black pepper

NUTRITIONAL FACTS (PER 1-CUP SERVING)

Calories: 211	Fat: 0.9 g	Protein: 18 g
Cholesterol: 15 mg	Fiber: 4.7 g	Sodium: 333 mg

You Save: Calories: 56 Fat: 6.4 g

FAT-FIGHTER'S GUIDE TO
Soups, Broths, and Bouillons

It's hard to find a quicker or easier meal than canned soup. But until recently, you often had to sacrifice nutrition for the sake of convenience. Fortunately, those days have passed. Several manufacturers now offer entire lines of no- and low-fat soups that contain 30 to 50 percent less sodium than traditional canned soups. Also available is a variety of low-sodium bouillons—a boon to the health-conscious cook who simply doesn't have time to prepare a homemade stock. Let's take a look at some of the products that may be available at your local grocery or health foods store.

CANNED SOUPS AND BROTHS

Looking for a tasty low-fat, low-sodium soup to accompany your lunch-time sandwich? Nowadays, your choices are greater than ever before. Look for brands like Campbell's Healthy Request, Hain 99% Fat Free, Health Valley, Healthy Choice, Progresso Healthy Classics, and Pritikin. For a hearty soup that is loaded with cholesterol-lowering soluble fiber, try bean, split pea, or lentil soup. To get your five-a-day of vegetables, choose a hearty tomato or vegetable soup. And if it's calcium you're looking for, choose a soup that's prepared with milk—and then use nonfat or 1-percent milk.

Every cook knows that canned soups are not only great-tasting dishes in themselves, but also wonderful ingredients in all kinds of recipes. Looking for a low-fat cream of mushroom or cream of celery soup to add to your favorite casserole? Try Campbell's Healthy Request. And for a convenient broth to serve as a base for your own homemade soups, look for brands like Campbell's Healthy Request, Swanson Natural Goodness, and Health Valley No Salt Added

chicken broths. Health Valley also makes a fat-free, low-sodium beef broth, and Swanson and Hain both make low-fat vegetable broths.

DRY BOUILLONS AND BASES

Dry bouillons, like canned soups, are great to have on hand for those days when there's no time to make soup stock from scratch. Available in beef, chicken, ham, vegetable, and onion flavors, bouillons can also add flavor to vegetable side dishes, casseroles, and many other culinary creations.

The good news is that most bouillons are fat-free. The bad news is that most contain a whopping 1,000 milligrams of sodium per teaspoon. Maggi instant bouillon granules, a widely available product, contains about 30-percent less sodium than the average bouillon. Also available are very low-sodium bouillons, including Featherweight and Lite-Line Low Sodium. These products contain only about 5 milligrams of sodium per serving. How can a flavorful bouillon be made without sodium? Most low-sodium bouillons are made with potassium chloride—the same ingredient found in salt substitutes—rather than sodium chloride (salt). However, if you are on a potassium-restricted diet, such products should be avoided.

Other products that can help you reduce your salt intake are Vogue soup bases. Made mostly of powdered vegetables, Vogue chicken, beef, onion, and vegetable bases contain about 300 milligrams of sodium per serving. Yet another reduced-sodium alternative is VegeX Brewer's Yeast Extract. Found in health foods stores, this product provides 250 milligrams of sodium per serving, and can be substituted for beef bouillon on a one-for-one basis.

Of course, whenever you want a low-sodium product to enhance your soup, you may need to look no further than your herb garden. Wisely used, herbs and spices add spark to soups, reducing the need for bouillons by as much as 25 to 50 percent. Another way to slash salt is to add a splash of lemon juice or vinegar to your finished soup. This gives the impression of saltiness.

When shopping for your low-sodium bouillon, keep in mind that most products do contain mono-sodium glutamate or the related substances, hydrolyzed vegetable protein and hydrolyzed yeast extract. If these are ingredients that you're trying to avoid, read the label carefully before tossing the product into your shopping cart.

DRY SOUP MIXES

The selection of low-fat, reduced-sodium dry soup offerings is a not nearly as good as that of canned soups, but at least three brands are definitely worth stocking in your pantry. Fantastic Foods, Nile Spice, and Health Valley make lines of dry soup mixes that are low in fat and contain less than 500 millgrams of sodium per serving. If 500 milligrams of sodium seems a bit high for a serving of soup, it is. But compared with the 1,000 or more milligrams of sodium in a traditional soup, 500 is pretty good—as long as you select lower-sodium foods to accompany your soup.

Mexican Bean Soup

1. Combine all of the ingredients in a 3-quart pot, and bring to a boil over high heat. Reduce the heat to low, cover, and simmer, stirring occasionally, for about 2 hours, or until the beans are soft and the liquid is thick. Add a little more water during cooking if the soup begins to dry out.

2. Ladle the soup into individual serving bowls, and serve hot.

NUTRITIONAL FACTS (PER 1-CUP SERVING)

Calories: 170	Fat: 1.5 g	Protein: 14 g
Cholesterol: 11 mg	Fiber: 8.6 g	Sodium: 311 mg

You Save: Calories: 60 Fat: 5.3 g

Yield: 7 servings

1½ cups dried pinto beans, cleaned and soaked (page 130)

1 can (14¼ ounces) Health Valley no salt added chicken broth

2½ cups water

1 medium Spanish onion, chopped

1 medium carrot, peeled, halved, and sliced

6 ounces diced Hormel Curemaster 96% fat-free ham

1 tablespoon chopped jalapeño pepper

2½ teaspoons chili powder

1 teaspoon ground cumin

Savory Bean Soup

Yield: *10 cups*

2 cups dried 15-bean mixture or
   navy beans, cleaned and
   soaked (page 130)

1½ cups diced peeled potatoes
   (about ¾ pound)

¾ cup sliced celery (include
   leaves)

¾ cup diced peeled carrots

1 medium yellow onion, chopped

8 ounces Healthy Choice smoked
   turkey sausage, diced

8 cups water

1 teaspoon crushed fresh garlic

2 teaspoons ground paprika

2 teaspoons Vogue instant
   chicken-flavored base

1 teaspoon dried savory

¼ teaspoon ground black pepper

1. Combine all of the ingredients in a 4-quart pot, and bring to a boil over high heat. Reduce the heat to low, cover, and simmer, stirring occasionally, for about 2 hours, or until the beans are soft and the liquid is thick. Add a little more water during cooking if the soup begins to dry out.

2. Ladle the soup into individual serving bowls, and serve hot.

NUTRITIONAL FACTS (PER 1-CUP SERVING)

Calories: 192	Fat: 1 g	Protein: 12 g
Cholesterol: 10 mg	Fiber: 9 g	Sodium: 254 mg

You Save: Calories: 55 Fat: 6.7 g

*Top: Fiesta Layered Salad (page 65), Center: Terrific Taco Salad (page 64),
With Tex-Mex Salad Dressing (page 56), Bottom: Old-Fashioned Macaroni Salad (page 58)*

Top: Split Pea Soup With Ham (page 81), Center: French Onion Soup (page 76),
Bottom: Mama Mia Minestrone (page 71)

Top: *Spinach, Ham, and Swiss Strudels (page 90)*, Bottom Left: *Crispy Shrimp With Sauce (page 94)*,
Bottom Right: *Chili-Cheese Potato Skins (page 92)*

Top: Submarine Finger Sandwiches (page 88), Bottom Left: Garden Artichoke Dip (page 98), Bottom Right: Asparagus Roll-Ups With Dressing (page 87)

5. Party-Perfect Hors D'oeuvres and Appetizers

For most of us, party foods spell fun and festivity—and fat. Cheesy dips, fried chips, and other high-fat fare make most special occasions a nightmare for anyone who's trying to eat healthfully.

If special occasions were few and far between, a once-in-a-while fat overdose would not be a problem. But when you add up all the holidays, birthdays, anniversaries, weddings, and other gatherings that crop up during the year, you may find that the amount of fat you get from parties is not a trivial matter. Besides, once you discover how delicious low-fat eating can be, and how great you look and feel on your slimmed-down diet, you will want to eat this way all year round.

Fortunately, adopting a low-fat lifestyle does not mean giving up your favorite party foods. For just about any high-fat ingredient you can think of, there is a low-fat or fat-free alternative. No- and low-fat cheeses, nonfat sour cream and mayonnaise, ultra-lean lunchmeats, and a host of other products can help take the fat out of your celebrations and get-togethers. You'll be amazed at the big fat difference a few simple ingredient substitu-

tions can make in traditional party favorites. For instance, a bowl of dip made with a cup of full-fat mayonnaise gets 1,582 calories and 186 fat grams from the mayonnaise alone. Prepare the same dip with a light mayonnaise, and you will cut the fat and calories by 50 to 80 percent. Use a nonfat mayonnaise, and you will eliminate *all* of the fat and 90 percent of the calories!

This chapter uses these and other healthful ingredients to create a wide range of hot and cold hors d'oeuvres, both plain and fancy. From Asparagus Roll-Ups to Submarine Finger Sandwiches, Italian Sausage-Stuffed Mushrooms, and Crispy Shrimp, you will find a wealth of festive, party-perfect foods. Add some trays of fresh vegetables, a selection of in-season fruit, and plenty of low-cal beverages, and your menu will be the life of the party.

To guide you in making fat-smart party-food choices, this chapter includes a Fat-Fighter's Guide to the many low- and no-fat chips, crackers, and other snack foods now available in your local grocery store (page 96). You'll be delighted to find that there are just as many healthy options for scooping up a dip as there are for making one. Other guides provide great tips on buying low-fat meats (page 140), dairy products (page 116), and condiments (page 52).

So send out the invitations, and get ready to treat friends and family to a menu that's high on satisfaction, yet remarkably low in fat. Your guests will appreciate this more than you know.

FAT-FIGHTER'S GUIDE TO
Peanut Butter

Who doesn't love peanut butter? This creamy treat is delicious in sandwiches, sauces, dressings, cookies, and more. Unfortunately, as every fat-fighter knows, peanut butter is loaded with fat and calories—about 100 calories and 8 grams of fat per tablespoon, to be exact. Does this mean that you should eliminate peanut butter from your diet? Not necessarily. Remember that you can and should eat some fat in order to get essential fatty acids. Peanut butter, like other nut and seed products, supplies some of these essential fats, and does so in a natural and healthful form.

But all peanut butters are not alike. To prevent the oil from separating and rising to the top, most leading brands contain small amounts of both partially and fully hydrogenated vegetable oils, as well as sugar and salt. And if you think that you can save calories by switching to a reduced-fat product, think again. Unlike reduced-fat margarine, which replaces fat with water, most reduced-fat brands of pea-

nut butter substitute corn syrup or similar products for part of the fat. The result is a peanut butter with about 25-percent less fat, but little or no difference in calories.

If your goal is to cut both fat *and* calories, your best bet is to switch to a whipped peanut butter, like Peter Pan Whipped. This product has about 25-percent less fat and calories than traditional versions of the spread. Your most natural choice, though, is a product made only from roasted peanuts, with no added hydrogenated fats. Two delicious examples are Smucker's Natural, which contains no added fats, and Arrowhead Mills Easy Spreading, which contains a small amount of lecithin. Lecithin, a nutritious by-product of soybean oil-refining, prevents the product from separating and makes it spread smoothly on bread.

So go ahead and include some peanut butter in your diet. As long as you let your fat budget be your guide, you can have your peanut butter and eat it too.

Asparagus Roll-Ups

1. To make the dressing, combine all of the dressing ingredients in a small bowl, and stir to mix well. Set aside.

2. Rinse the asparagus with cool running water, and snap off the tough stem ends. Arrange the asparagus spears in a microwave or conventional steamer. Cover and cook at high power or over medium-high heat for about 3 minutes, or just until the spears are crisp-tender.

3. Drain the asparagus, and plunge them into a large bowl of ice water to stop the cooking process. Drain the spears, and pat dry.

4. Lay one slice of turkey on a flat surface, and place one asparagus spear on the lower end of the slice. Roll the asparagus spear up in the turkey slice, and secure with a wooden toothpick. Repeat with the remaining turkey slices and asparagus spears.

5. Arrange the roll-ups on a serving platter, and serve, accompanied by the bowl of dressing.

Yield: 30 appetizers

30 fresh asparagus spears (about 1 pound)

30 thin slices (about 6 ounces) Butterball honey roasted turkey breast

DRESSING

½ cup Hellmann's low-fat mayonnaise

½ cup Sealtest Free nonfat sour cream

¼ cup Dijon mustard

1 tablespoon plus 1 teaspoon honey

NUTRITIONAL FACTS (PER APPETIZER)

Calories: 29	Fat: 0.5 g	Protein: 2.2 g
Cholesterol: 4 mg	Fiber: 0.4 g	Sodium: 141 mg

You Save: Calories: 31 Fat: 4.3 g

Submarine Finger Sandwiches

Yield: *14 appetizers*

1 loaf French bread (14 x 2½ inches)

1 tablespoon plus 1 teaspoon Smart Beat nonfat mayonnaise

1 tablespoon plus 1 teaspoon spicy mustard

1½ cups shredded romaine lettuce, divided

2 ounces Healthy Choice thinly sliced fat-free skinless turkey breast

2 ounces Healthy Choice thinly sliced 97% fat-free honey ham

2 ounces thinly sliced Alpine Lace reduced-fat provolone or Cheddar cheese

1 plum tomato, thinly sliced

3 very thin onion slices, separated into rings

6 very thin green bell pepper rings

3 tablespoons canned hot banana pepper rings

1 tablespoon plus 1 teaspoon Kraft Free Italian salad dressing

1. Using a serrated knife, cut the bread in half lengthwise. Using your fingers, remove and discard the top ½ inch of bread from the center of each half to form a slight depression.

2. Spread the mayonnaise over the bottom piece of bread, and the mustard over the top piece. Lay the bottom of the loaf on a flat surface, and arrange ½ cup of the lettuce over the bread. Layer the turkey, ham, and cheese over the lettuce. Top with the tomato, onion, green pepper, and banana pepper, and the remaining lettuce. Drizzle the Italian dressing over the lettuce, and replace the top of the loaf.

3. Cut the sandwich into 1-inch slices, and secure each piece with a toothpick. Arrange the appetizers on a serving platter, and serve immediately, or cover with plastic wrap and refrigerate for up to 3 hours.

NUTRITIONAL FACTS (PER APPETIZER)

Calories: 68	Fat: 1.4 g	Protein: 4.2 g
Cholesterol: 6 mg	Fiber: 0.7 g	Sodium: 204 mg

You Save: Calories: 57   Fat: 6.5 g

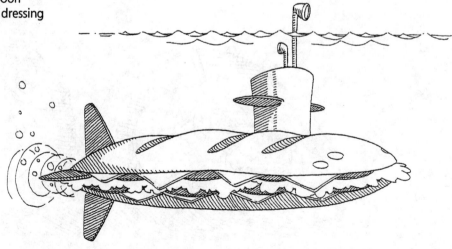

Sausage and Artichoke Bruschetta

1. Combine the artichoke hearts, tomatoes, sausage, mozzarella, and Parmesan in a medium-sized bowl, and stir to mix well.

2. Slice the bread into 48 ($\frac{1}{2}$-inch) slices, and arrange the slices on a baking sheet. Top each slice with 1 tablespoon of the artichoke mixture.

3. Bake at 400°F for 5 minutes, or until the cheese is melted and lightly browned. Arrange the appetizers on a serving platter, and serve hot.

Yield: 48 appetizers

1 cup plus 2 tablespoons finely chopped frozen (thawed) or canned (drained) artichoke hearts

$\frac{3}{4}$ cup finely chopped plum tomatoes

6 ounces Turkey Italian Sausage (page 182), cooked, crumbled, and drained

1$\frac{1}{4}$ cups Sargento Light fancy shredded natural mozzarella cheese

2 tablespoons Alpine Lace fat-free grated Parmesan cheese

1 long, thin loaf sourdough French bread (24 x 2 inches)

NUTRITIONAL FACTS (PER APPETIZER)		
Calories: 34	Fat: 0.7 g	Protein: 2.4 g
Cholesterol: 3 mg	Fiber: 0.4 g	Sodium: 72 mg

You Save: Calories: 32 Fat: 3.6 g

Italian Sausage-Stuffed Mushrooms

1. Wash the mushrooms and pat dry. Remove the stems, and finely chop. Combine the chopped stems with the Italian sausage in a medium-sized bowl, and mix thoroughly.

2. Coat a shallow baking pan with nonstick cooking spray. Place a heaping teaspoonful of stuffing in each mushroom cap, and arrange the mushrooms on the prepared pan.

3. Bake at 375°F for 15 minutes, or until sausage is no longer pink inside. Transfer the mushrooms to a serving platter, and serve hot.

Yield: 40 appetizers

40 medium-large fresh mushrooms (about 1$\frac{1}{4}$ pounds)

1 pound Turkey Italian Sausage (page 182)

NUTRITIONAL FACTS (PER APPETIZER)		
Calories: 17	Fat: 0.4 g	Protein: 2.9 g
Cholesterol: 7 mg	Fiber: 0.2 g	Sodium: 34 mg

You Save: Calories: 26 Fat: 3.2 g

Spinach, Ham, and Swiss Strudels

Yield: *32 appetizers*

3 cups packed chopped fresh spinach

1 cup shredded Jarlsberg Lite Swiss cheese

¾ cup finely chopped Hormel Curemaster 96% fat-free ham (about 3½ ounces)

2 teaspoons spicy brown mustard

¼ cup Scramblers egg substitute

12 sheets Athens Foods phyllo dough (about 10 ounces)

PAM® Butter Flavor No Stick Cooking Spray

NUTRITIONAL FACTS
(PER APPETIZER)

Calories: 39	Fiber: 0.2 g
Chol: 3 mg	Protein: 2.6 g
Fat: 0.9 g	Sodium: 88 mg

You Save: Calories: 42 Fat: 5 g

Making Spinach, Ham, and Swiss Strudels

1. Coat a medium-sized nonstick skillet with nonstick cooking spray, and place over medium heat. Add the spinach, and stir-fry for about 2 minutes, or just until wilted. Remove the skillet from the heat, and let the spinach cool to room temperature.

2. Add the cheese and ham to the cooled spinach, and toss to mix well. Combine the mustard and egg substitute in a small bowl, and add to the spinach mixture, tossing to mix well. Set aside.

3. Spread the phyllo dough out on a clean dry surface. You should have a 14-x-18-inch sheet that is 12 layers thick. Cover the phyllo dough with plastic wrap to prevent it from drying out as you work. (Remove sheets as you need them, being sure to recover the remaining dough.)

4. Remove 1 sheet of phyllo dough, and lay it flat on a clean dry surface with the short end near you. Spray the strip lightly with the cooking spray. Top with another phyllo sheet, and spray lightly with cooking spray. Repeat with a third sheet.

5. Spread a fourth of the filling over the lower third of the stacked sheets, leaving a 4-inch margin on each side. Fold the left and right edges inward to enclose the filling, and roll the sheet up from the bottom, jelly-roll style. Repeat with the remaining dough and filling to make 4 rolls.

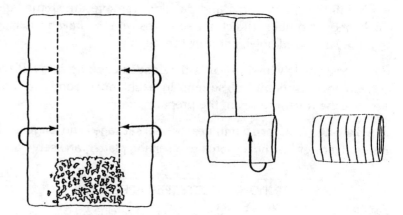

a. Spread the filling over the dough, and fold the left and right edges. inward over the filling

b. Roll the folded sheet up.

c. Score each roll at 1-inch intervals.

6. Coat a baking sheet with nonstick cooking spray. Place the rolls seam side down on the sheet, and spray the tops lightly with the cooking spray. Score the rolls with a sharp knife at 1-inch intervals, cutting through just the outer layer of phyllo. (This will keep the baked phyllo from shattering when you slice it.)

7. Bake at 350°F for 25 minutes, or until light golden brown. Remove the rolls from the oven, and allow to cool for 5 minutes. Slice along the score lines, and serve hot.

Chicken Tortilla Crisps

1. Coat several baking sheets with nonstick cooking spray, and arrange the tortillas on the sheets. Bake at 350°F for about 6 minutes, or until lightly browned.

2. While the tortillas are baking, combine the chicken, salsa, and chili powder in a small bowl, and stir to mix well. Set aside.

3. Remove the tortillas from the oven, and sprinkle ¼ cup of the cheese over each tortilla. Top each tortilla with a fourth of the chicken mixture, 1 tablespoon of olives, and 1 tablespoon of scallions. Sprinkle with 2 tablespoons of the cheese.

4. Return the tortillas to the oven for 5 to 7 minutes, or until the cheese is melted and the tortillas are crisp. While the tortillas are baking, place the sour cream in a small serving bowl. Cut each tortilla into 8 wedges, and arrange the wedges on a serving platter accompanied by the sour cream. Serve immediately.

Yield: 32 appetizers

4 Buena Vida fat-free flour tortillas (8-inch rounds) or other fat-free tortillas

1 cup shredded cooked chicken breast (about 5 ounces) or 1 cup (drained) Swanson premium chunk white chicken in water

½ cup Enrico's no salt added chunky style salsa

2 teaspoons chili powder

1½ cups Healthy Choice fancy shredded fat-free pizza cheese, divided

¼ cup sliced black olives

¼ cup sliced scallions

½ cup plus 2 tablespoons Naturally Yours nonfat sour cream

NUTRITIONAL FACTS (PER APPETIZER)

Calories: 33	Fat: 0.1 g	Protein: 3.3 g
Cholesterol: 4 mg	Fiber: 0.3 g	Sodium: 95 mg

You Save: Calories: 22 Fat: 3.2 g

Chili-Cheese Potato Skins

Yield: *12 appetizers*

6 small baking potatoes (about 4 ounces each)

¾ cup Health Valley fat-free chili with black beans or Hormel 99% fat-free turkey chili

½ cup Healthy Choice fancy shredded fat-free pizza cheese

PAM® Olive Oil No Stick Cooking Spray

½ cup Breakstone's Free nonfat sour cream

¼ cup thinly sliced scallions

1. If using a conventional oven, wrap the potatoes in aluminum foil, and bake at 400°F for about 35 minutes, or until tender. If using a microwave oven, pierce each potato in several places with a fork, and microwave on high power for about 12 minutes, or until tender. Set aside to cool.

2. Cut the potatoes in half lengthwise. Scoop out and discard the pulp, leaving a ¼-inch-thick shell. Place 1 tablespoon of chili in each skin, and top with 2 teaspoons of cheese. Spray the tops of the stuffed potatoes lightly with the cooking spray.

3. Place the potato skins on a baking sheet, and bake at 450°F for 12 minutes, or until the filling is hot and the cheese is bubbly. Transfer the skins to a serving platter, top each skin with 2 teaspoons of sour cream and a sprinkling of scallions, and serve hot.

NUTRITIONAL FACTS (PER APPETIZER)		
Calories: 71	Fat: 0.4 g	Protein: 3.3 g
Cholesterol: 1 mg	Fiber: 1.8 g	Sodium: 61 mg

You Save: Calories: 77 Fat: 9 g

Chicken Fingers
With Tangy Apricot Sauce

1. Rinse the chicken with cool water, and pat it dry with paper towels. Cut each piece into 5 long strips, and set aside.

2. Place the corn flakes, poultry seasoning, ginger, and pepper in a blender or food processor, and process into crumbs. (You should get about $\frac{3}{4}$ cup of crumbs. Adjust the amount if necessary.) Transfer the mixture to a shallow dish, stir in the sesame seeds, and set aside.

3. Place the egg substitute in another shallow dish, and set aside.

4. Coat a large baking sheet with nonstick cooking spray. Dip each chicken strip first in the egg substitute and then in the crumb mixture, turning to coat well. Arrange the strips in a single layer on the prepared sheet.

5. Spray the tops of the strips lightly with the cooking spray, and bake at 400°F for 15 minutes, or until the strips are golden brown and no longer pink inside.

6. While the chicken is baking, place all of the sauce ingredients in a blender, and process until smooth. Pour the mixture into a small saucepan, and cook over medium heat for several minutes, or until just heated through. Transfer the sauce to a small dish.

7. Arrange the chicken strips on a serving platter, and serve hot, accompanied by the dish of warm sauce.

Yield: 20 appetizers

1 pound boneless skinless chicken breasts (about 4 halves)

3 cups Kellogg's corn flakes

¼ teaspoon poultry seasoning

¼ teaspoon ground ginger

¼ teaspoon ground white pepper

2 tablespoons sesame seeds

½ cup Better'n Eggs egg substitute

Wesson No Stick cooking spray

SAUCE

½ cup Smucker's Simply Fruit apricot spread

¼ cup plus 2 tablespoons Swanson Natural Goodness chicken broth

1 tablespoon Marukai seasoned rice vinegar

¼ teaspoon crushed fresh garlic

¼ teaspoon ground ginger

NUTRITIONAL FACTS (PER APPETIZER)

Calories: 67	Fat: 0.8 g	Protein: 6.3 g
Cholesterol: 13 mg	Fiber: 0.2 g	Sodium: 76 mg

You Save: Calories: 47 Fat: 5.2 g

Crispy Shrimp

Yield: *40 appetizers*

40 large raw shrimp (about 1 pound), peeled and deveined

¼ cup plus 2 tablespoons unbleached flour

¼ cup plus 2 tablespoons Scramblers egg substitute

¼ cup orange juice

4 cups Arrowhead Mills corn flakes

¼ cup Kretschmer toasted wheat germ or finely ground pecans

½ teaspoon coarsely ground black pepper

Wesson No Stick cooking spray

SAUCE
½ cup Miracle Whip Free nonfat dressing

2 tablespoons spicy brown mustard

¼ cup orange juice

For variety, substitute bite-sized pieces of chicken breast for the shrimp.

1. Rinse the shrimp with cool water, and pat them dry with paper towels. Set aside.

2. In a shallow bowl, combine the flour, egg substitute, and orange juice, and stir with a wire whisk until smooth. Set aside.

3. Place the corn flakes in a blender, and process into crumbs. (You should get about 1 cup of crumbs. Adjust the amount if necessary.) Transfer the crumbs to a shallow dish, and stir in the wheat germ or pecans and the pepper.

4. Coat a large baking sheep or Crispy Crust pizza pan with nonstick cooking spray. Dip the shrimp first in the crumb mixture, then in the egg mixture, and once again in the crumb mixture, turning to coat well. Arrange the shrimp in a single layer on the prepared pan.

5. Spray the shrimp lightly with the cooking spray, and bake at 400°F for about 12 minutes, or until the shrimp are nicely browned on the outside and opaque on the inside.

6. While the shrimp are baking, make the sauce by combine the nonfat dressing and mustard in a small dish. Stir to mix well. Stir in the orange juice.

7. Arrange the shrimp on a serving platter, and serve hot, accompanied by the dish of sauce.

NUTRITIONAL FACTS (PER APPETIZER)
Calories: 34	Fat: 0.3 g	Protein: 31 g
Cholesterol: 17 mg	Fiber: 0.3 g	Sodium: 71 mg

You Save: Calories: 40 Fat: 4 g

Cashew Chicken Salad Finger Sandwiches

1. Combine the chicken or turkey, cashews, celery, and red pepper in a medium-sized bowl, and toss to mix well. Add the mayonnaise, sour cream, and white pepper, and stir to mix well.

2. Arrange 9 of the bread slices on a flat surface. Spread $\frac{1}{4}$ cup plus 1 tablespoon of the filling on each slice, and top each with a remaining slice. Trim the crusts from the bread, and cut each sandwich into 4 fingers.

3. Arrange the sandwiches on a serving platter, and serve immediately, or cover with plastic wrap and refrigerate for up to 3 hours.

Yield: 36 appetizers

2 cups finely chopped cooked chicken or turkey breast (about 10 ounces)

$\frac{1}{2}$ cup chopped Fisher dry-roasted cashews

$\frac{1}{2}$ cup finely chopped celery

$\frac{1}{4}$ cup finely chopped red bell pepper

$\frac{1}{2}$ cup Weight Watchers fat-free mayonnaise

$\frac{1}{4}$ cup Sealtest Free nonfat sour cream

$\frac{1}{8}$ teaspoon ground white pepper

18 slices Brownberry natural wheat bread

NUTRITIONAL FACTS (PER APPETIZER)

Calories: 55	Fat: 1.3 g	Protein: 4.7 g
Cholesterol: 6 mg	Fiber: 1.7 g	Sodium: 96 mg

You Save: Calories: 35 Fat: 4.2 g

Bacon, Cheddar, and Pecan Spread

1. Combine the cream cheese, sour cream, mayonnaise, onion, and pepper in a food processor, and process until smooth. Add the Cheddar cheese, bacon, and pecans, and process just until well mixed. Transfer the spread to a serving dish, cover, and chill for several hours or overnight.

2. Serve with whole grain crackers, sliced bagels, and fresh-cut vegetables, or use as a stuffing for celery or as a finger-sandwich filling.

Yield: 2$\frac{2}{3}$ cups

1 block (8 ounces) Philadelphia Free nonfat cream cheese

1 cup Breakstone's Free nonfat sour cream

$\frac{1}{2}$ cup Kraft Free mayonnaise

2 tablespoons chopped onion

$\frac{1}{8}$ teaspoon ground white pepper

1 cup Healthy Choice fancy shredded fat-free Cheddar cheese

4 slices Mr. Turkey Bacon, cooked, drained, and crumbled

$\frac{1}{4}$ cup chopped toasted pecans (page 191)

NUTRITIONAL FACTS (PER TABLESPOON)

Calories: 24	Fat: 0.7 g	Protein: 2 g
Cholesterol: 2 mg	Fiber: 0 g	Sodium: 88 mg

You Save: Calories: 44 Fat: 6 g

Until recently, dedicated fat-fighters had few options in the snack aisle. But all that has changed. These days, there are plenty of excellent low- and no-fat chips, pretzels, and other fun foods that take the guilt out of snacking while leaving in the flavor and crunch. Let's take a look at some of the many products that await you at your local grocery store.

CHIPS

To the delight of chip lovers everywhere, several brands of low-fat and fat-free potato chips are now widely available. These crispy chips—which are baked, not fried—make a nutritious and tasty snack. Look for brands like Baked Lay's, Childer's Fat Free, Fit Foods Fat Free, and Louise's Fat Free. If tortilla chips are more to your liking, try a brand like Baked Tostitos, Guiltless Gourmet, Louise's, or Smart Temptations. In each case, you will save about 10 grams of fat and 60 calories per ounce of chips. And most brands of fat-free chips have surprisingly little sodium—about 100 to 200 milligrams per 1-ounce serving. Unsalted brands are also available.

POPCORN

It's hard to beat air-popped popcorn as a snack food. For buttery flavor, spray your air-popped treat with a little Weight Watchers Butter Spray or I Can't Believe It's Not Butter! spray. In the microwave popcorn department, look for brands like Orville Redenbacher's Smart Pop, Weight Watchers Smart Snackers Microwave Popcorn, or Betty Crocker Pop Secret by Request.

PRETZELS

While these crunchy treats have always been low in fat, most pretzels are little more than refined white flour and salt. And with up to 600 milligrams of sodium per 1-ounce serving, your average pretzel is not the most nutritious snack-food choice.

Fortunately, some unsalted and reduced-salt brands are available, including Bachman unsalted and Quinlan unsalted. And some pretzels do contain whole grain flour. One good choice is Wege Honey Wheat pretzels. Made with part whole wheat flour and coated with sesame seeds, these pretzels make a satisfying snack that is low in both fat and salt. Yet another excellent product is Barbara's Organic Whole Wheat Pretzels.

CRACKERS

Although plenty of fat-free and low-fat options abound in the cracker aisle, your best bets are crackers that are both low in fat and high in whole grains. Brands like Finn Crisp, Health Valley, Hol Grain, Kavli, Rye Krisp, Rye Vita, and Wasa are among the most healthful choices. Other good options are rice and popcorn cakes, most of which are made with whole grains and little or no added fat. Reduced Fat Triscuits and Reduced Fat Wheat Thins also provide some fiber, but with a little more fat.

Next in line are crackers that are fat-free or low in fat, but contain mostly refined white flour or refined grains. These include Mr. Phipps Fat-Free Pretzel Chips, Jacobsen's Snack Toast, SnackWell's, Stoned Wheat Thins, and melba toast.

As a hearty and nutritious alternative to crackers and rice cakes, accompany your favorite dips and spreads with wedges of whole grain pita bread, slices of firm whole wheat or rye bread, or slices of whole grain bagels.

SALSA

Once you have selected a bag of low-fat chips or a box of low-fat crackers, you may be faced with a real challenge—finding a healthy dip in a sea of high-fat, high-sodium products. Try salsa, which has always been fat-free. Compare brands, though, and choose those with the lowest sodium counts. Green Mountain Gringo, Louise's, and Guiltless Gourmet salsas tend to be lower in sodium than most other brands. Enrico's and Millina's Finest both offer salsas made with no added salt. And don't forget that for a creamy guilt-free treat, you can easily prepare your favorite chip dip using nonfat sour cream.

Peanut Butter-Hot Fudge Fruit Dip

1. Place the cocoa, sugar, and cornstarch in a 1½-quart pot, and stir to mix well. Using a wire whisk, slowly stir in the milk and the evaporated milk. Place the pot over medium heat, and cook, stirring constantly, for 5 minutes, or just until the mixture comes to a boil.

2. Reduce the heat to low, add the peanut butter, and cook and stir for 2 minutes, or until the peanut butter has melted into the chocolate mixture. Remove the pot from the heat, and stir in the vanilla extract.

3. Transfer the mixture to a small chafing dish or Crock-Pot heated casserole dish to keep warm, and serve with chunks of angel food cake, whole fresh strawberries, and chunks of bananas, pineapples, apples, and pears.

Yield: 2¼ cups

½ cup Hershey's Dutch Processed European Style cocoa powder

¾ cup sugar

1 tablespoon plus 1 teaspoon cornstarch

1 cup skim milk

½ cup Carnation Lite evaporated skimmed milk

3 tablespoons Smucker's natural creamy peanut butter

2 teaspoons vanilla extract

NUTRITIONAL FACTS (PER TABLESPOON)

Calories: 33	Fat: 0.8 g	Protein: 1 g
Cholesterol: 0 mg	Fiber: 0.5 g	Sodium: 14 mg

You Save: Calories: 40   Fat: 2 g

Garden Artichoke Dip

Yield: *4 cups*

2 cups Land O Lakes no-fat sour
  cream

½ cup Hellman's low-fat
  mayonnaise

1 package (1.4 ounces) Knorr dry
  vegetable soup mix

1 package (9 ounces) frozen
  (thawed) or canned (drained)
  artichoke hearts, chopped

1 can (8 ounces) sliced water
  chestnuts, drained and
  chopped

⅓ cup chopped red bell pepper

¼ cup chopped scallions

1. Combine the sour cream, mayonnaise, and vegetable soup mix in a large bowl, and stir to mix well. Add the artichokes, water chestnuts, red pepper, and scallions, and stir to mix well. Transfer the dip to a serving dish, cover, and chill for several hours.

2. Serve with whole grain crackers, thinly sliced bagels, and fresh-cut vegetables.

NUTRITIONAL FACTS (PER TABLESPOON)

Calories: 16	Fat: 0.2 g	Protein: 0.5 g
Cholesterol: 0 mg	Fiber: 0.3 g	Sodium: 69 mg

You Save: Calories: 17 Fat: 3 g

Spicy Black Bean Dip

Yield: *1¾ cups*

1 can (15 ounces) Progresso black
  beans, drained

¾ cup diced plum tomatoes

2 scallions, sliced

3 tablespoons chopped fresh
  cilantro

1–2 tablespoons chopped
  jalapeño peppers

1 tablespoon Progresso
  garlic-flavored wine vinegar

2 teaspoons chili powder

¼ teaspoon ground cumin

Many bean dips are already fat-free or quite low in fat, but this one has garden-fresh flavor and less than half the sodium of most commercial brands.

1. Combine all of the ingredients in a food processor or blender, and process until well mixed, but slightly chunky. Transfer the dip to a serving dish.

2. Serve at room temperature with baked tortilla chips.

NUTRITIONAL FACTS (PER TABLESPOON)

Calories: 11	Fat: 0 g	Protein: 0.7 g
Cholesterol: 0 mg	Fiber: 0.7 g	Sodium: 42 mg

You Save: Calories: 8 Fat: 1 g

6. Savory Side Dishes

Side dishes often pose a dilemma when people first adopt a low-fat lifestyle. Noodles swimming in creamy sauces, rice dishes made with butter or margarine, and casseroles laden with sour cream and cheese are side dish specialties in many households. It may come as no surprise that many of these dishes have as much or more fat than the entrée they're accompanying.

Part of the problem is that so many people have come to rely on side dish mixes, especially on busy week nights. If they were to read the labels on their favorite mixes, they would find that most of these products, when prepared, not only are loaded with fat, but also contain a staggering amount of sodium.

So what *can* you serve alongside your favorite entrée? Fresh vegetables and whole grains are the best choices by far. Busy cooks will be happy to know that the less you do to vegetables in the way of cooking, the better off your side dish will be nutritionally. Simple methods like steaming and stir-frying are superb techniques for preserving nutrients, flavor, and color. Or cook your vegetables in a covered skillet with a few tablespoons of water, broth, or wine.

It is equally easy to base your side dishes on whole grains like brown rice, barley, bulgur wheat, and whole wheat couscous. Your grocery store has many flavorful, nutrient-rich brands of quick-cooking brown rice and barley. And bulgur wheat and couscous have always been a snap to fix. Serve these grains alone, or combine them with vegeta-

bles for super-delicious side dishes that are special enough for any occasion.

The recipes in this chapter use garden-fresh vegetables, whole grains, zesty herbs and spices, and a variety of terrific no- and low-fat products to make a wide range of tantalizing side dishes. If you feared that you'd have to give up favorites like cheese-topped stuffed potatoes and fried rice to follow a low-fat diet, take heart. The following pages will prove to you once and for all that wholesome doesn't have to mean boring.

To help you make the best ingredient choices, this chapter includes two great Fat-Fighter's Guides. The first guide (page 100) will steer you toward the freshest, ripest produce available—and steer you away from the produce aisle's "fat traps." The second guide (page 111) will help you choose low-fat side dish mixes and frozen side dishes, and will explain how you can easily turn regular mixes into tempting low-fat creations. Additionally, the Fat-Fighter's Guide on page 116 highlights the best low-fat and fat-free dairy products—products that make it possible to add great taste to a variety of side dishes *without* adding extra fat.

So take out your skillet, a selection of whole grains, and the freshest vegetables available, and treat your family to savory side dishes that are sure to please. You'll be delighted to learn that even crisp-coated onion rings can take their place on a low-fat table—once you know the secrets of low-fat cooking.

FAT-FIGHTER'S GUIDE TO
The Produce Section

This is one part of the supermarket where we should all spend more time. Why? To maximize your health, nothing is more important than eating at least five servings of fruits and vegetables each day. With a few exceptions, produce is fat-free. Moreover, all produce is cholesterol-free and rich in the fiber and nutrients that help ward off cancer, heart disease, and many other disorders.

Contrary to popular belief, produce is fast food—or, at least, it should be. The fact is that the less you do to fresh fruits and vegetables in the way of cooking, the more nutritious they are. Vegetables served raw in salads, steamed, or stir-fried only until crisptender are just what the doctor ordered. Prepared in these ways, produce requires very little time. And what could be a faster snack than a piece of fresh fruit eaten out of hand?

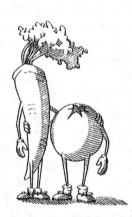

Although all produce provides fiber and nutrients for very few calories, some fruits and vegetables are especially rich in nutrients. Some of the best vegetable selections include those in the cabbage family, such as broccoli, bok choy, cabbage, cauliflower, kale, and greens. Carrots, sweet peppers, sweet potatoes, tomatoes, and winter squash are other nutrient-packed choices. Supernutritious fruits include oranges, mangoes, cantaloupes, kiwi, and strawberries. Try to eat these foods often.

SELECTING PRODUCE

Buy fresh, locally grown produce whenever possible. This will help ensure that the produce you buy is more nutritious, and grown with fewer pesticides and chemicals. If local produce is not available, domestically grown produce is a better choice than imported produce. Why? Most other countries are allowed to use harmful pesticides and other chemicals that are banned in the United States. Of course, your best option, whenever possible, is to purchase organic produce, which is grown without chemical fertilizers and pesticides of any kind. It is also a very good idea to purchase fruits and vegetables in season. By doing this, you will be much more likely to get a juicy, flavorful, and nutritious product for the best value.

Is fresh always best? Yes—if the produce has been properly handled. Beware, though. If fresh produce was picked when underripe, mishandled during shipping, and then stored for several days before being sold, frozen vegetables are a better option. Frozen vegetables are picked close to their peak of ripeness and then quickly processed, allowing them to retain more nutrients than poorly handled fresh produce. Even canned vegetables may be more nutritious than some fresh vegetables.

As you walk through the produce section of your grocery store, you will often see people squeezing, thumping, shaking, and sniffing the merchandise, checking for ripeness and freshness. How can you choose the best produce? Look for vegetables and fruits that are plump and heavy for their size. This indicates that the produce is juicy, rather than dried out. Avoid any produce that looks shriveled or wilted, and therefore past its prime. Also avoid produce that is overly large, as this may indicate a stringy texture and bitter taste. Finally, check the item for fragrance. Fruit that has a sweet smell is at its peak of ripeness and flavor. Fruits such as strawberries and blueberries should be purchased when fully mature and ripe. Fruits such as bananas, pears, kiwi, cantaloupes, plums, peaches, and nectarines may be purchased slightly underripe and allowed to finish ripening at room temperature at home. Place the produce in a closed paper bag to hasten the process. Avoid fruits that are very firm or hard and have a greenish color, as these were probably picked when immature and will never ripen properly.

AVOIDING THE FAT TRAPS

Although you can make most of your purchases in the produce department without fear of fat, there are a few exceptions. Coconut and avocados are two fruits that are loaded with fat. In the case of coconut, the fat is of the highly saturated, artery-clogging kind. This is not to say that you should entirely eliminate coconut from your diet—rather, use it sparingly. Try adding

some coconut-flavored extract to cakes, cookies, muffins, and other baked goods to reduce the need for flaked or shredded coconut. A few tablespoons of coconut may then be all that is needed.

As for avocados, their fat is mostly monounsaturated, which has no harmful health effects other than being high in calories like all fats. Moreover, these velvety fruits are rich in vitamin E, potassium, folate, vitamin B_6, and other nutrients. So if you like avocados, by all means, work them into your fat budget. Even with 11.5 grams of fat and 121 calories per half cup, the avocado is certainly a better fat choice than a tablespoon of butter, margarine, or oil, which provides about the same amount of fat and calories.

Nuts are another food that can lure you into the fat trap. These tasty morsels add crunch and flavor to a variety of dishes. Unfortunately, they also add fat and calories—about 80 grams of fat and 800 calories per cup. But take heart. Like avocados, nuts are high in monounsaturated fats, and so do not promote heart disease. In fact, some studies show that people who eat nuts on a regular basis actually *lower* their risk of heart disease. The reason for this may be that the fat in nuts—unlike the fat in refined oils—still contains all of its vitamin E and other essential nutrients. So if you like nuts, feel free to spend some of your fat budget on them. Instead of eating them by the handful, though, sprinkle a few over salads, add some to casseroles, or stir 3 or 4 tablespoons into muffin, quick bread, and cake batters.

To get the most out of nuts, try toasting them. Toasting intensifies the flavor of nuts so much that you can often halve the amount used. (See the inset on page 191 for details.) When used wisely, nuts will add flavor and a nutritious crunch to your dishes *without* blowing your fat budget.

PREPARING PRODUCE

Once you've brought your produce home, you'll want to prepare it in a way that maximizes taste and nutrition. If your produce is not organic, be sure to peel or thoroughly wash it before using. If any of your produce is waxed—and many apples, cucumbers, eggplants, and other fruits and vegetables are—peeling will be your best bet, as waxes cannot be washed away. For maximum freshness and nutritional value, wash and cut your vegetables just before cooking. Washing and cutting hours before use can destroy nutrients.

Finally, to preserve vitamins and minerals, eat vegetables raw, or cook them in a steamer or microwave oven just until crisp-tender. Vegetables that are cooked just until done retain not only their nutrients, but also their appealing color and fresh taste.

Broccoli With Spicy Mustard Sauce

Yield: 6 servings

1 medium head broccoli (1¼ pounds)

¾ cup Spicy Mustard Sauce (page 107)

NUTRITIONAL FACTS (PER SERVING)

Calories: 75   Fiber: 3 g
Chol: 0 mg   Protein: 3 g
Fat: 1.9 g   Sodium: 278 mg

You Save: Calories: 99 Fat: 13.3 g

1. Trim the tough stem end from the broccoli. Rinse the broccoli under cool running water, and separate it into stalks.

2. Arrange the broccoli in a microwave or conventional steamer. Cover and cook at high power or over high heat for 4 to 6 minutes, or just until tender.

3. While the broccoli is cooking, place the Spicy Mustard Sauce in a small saucepan. Place over medium heat, and cook, stirring constantly, just until the sauce is heated through.

4. Drain the broccoli, and transfer it to a serving dish. Drizzle the sauce over the broccoli, and serve hot.

Parmesan Peas and Noodles

Yield: 8 servings

6 ounces No Yolks cholesterol-free extra broad noodles

1½ cups frozen (unthawed) green peas

¾ cup Pet evaporated skimmed milk

½ cup Land O Lakes no-fat sour cream

¼ teaspoon ground white pepper

½ cup Kraft Free nonfat grated Parmesan topping

1. Cook the noodles according to package directions for 5 minutes. Add the peas to the boiling noodles, and cook for 5 to 7 additional minutes, or until the noodles are al dente and the peas are tender.

2. While the noodles are cooking, combine the evaporated milk, sour cream, and pepper in a small bowl, and stir to mix well. Set aside.

3. Drain the noodles and peas well, and return them to the pot. Add the evaporated milk mixture, and cook over low heat for about 1 minute, tossing gently until the sauce is heated through. Add the Parmesan topping, and toss to mix well. Serve hot.

NUTRITIONAL FACTS (PER ⅔-CUP SERVING)

Calories: 156   Fat: 0.5 g   Protein: 9 g
Cholesterol: 4 mg   Fiber: 1.8 g   Sodium: 177 mg

You Save: Calories: 80 Fat: 13.1 g

Crispy Onion Rings

1. Cut the onions into $\frac{1}{2}$-inch-thick slices. Separate the slices into rings, and set aside.

2. Combine all of the egg coating ingredients in a shallow bowl, and stir with a wire whisk until smooth. Set aside.

3. Place all of the corn flake coating ingredients in a food processor or blender, and process into fine crumbs. Transfer the corn flake mixture to a shallow dish.

4. Coat a large baking sheet with nonstick cooking spray. Dip the onion rings first in the egg mixture, turning to coat well, and then in the corn flake mixture. Arrange the rings in a single layer on the prepared sheet, and spray them lightly with the cooking spray.

5. Bake at 400°F for 10 to 12 minutes, or until the onion rings are crisp and nicely browned. Serve hot.

Yield: 5 servings

2 medium-large sweet onions (about 8 ounces each)

PAM® No Stick Cooking Spray

EGG COATING
$\frac{1}{4}$ cup plus 2 tablespoons Gold Medal unbleached flour

$\frac{1}{4}$ cup plus 2 tablespoons Egg Beaters egg substitute

$\frac{1}{4}$ cup skim milk

CORN FLAKE COATING
$3\frac{1}{2}$ cups Arrowhead Mills corn flakes

$\frac{1}{4}$ cup Kraft Free nonfat grated Parmesan topping

$\frac{1}{4}$ teaspoon dried thyme

$\frac{1}{4}$ teaspoon ground black pepper

NUTRITIONAL FACTS (PER SERVING)

Calories: 169	Fat: 0.2 g	Protein: 8 g
Cholesterol: 2 mg	Fiber: 2.7 g	Sodium: 156 mg

You Save: Calories: 385 Fat: 36 g

Veggie Fried Rice

Yield: 7 *servings*

1 boil-in-bag Success brown rice

1½ teaspoons sesame oil

1 teaspoon crushed fresh garlic

2½ cups finely chopped fresh broccoli

1 cup sliced fresh mushrooms

½ cup finely chopped carrot

2 tablespoons La Choy Lite soy sauce

⅛ teaspoon ground white pepper

You Save: Cal: 51 Fat: 5.9 g

1. Cook the rice according to package directions. Drain, and set aside.

2. Place the oil in a large nonstick skillet, and preheat over medium-high heat. Add the garlic, and stir-fry for 30 seconds. Add the vegetables, and stir-fry for 3 minutes, or until crisp-tender.

3. Reduce the heat to low, and add the rice, soy sauce, and pepper to the vegetable mixture. Stir-fry for another minute or 2, or until the rice and vegetables are well mixed and heated through. Add a tablespoon of water or broth if the skillet becomes too dry. Serve hot.

NUTRITIONAL FACTS (PER ¾-CUP SERVING)		
Calories: 103	Fat: 1.7 g	Protein: 3.2 g
Cholesterol: 0 mg	Fiber: 2.6 g	Sodium: 163 mg

Crispy Oven Fries

Yield: 6 *servings*

1½ pounds unpeeled baking potatoes (about 3 large)

3 tablespoons Scramblers egg substitute

PAM® No Stick Cooking Spray

COATING

⅓ cup Kraft Free nonfat grated Parmesan topping

¼ teaspoon ground black pepper

½ teaspoon dried thyme or rosemary (optional)

You Save: Cal: 263 Fat: 21.5 g

1. Combine the coating ingredients in a small dish. Stir to mix well, and set aside.

2. Scrub the potatoes, dry well, and cut into ⅜-inch-thick strips. Place the potatoes in a large bowl, drizzle the egg substitute over the potatoes, and toss to coat well. Sprinkle the prepared coating mixture over the potatoes, and toss again to coat.

3. Coat a large baking sheet with nonstick cooking spray, and arrange the potatoes in a single layer on the sheet, making sure that the strips are not touching one another. Spray the tops lightly with the cooking spray, and bake at 400°F for 15 minutes. Turn the potatoes with a spatula, and bake for 10 to 15 additional minutes, or until nicely browned and tender. Serve hot.

NUTRITIONAL FACTS (PER SERVING)		
Calories: 148	Fat: 0.3 g	Protein: 6.3 g
Cholesterol: 2 mg	Fiber: 2.7 g	Sodium: 112 mg

Cheddar-Stuffed Potatoes

Yield: 4 servings

1. If using a conventional oven, wrap each potato in aluminum foil, and bake at 400°F for 45 minutes, or until the potatoes can be pierced easily with a sharp knife. If using a microwave oven, pierce each potato with a fork in several places, and microwave at high power for 15 minutes. Allow the potatoes to cool until they can be handled easily.

2. Cut a $\frac{1}{2}$-inch lengthwise slice from the top of each potato, and carefully scoop out the pulp, leaving a $\frac{1}{4}$-inch-thick shell. Place the scooped-out potato flesh and the milk in a medium-sized bowl, and mash with a fork. Add the onion, sour cream, cheese, pepper, and parsley, and stir to mix well. Add a little more milk if the mixture seems too dry.

3. Spoon the filling back into the potato skins. Arrange the potatoes in an 8-x-8-inch baking dish, and sprinkle some paprika over the top of each. Bake at 350°F for 25 to 30 minutes, or until the filling is heated through and the top is lightly browned. Serve hot.

4 medium-sized baking potatoes (about 6 ounces each)

2 tablespoons skim milk

3 tablespoons finely chopped onion

$\frac{1}{2}$ cup Land O Lakes no-fat sour cream

$\frac{1}{2}$ cup Kraft $\frac{1}{3}$ Less Fat shredded Cheddar cheese

$\frac{1}{8}$ teaspoon ground white pepper

1 tablespoon finely chopped fresh parsley, chives, or dill

Ground paprika

NUTRITIONAL FACTS (PER SERVING)

Calories: 231	Fat: 2.9 g	Protein: 9.2 g
Cholesterol: 10 mg	Fiber: 3.6 g	Sodium: 161 mg

You Save: Calories: 100 Fat: 14 g

Sauce It Up!

Vegetables blanketed with high-fat cheese or butter sauces are *not* what the doctor ordered. Made properly, though, creamy, rich-tasting sauces can still adorn your favorite veggies. Here are some ideas for fabulously flavorful low-fat and fat-free toppings.

Spicy Peanut Sauce

Yield: ³/₄ cup

½ cup Campbell's Healthy Request chicken broth

2 tablespoons Arrowhead Mills easy spreading peanut butter

2 tablespoons Pet evaporated skimmed milk

2 teaspoons La Choy Lite soy sauce

1 tablespoon light brown sugar

2 teaspoons cornstarch

¼ cup finely chopped onion

³/₄ teaspoon crushed fresh garlic

½ teaspoon curry powder

¼ teaspoon ground ginger

1. Combine the broth, peanut butter, evaporated milk, soy sauce, brown sugar, and cornstarch in a blender, and process until smooth. Set aside.

2. Coat a small nonstick skillet with nonstick cooking spray, and preheat over medium-high heat. Add the onion and garlic, and stir-fry for about 1 minute, or until the onion is tender and starts to brown.

3. Reduce the heat under the skillet to medium, and add the curry powder and ginger. Stir-fry for about 30 seconds, or until the onions are coated with the spices. Add the broth mixture, and cook and stir for another 2 minutes, or until the mixture is thickened and bubbly.

4. Serve hot over steamed broccoli, cauliflower, green beans, asparagus, or other vegetables.

NUTRITIONAL FACTS (PER TABLESPOON)

Calories: 25	Fat: 1.2 g	Protein: 1 g
Cholesterol: 0 mg	Fiber: 0.2 g	Sodium: 60 mg

You Save: Calories: 40 Fat: 4.3 g

Spicy Mustard Sauce

1. Place all of the ingredients in a small saucepan, and stir to mix well. Place the pan over medium heat, and cook, stirring constantly, until the sauce is heated through.

2. Serve hot over steamed broccoli, cauliflower, green beans, Brussels sprouts, asparagus, or other vegetables.

Yield: 1 1/8 cups

3/4 cup Hellmann's low-fat mayonnaise

3 tablespoons spicy mustard

3 tablespoons lemon juice

1 tablespoon plus 1 1/2 teaspoons honey

NUTRITIONAL FACTS (PER TABLESPOON)

Calories: 23	Fat: 0.7 g	Protein: 0.1 g
Cholesterol: 0 mg	Fiber: 0 g	Sodium: 116 mg

You Save: Calories: 45 Fat: 6.3 g

Sour Cream-Dill Sauce

1. Place the mayonnaise, sour cream, water, lemon juice, and pepper in a small saucepan, and stir with a wire whisk to mix well. Place the pan over medium heat, and cook, stirring constantly, until the sauce is heated through.

2. Stir the dill into the sauce, and remove the pot from the heat. Serve hot over steamed cauliflower, asparagus, green beans, potatoes, or other vegetables.

Yield: 1 1/8 cups

1/2 cup plus 1 tablespoon Kraft Free mayonnaise

1/2 cup plus 1 tablespoon Breakstone's Free nonfat sour cream

1 tablespoon plus 1 1/2 teaspoons water

1 tablespoon lemon juice

1/8 teaspoon ground white pepper

2 tablespoons finely chopped fresh dill

NUTRITIONAL FACTS (PER TABLESPOON)

Calories: 12	Fat: 0 g	Protein: 0.2 g
Cholesterol: 0 mg	Fiber: 0 g	Sodium: 56 mg

You Save: Calories: 47 Fat: 6.3 g

Streusel Sweet Potatoes

Yield: *8 servings*

2 pounds sweet potatoes (about 4 medium-large)

2 cups Tree Top 100% apple juice

2 tablespoons light brown sugar

¾ teaspoon ground cinnamon

¼ teaspoon ground nutmeg

½ cup Egg Beaters egg substitute

TOPPING

⅓ cup Post Grape-Nuts cereal

2 tablespoons Pillsbury's Best whole wheat flour

3 tablespoons light brown sugar

2 tablespoons Kretschmer toasted wheat germ or finely chopped pecans

1 tablespoon Tree Top frozen (thawed) 100% apple juice concentrate

1. Peel the potatoes, and cut them into ¾-inch pieces. Place the potatoes and the juice in a 3-quart pot, and bring to a boil over high heat. Reduce the heat to low, cover, and simmer for 25 to 30 minutes, or until the potatoes are very soft.

2. Drain all but ½ cup of juice from the potatoes. Add the brown sugar, cinnamon, and nutmeg to the potatoes, and, using a potato masher, mash the mixture until smooth.

3. Stir the egg substitute into the potato mixture. Coat an 8-inch square pan with nonstick cooking spray, and spread the mixture evenly in the dish.

4. To make the topping, combine the cereal, flour, brown sugar, and wheat germ or pecans in a small bowl, and stir to mix well. Add the juice concentrate, and stir until the mixture is moist and crumbly. Sprinkle the topping over the sweet potato mixture.

5. Bake at 350°F for 40 minutes, or until a sharp knife inserted in the center of the dish comes out clean. If the top starts to brown too quickly, loosely cover the dish with aluminum foil during the last 10 minutes of baking. Remove the dish from the oven, and let sit for 5 minutes before serving.

NUTRITIONAL FACTS (PER ⅔-CUP SERVING)

Calories: 173	Fat: 0.6 g	Protein: 4.5 g
Cholesterol: 0 mg	Fiber: 3.2 g	Sodium: 73 mg

You Save: Calories: 184   Fat: 18.5 g

Savory Acorn Squash

1. Cut each squash in half crosswise, and scoop out and discard the seeds. If necessary, trim a small piece off the bottom of each half to allow it to sit upright.

2. Combine the bulgur wheat and broth in a 1½-quart pot, and bring to a boil over high heat. Stir the mixture, cover, and remove from the heat. Set aside for 30 minutes, or until the liquid has been absorbed.

3. Stir the apple, raisins or cranberries, celery, savory or rosemary, and, if desired, the nuts into the bulgur.

4. Coat a 7-x-11-inch pan with nonstick cooking spray. Spoon the bulgur mixture into the squash shells, mounding the tops slightly. Arrange the squash in the prepared dish.

5. Cover the dish with aluminum foil, and bake at 350°F for 50 minutes, or until the squash are tender. Serve hot.

Yield: 4 servings

2 medium acorn squash (about 1 pound each)

½ cup Good Shepherd bulgur wheat

¾ cup plus 2 tablespoons Hain fat-free vegetable broth

¾ cup chopped tart apple

3 tablespoons dark raisins or dried cranberries

3 tablespoons finely chopped celery

¾ teaspoon dried savory or rosemary leaves, or 2¼ teaspoons fresh

2 tablespoons chopped toasted pecans or walnuts (page 191) (optional)

NUTRITIONAL FACTS (PER SERVING)		
Calories: 192	Fat: 0.6 g	Protein: 4.5 g
Cholesterol: 0 mg	Fiber: 10.8 g	Sodium: 149 mg

You Save: Calories: 75 Fat: 8.3 g

Country-Style Collards

1. Combine all of the ingredients in a 2-quart pot, and bring to a boil over high heat. Stir to mix well, reduce the heat to medium-low, and cover.

2. Simmer the greens, stirring occasionally, for about 20 minutes, or until tender. Serve hot.

Yield: 5 servings

1 pound frozen (unthawed) chopped collard or turnip greens

¾ cup water

½ cup diced Butterball turkey ham

¾ teaspoon dry mustard

NUTRITIONAL FACTS (PER ⅔-CUP SERVING)		
Calories: 48	Fat: 0.8 g	Protein: 5.3 g
Cholesterol: 6 mg	Fiber: 3 g	Sodium: 177 mg

You Save: Calories: 32 Fat: 4.7 g

Summer Squash Casserole

Yield: *6 servings*

1½ pounds fresh yellow squash (about 8–10 medium)

½ cup finely chopped onion

3 tablespoons Gold Medal unbleached flour

¼ teaspoon coarsely ground black pepper

¾ cup Light n' Lively nonfat cottage cheese

¾ cup Egg Beaters egg substitute

¾ cup Sargento Light fancy shredded natural Cheddar cheese

2 slices Louis Rich turkey bacon, cooked, crumbled, and drained (optional)

2 tablespoons finely ground SnackWell's Cracked Pepper crackers (about 5 crackers)

PAM® Butter Flavor No Stick Cooking Spray

1. Cut each squash into fourths lengthwise. Then cut into ¼-inch-wide slices. (There should be about 5 cups of squash. Adjust the amount if necessary.)

2. Combine the squash and onion in a large bowl. Add the flour and pepper, and toss to mix well. Add the cottage cheese and egg substitute, and stir to mix well. Stir in the Cheddar and, if desired, the bacon.

3. Coat an 8-inch square casserole dish with nonstick cooking spray, and spread the squash mixture evenly in the dish. Sprinkle the cracker crumbs over the top, and spray the top lightly with the cooking spray.

4. Bake at 375°F for 55 minutes, or until the top is nicely browned and the edges are bubbly. Remove the dish from the oven, and let sit for 10 minutes before serving.

NUTRITIONAL FACTS (PER ¾-CUP SERVING)

Calories: 101	Fat: 2.6 g	Protein: 10 g
Cholesterol: 61 mg	Fiber: 2.1 g	Sodium: 227 mg

You Save: Calories: 170   Fat: 19.6 g

FAT-FIGHTER'S GUIDE TO
Packaged and Frozen Side Dishes

Many busy people love the convenience of boxed side dish mixes. Whether the dish is macaroni and cheese, potatoes au gratin, or rice pilaf, most of the ingredients are in the box, and with a minimum of effort, you can enjoy a tasty dish in just a few minutes. Similarly, the frozen food case of the grocery store has a dazzling selection of frozen side dishes, from French fried potatoes to broccoli with cheese sauce.

The bad news is that while side dish mixes are convenient, most are highly processed, and therefore high in sodium and artificial ingredients. In fact, a half-cup serving of most mixes provides 500 to 700 milligrams of sodium. Most rice and pasta side dish mixes are made with white rice and refined pasta, so that they contain significantly less fiber, vitamins, and minerals than whole grain products. And if your family loves mashed potatoes made from potato flakes, or other dishes made with dehydrated potatoes, keep in mind that processing has robbed these potatoes of most of their vitamin C.

Are frozen side dishes any better? Many of these products, too, provide far too much sodium, as well as a generous dose of fat.

Fortunately, side-by-side with these high-sodium and high-fat products are a number of excellent packaged and frozen side dishes that are easy to make, low in fat, and just as delicious as their higher-sodium and -fat counterparts. Moreover, a number of regular side dish mixes can be made low-fat with just a few ingredient substitutions. This Fat-Fighter's Guide will show you how.

BOXED SIDE DISH MIXES

Most grocery and health foods stores offer a number of healthful packaged side dishes. Arrowhead Mills, for instance, makes a variety of quick-cooking brown rice pilafs—products that provide lots of flavor and nutrition with far less sodium than most brands. Lundberg Farms, Near East, Fantastic Foods, and De Bole's also make a range of whole grain side dish mixes, from macaroni and cheese to brown rice and lentil pilafs.

When whipping up side dishes with *any* mix, it's easy to make a healthier dish by modifying the manufacturer's directions. In fact, many mixes, as packaged, contain very little fat. Most of the finished dish's fat is added during preparation.

When preparing your favorite packaged mix, simply replace the full-fat products called for with their no- or low-fat counterparts. For instance, if the directions on a box of macaroni and cheese instruct you to add milk and margarine to the sauce packet, substitute skim milk and reduced-fat margarine. Or, even better, use only the skim milk, and leave out the margarine entirely. If the resulting sauce seems a little dry, add a few more tablespoons of milk until the sauce has the desired consistency. You'll soon learn the best way to prepare the mix so that the dish is both healthy and tasty.

FROZEN SIDE DISHES

When choosing frozen side dishes, your best bet is to stick with plain frozen vegetables, and then add your own low-fat seasonings and sauces. (See the inset on page 106 for some low-fat sauce ideas.)

Looking for low-fat frozen fries? Think big. The larger the cut, the less surface area there is to soak up fat. Large-cut fries like Ore Ida Potato Wedges With Skins have only 2.5 grams of fat per serving, rather than the 5 or 6 fat grams found in a serving of thinner-cut shoestring fries. Finally, to keep the fat count low, be sure to bake those fries in the oven instead of deep-frying them.

Spinach-Stuffed Tomatoes

Yield: *8 servings*

4 large tomatoes (about 8 ounces each)

1 cup Fantastic Foods whole wheat couscous

1½ cups Hain fat-free vegetable broth

1½ teaspoons crushed fresh garlic

3 cups (packed) chopped fresh spinach

¼ cup finely chopped fresh basil

¼ cup Alpine Lace fat-free grated Parmesan cheese

½ cup Sargento Light fancy shredded natural mozzarella cheese

1. Cut each tomato in half crosswise, and scoop out the pulp, leaving just the shell. Discard the pulp or reserve it for another use, and set the tomato shells aside.

2. Place the couscous and broth in a 1-quart pot, and bring to a boil over high heat. Stir the mixture, reduce the heat to low, and cover. Simmer for 3 to 5 minutes, or until the liquid is absorbed and the couscous is tender. Remove the pot from the heat, and set aside to cool slightly.

3. Coat a large nonstick skillet with nonstick cooking spray, and preheat over medium heat. Add the garlic, and stir-fry for about 1 minute, or until the garlic is browned. Add the spinach, and stir-fry for another minute or 2, or until the spinach is wilted.

4. Remove the skillet from the heat, and add the couscous, basil, and Parmesan. Toss to mix well.

5. Coat a 7-x-11-inch pan with nonstick cooking spray. Spoon the spinach mixture into the tomato shells, mounding the tops slightly, and arrange the tomatoes in the prepared pan. Sprinkle 1 tablespoon of mozzarella over the top of each tomato.

6. Bake at 350°F for 25 minutes, or until the tomatoes are tender, the filling is heated through, and the cheese is melted. Serve hot.

NUTRITIONAL FACTS (PER SERVING)

Calories: 105	Fat: 1.4 g	Protein: 6 g
Cholesterol: 3 mg	Fiber: 3.2 g	Sodium: 109 mg

You Save: Calories: 78 Fat: 8.6 g

Santa Fe Stuffed Zucchini

1. Slice each zucchini in half lengthwise, and slice a thin strip off the bottom of each half so that the halves sit upright. Using a spoon, scoop the flesh out of the center of each zucchini half, leaving a $\frac{1}{4}$-inch-thick shell. Chop the scooped-out zucchini flesh, and set aside.

2. Coat a large skillet with nonstick cooking spray, and preheat over medium heat. Add the cumin, and cook, stirring constantly, for about 2 minutes, or until the cumin smells toasted and fragrant. Add the chopped zucchini, tomato, onion, and pepper to the skillet. Cover and cook for about 5 minutes, or until the vegetables are soft.

3. Remove the skillet from the heat, and allow the mixture to cool slightly. Stir in first the corn, and then the cheese.

4. Coat a 9-x-13-inch pan with nonstick cooking spray. Spoon the mixture into the hollowed-out zucchini halves, and arrange the halves in the prepared pan. Bake at 350°F for about 20 minutes, or until the shells are tender and the cheese is melted. Serve hot.

Yield: 8 servings

4 large zucchini (about 8 ounces each)

1 teaspoon whole cumin seeds

1 cup chopped plum tomatoes (about 3 medium)

$\frac{1}{4}$ cup chopped onion

$\frac{1}{8}$ teaspoon ground black pepper

1 cup frozen (thawed) whole kernel corn

1 cup Sargento Light fancy shredded natural Cheddar cheese

NUTRITIONAL FACTS (PER SERVING)		
Calories: 74	Fat: 2.5 g	Protein: 6.1 g
Cholesterol: 5 mg	Fiber: 2.2 g	Sodium: 106 mg

You Save: Calories: 66 Fat: 6.5 g

Barley, Spinach, and Mushroom Pilaf

Yield: *5 servings*

1 cup Mother's quick-cooking
  barley

2 cups Hain fat-free vegetable
  broth

1½ teaspoons crushed fresh garlic

1½ cups sliced fresh mushrooms

½ teaspoon dried thyme

⅛ teaspoon ground black pepper

1½ cups packed chopped fresh
  spinach

1. Combine the barley and broth in a 1-quart pot, and bring to a boil over high heat. Reduce the heat to low, cover, and simmer for 10 to 12 minutes, or until the liquid is absorbed and the barley is tender. Remove the pot from the heat, and set aside.

2. Coat a large nonstick skillet with olive oil cooking spray, and preheat over medium-high heat. Add the garlic, and stir-fry for about 30 seconds, or until the garlic starts to brown. Add the mushrooms, thyme, and pepper, and stir-fry for about 2 minutes, or until the mushrooms are tender. Add the spinach, and stir-fry for about 1 additional minute, or just until the spinach is wilted. Add a little water or broth if the skillet becomes too dry.

3. Add the barley to the skillet, and stir-fry for another minute, or until well mixed and heated through. Serve hot.

NUTRITIONAL FACTS (PER ⅔-CUP SERVING)

| Calories: 126 | Fat: 0.7 g | Protein: 4.3 g |
| Cholesterol: 0 mg | Fiber: 3.8 g | Sodium: 258 mg |

You Save: Calories: 54   Fat: 6 g

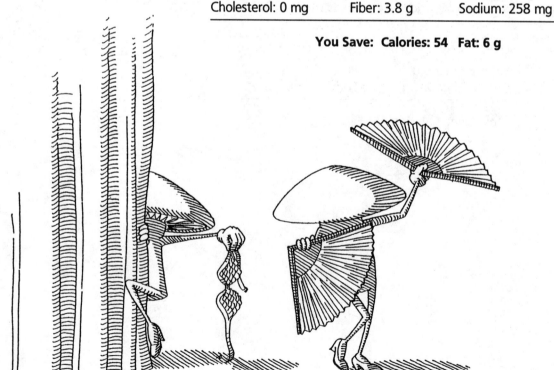

7. Meatless Main Dishes

What's one of the best ways to get the fat out of your diet and boost your intake of fiber? Eat more meatless meals. The vegetables, legumes, and grains featured in vegetarian cuisine are naturally low in fat and rich in fiber. And as vegetarians have long known, these foods are also powerful preventive medicine against cancer, heart disease, high blood pressure, obesity, and many other health problems.

There is one catch, though. Meatless meals made with whole milk cheeses, full-fat sour cream, and other high-fat dairy products, or with excessive amounts of oil, are no more healthful than meat-based meals. If this is hard to believe, consider this: Just one ounce of full-fat cheese, such as Cheddar or Swiss, contains almost twice as much fat as a three-ounce serving of top beef round, and more than three times as much fat as a three-ounce portion of skinless chicken breast! Fortunately, the vast selection of low-fat and nonfat dairy products now available makes it possible to eliminate much of the fat from vegetarian fare. In addition, the vegetable oil, butter, and margarine used in most recipes can be greatly reduced or even eliminated.

Will your low-fat meatless meals be bland and boring? Never! In the recipes that follow, vegetable broths, garlic, herbs, and other savory seasonings enhance the natural flavors of fresh vegetables, hearty beans, and whole grains. The result is an array of tantalizing dishes that provide a welcome change of pace from the typical meat-starch-vegetable routine.

To make your next visit to the grocery store a breeze, this chapter includes a terrific Fat-Fighter's Guide to the Dairy Case (page 116). This guide introduces a host of delicious low-fat and fat-free products, including cheeses, sour cream, yogurt, and more. Additionally, the Fat-Fighter's Guide on page 28 acquaints you with the many wonderful egg substitutes now available, and explains how these substitutes, as well as egg whites, can be used successfully in the preparation of low-fat dishes.

When scanning this chapter for dinner ideas, you'll want to keep your "audience" in mind. If your family is skeptical about vegetarian dishes, a south-of-the-border entrée such as Black Bean Quesadillas or Enchilada Pie will make a perfect introduction to vegetarian cuisine. In fact, these festive stick-to-your ribs dishes—prepared with spicy beans, nonfat and low-fat cheeses, and nonfat sour cream—may even pass as "junk food." If your family is a bit more adventurous, try a more sophisticated dish, such as Spicy Vegetable Stew, savory Orzo and Vegetable Pie, or flavorful Fantastic Falafel. Then warm some crusty whole grain bread, toss together a crisp green salad, and get ready to experience the many pleasures and rewards of low-fat vegetarian cuisine.

FAT-FIGHTER'S GUIDE TO
The Dairy Case

In the dairy case, you will find a dazzling assortment of reduced-fat, low-fat, and nonfat products—all great ways to make your diet leaner and healthier. This Fat-Fighter's Guide highlights some of the available products, and provides simple guidelines for choosing and using dairy foods.

Bear in mind that unlike most areas of the food industry, the dairy business is partially constituted of local and regional manufacturers. Therefore, each part of the country has many fine brands that are specific to that region. By comparing your local products with the national brands highlighted in this guide, you will be able to choose those foods that best meet your nutritional needs, your cooking needs, your tastes, and your budget.

CHEESE

Nearly everyone loves cheese. Fortunately, whether you like your cheese "straight" with crackers or whipped into a creamy cheesecake filling, you can now find a variety of low- and no-fat products that will allow you to lose the fat without losing the taste.

When selecting dairy products, be aware that these items are quite perishable. For this reason, it's important to check the date stamp on all packages and to buy the freshest products available.

Firm and Hard Cheeses

Both reduced-fat and nonfat cheeses of many types—including Swiss, Cheddar, Monterey jack, and mozzarella—are widely available in grocery stores. Reduced-fat cheeses generally have 60 to 80 calories and 3 to 6 grams of fat per ounce, while nonfat cheeses contain about 40 calories per ounce, and no fat at all. Compare this with whole milk varieties, which contain 8 to 10 grams of fat and 100 to 110 calories per ounce, and you'll realize your savings in fat and calories.

Firm and hard cheeses can be grouped in one of two categories—natural or process. Natural cheeses generally contain 30 to 50 percent less salt than process brands. They also contain few or no artificial ingredients. Process cheeses, on the other hand, tend to be high in both salt and artificial ingredients. Process cheeses—which are so labelled for easy identification—do melt exceptionally well, though, and so are your best bet for making recipes like cheese sauces.

The following table presents nutrition information for some commonly available nonfat, low-fat, and reduced-fat firm and hard cheeses. For regular use, try to select brands with no more than 3 grams of fat and 200 milligrams of sodium per ounce. Higher-fat, higher-sodium brands should be used with moderation.

Some Commonly Available Nonfat, Low-Fat, and Reduced-Fat Firm and Hard Cheeses

Brand	Serving Size	Calories	Fat	Sodium
Alpine Lace Fat-Free Grated Parmesan	2 teaspoons	10	0 g	65 mg
Alpine Lace Fat-Free Pasteurized Process Cheddar Cheese Product (block or shredded)	1 ounce	45	0 g	280 mg
Alpine Lace Reduced-Fat Cheddar (block)	1 ounce	80	4.5 g	95 mg

Brand	Serving Size	Calories	Fat	Sodium
Alpine Lace Reduced-Fat Provolone (block)	1 ounce	70	5 g	85 mg
Borden Fat-Free Singles Process Cheese Product	$2/3$ ounce	25	0 g	280 mg
Borden Low-Fat Process Cheese Product (slices)	$2/3$ ounce	30	1 g	260 mg
Borden Light Singles Pasteurized Process Cheese Product	$3/4$ ounce	45	2.5 g	300 mg
Cracker Barrel $1/3$ Less Fat Sharp Cheddar (block)	1 ounce	90	6 g	240 mg
Healthy Choice Shredded Fat-Free Cheddar, Mozzarella, or Pizza Cheese	1 ounce	45	0 g	200 mg
Healthy Choice Fat-Free Pasteurized Process Cheese Product	1 ounce	35	0 g	390 mg
Healthy Choice Fat-Free String Cheese	1 ounce	45	0 g	200 mg
Jarslberg Lite Swiss (block)	1 ounce	70	3.5 g	130 mg
Kraft Free Nonfat Grated Parmesan Topping	2 teaspoons	15	0 g	65 mg
Kraft Free Singles Nonfat Pasteurized Process Sharp Cheddar	$3/4$ ounce	35	0 g	310 mg
Kraft $1/3$ Less Fat American Pasteurized Process Cheese Product (slices)	$3/4$ ounce	50	3 g	330 mg
Kraft 1/3 Less Fat Cheddar, Sharp Cheddar, Colby, or Monterey Jack (block or shredded)	1 ounce	90	6 g	240 mg
Lifetime Nonfat Process Cheddar or Sharp Cheddar (block)	1 ounce	40	0 g	220 mg
Moo Town Snackers Light String Cheese	1 ounce	60	3 g	200 mg
Polly-O Free Natural Nonfat Mozzarella (block)	1 ounce	35	0 g	220 mg
Sargento Light Shredded Natural Cheddar	1 ounce	70	4.5 g	200 mg
Sargento Light Shredded Natural Mozzarella	1 ounce	70	3.5 g	140 mg
Sargento Preferred Light Wafer Thin Sliced Reduced-Fat Swiss	1 ounce	80	4 g	50 mg
Smart Beat Fat Free Nondairy Slices	$2/3$ ounce	25	0 g	180 mg
Velveeta Light Pasteurized Process Cheese Product	1 ounce	60	3 g	420 mg
Weight Watchers Fat-Free Parmesan	1 tablespoon	20	0 g	60 mg
Weight Watchers Fat-Free Swiss Process Cheese Product (slices)	$3/4$ ounce	30	0 g	280 mg

Cooking With Firm and Hard Cheeses

If you have been cooking with nonfat cheeses for a while, you may have noticed that some brands do not melt as well as their full-fat counterparts. So what do you do when you want to prepare a cheese sauce, a cheese soup, or another smooth and creamy cheese dish? One option is to use a finely shredded brand of nonfat cheese. Usually referred to on the package label as "fancy" shredded cheese, finely shredded nonfat cheeses melt better than coarsely shredded brands—although they still may not melt completely. Or use a process nonfat cheese. Process cheeses are specially made to melt, so they will work in any sauce recipe. Most process cheeses tend to be quite high in sodium, but you can avoid a sodium overload when using these cheeses by leaving out the salt and avoiding the use of other high-sodium ingredients in your recipe. What about reduced-fat cheeses? Most brands melt nicely, and can be substituted for full-fat brands in any sauce recipe, with very little difference in taste or texture.

What's your best choice for casseroles, lasagna, and pizza? Both nonfat and low-fat brands can be used, although low-fat brands like Sargento Preferred Light Fancy Shredded Mozzarella seem to have more "stretch" as a pizza topping. As for topping salads, tacos, or a bowl of chili or black bean soup, any of the nonfat or low-fat shredded brands work nicely. Only your waistline will know the difference!

Soft Cheeses

Low-fat and nonfat cottage cheese, cream cheese, ricotta, and farmer cheese make possible a wide range of healthy delights, from onion dip to cheesecake. By understanding the differences between the various products on the market, you'll be able to pick the one that best suits your needs. (For a quick overview of some of the products now available, see the table on page 119.)

Cottage Cheese

Although often thought of as a diet food, full-fat cottage cheese has 5 grams of fat per 4-ounce serving, making it far from diet fare. Instead, choose nonfat or 1-percent low-fat cottage cheese, both of which are versatile cooking ingredients. Puréed until smooth, these products make a great base for dips, spreads, and salad dressings. Cottage cheese also adds richness and body to casseroles, quiches, cheesecakes, and many other recipes. Most brands of cottage cheese are quite high in sodium, with about 400 milligrams per half cup, so it's best to avoid adding salt when this cheese is a recipe ingredient. As an alternative, use unsalted cottage cheese, which is available in some stores.

Another option when buying cottage cheese is dry curd cottage cheese. This nonfat version is made without the "dressing" or creaming mixture. Minus the dressing, cottage cheese has a drier consistency; hence its name, "dry curd." Unlike most cottage cheese, dry curd is very low in sodium. Use dry curd cottage cheese as you would nonfat cottage cheese in casseroles, quiches, dips, spreads, salad dressings, and cheesecakes.

Cream Cheese

Regular full-fat cream cheese contains 10 grams of fat per ounce, making this popular spread a real menace if you're trying to reduce dietary fat. A tasty alternative is light cream cheese, which has only 5 grams of fat per ounce. Another reduced-fat alternative is Neufchatel cheese, which contains 6 grams of fat per ounce. And, of course, nonfat cream cheese contains no fat at all. Like light cream cheese and Neufchatel, nonfat cream cheese may be used in dips, spreads, and sauces. Look for brands like Philadelphia Free and Healthy Choice, and use the block-style cream cheese for best results when following recipes. The softer tub-style cream cheese should be reserved for spreading on bagels and other foods.

When substituting nonfat cream cheese for the full-fat version in cheesecakes, you may find that the texture of the cake is softer—more pudding-like—than that of traditional cheesecake. If this happens, try adding a tablespoon of flour to the batter for each 8-ounce block of nonfat cream cheese used. This should produce a firm, nicely-textured cake that is remarkably low in calories and fat.

Ricotta Cheese

Ricotta is a mild, slightly sweet, creamy cheese that may be used in dips, spreads, and traditional Italian dishes like lasagna. As the name implies, nonfat ricotta contains no fat at all. Low-fat and light ricottas, on the other hand, have 1 to 3 grams of fat per ounce, while whole milk ricotta has 4 grams of fat per ounce. Look for brands like Frigo Fat-Free, Polly-O Free, Maggio Nonfat, Sorrento Fat-Free, and Sargento Preferred Light.

Many stores and regional dairies offer their own fat-free brands as well.

Soft Curd Farmer Cheese

This soft, spreadable white cheese makes a good low-fat substitute for cream cheese. Brands made with skim milk have about 3 grams of fat per ounce compared with cream cheese's 10 grams. Soft curd farmer cheese may be used in dips, spreads, and cheesecakes, and as a filling for blintzes. Some brands are made with whole milk, so read the label before you buy. Look for a brand like Friendship Farmer Cheese.

Nondairy Cheese Alternatives

If you choose to avoid dairy products because of a lactose intolerance or for another reason, you'll be glad to know that low-fat cheeses made from

Some Commonly Available Nonfat, Low-Fat, and Reduced-Fat Soft Cheeses

Cheese	Serving Size	Calories	Fat	Sodium
Cottage Cheese				
Breakstone's Free Cottage Cheese	4 ounces	80	0 g	430 mg
Friendship 1% No Added Salt Cottage Cheese	4 ounces	90	1 g	40 mg
Light n' Lively Nonfat Cottage Cheese	4 ounces	80	0 g	440 mg
Cream Cheese				
Healthy Choice Fat-Free Cream Cheese (block)	2 tablespoons	25	0 g	200 mg
Philadelphia Free Nonfat Cream Cheese (block)	2 tablespoons	25	0 g	135 mg
Philadelphia Free Nonfat Cream Cheese (tub)	2 tablespoons	35	0 g	180 mg
Philadelphia Light Cream Cheese (tub)	2 tablespoons	70	5 g	150 mg
Farmer Cheese				
Friendship Farmer Cheese	1 ounce	50	2.5 g	120 mg
Friendship No Added Salt Farmer Cheese	1 ounce	50	2.5 g	10 mg
Ricotta				
Frigo Fat-Free Ricotta	2 ounces	45	0 g	120 mg
Maggio Nonfat Riccotta	2 ounces	50	0 g	170 mg
Polly-O Free Ricotta	2 ounces	50	0 g	85 mg
Sorrento Nonfat Ricotta	2 ounces	60	0 g	60 mg

soymilk, almond milk, and Brazil nut milk are now available in a variety of flavors. Look for brands like AlmondRella, VeganRella, TofuRella, Soya Kaas, Nu Tofu, and Smart Beat Fat Free Nondairy Slices. Be aware that some of these brands do contain casein, a milk protein that you may want to avoid.

Measuring Cheese

Throughout the recipes in this book, I have usually expressed the amount of cheese needed in cups. For instance, a recipe may call for 1 cup of cottage cheese or ¼ cup of grated Parmesan. Since you will sometimes buy cheese in chunks and grate it in your own kitchen, or buy packages marked in ounces when the recipe calls for cups, it is useful to understand that the conversion of cheese from ounces (weight) to cups (volume) varies, depending on the texture of the cheese. When using the recipes in *The Brand Name Fat-Fighter's Cookbook,* the following table should help take the guesswork out of these conversions.

Cheese Equivalency Amounts

Cheese	Weight	Equivalent Volume
Cheddar	8 ounces	2 cups shredded or crumbled
Cottage Cheese	8 ounces	1 cup
Cream Cheese	8 ounces	1 cup
Farmer Cheese	8 ounces	1 cup
Mozzarella	8 ounces	2 cups shredded
Parmesan	8 ounces	2¼ cups grated
Ricotta	8 ounces	1 cup

OTHER LOW-FAT AND NONFAT DAIRY PRODUCTS

Of course, cheese isn't the only dairy product you buy at the supermarket. How about the sour cream you use to make dips and sauces, the yogurt you have at lunch time, and the milk you add to your coffee or cereal? Fortunately, there are low-fat and nonfat versions of these and other dairy products as well.

Buttermilk

Buttermilk adds a rich flavor and texture to baked goods like biscuits, muffins, and cakes, and lends a "cheesy" taste to sauces, cheesecakes, and casseroles. Originally a by-product of butter making, this product should perhaps be called "butterless" milk. Most brands of buttermilk are from 0.5 to 2 percent fat by weight, but some brands are as much as 3.5 percent fat. Choose brands that are no more than 1 percent milkfat.

If you do not have buttermilk on hand, a good substitute can be made by mixing equal parts of nonfat yogurt and skim milk. Alternatively, place a tablespoon of vinegar or lemon juice in a one-cup measure, and fill to the one-cup mark with skim milk. Let the mixture sit for five minutes before using.

Evaporated Skimmed Milk

This ingredient, which will be found with the canned goods, is included in this section because it can be substituted for cream in quiches, sauces, cream soups, custards, puddings, and other dishes. A wonderful cooking aid, this product adds creamy richness but no fat. It even makes a good creamer for coffee, where it will add some calcium, rather than the sugar and fat found in most nondairy creamers.

Milk

Whole milk, the highest-fat milk available, is 3.5 percent fat by weight and has 8 grams—almost 2 teaspoons—of fat per cup. Instead, choose skim (nonfat) milk, which, with all but a trace of fat removed, has only about 0.5 gram of fat per cup. Another good choice is 1-percent low-fat milk, which, as the name implies, is 1 percent fat by weight and contains 2 grams of fat per cup.

What about 2-percent low-fat milk? By legal definition, a low-fat product can have no more than 3 grams of fat per serving. Milk, however, is exempt from this rule. So 2-percent milk can be called low-fat even though each cup contains 5 grams of fat—the equivalent of 1 teaspoon of butter. Clearly, skim and 1-percent milk are the better choices.

People who cannot tolerate milk sugar—lactose—will be glad to know that most supermarkets stock Lactaid milk in a nonfat version. Nonfat Lactaid milk may be used in place of milk in any recipe. Some excellent nondairy alternatives to milk are also available. One tasty alternative is Rice Dream. This product, made from brown rice, has a creamy, slightly sweet taste that is similar to that of milk. Plain, unflavored Rice Dream is good for topping cereal and for cooking. Rice Dream is also available in several flavors. Whatever flavor you choose, be sure to get the 1-percent low-fat, calcium-fortified version. Several brands of low-fat calcium-fortified soy milk are also available. Look for brands like West Soy Low-Fat.

Nonfat Dry Milk Powder

Like evaporated skim milk, this product is not found in the dairy case. But because it is so indispensable in low-fat and fat-free cooking, nonfat dry milk powder is well worth mentioning. The addition of this handy powder to quiches, cream soups, sauces, custards, and puddings adds creamy richness, while boosting nutritional value. One cup of skim milk mixed with $1/3$ cup of nonfat dry milk powder can replace cream in most recipes. This product may also be added to fat-free cookies and brownies to enhance flavor and browning. And here's one more idea—try nonfat dry milk in coffee instead of powdered nondairy creamers. (Use about 1 tablespoon of milk powder to replace a teaspoon of nondairy creamer.) For best results, always buy *instant* nonfat dry milk powder, as this product will not clump. Look for brands like Carnation instant nonfat dry milk and Milkman instant low-fat dry milk.

Sour Cream

As calorie- and fat-conscious people know, full-fat sour cream can contain almost 500 calories and about 48 grams of fat per cup! Use nonfat sour cream, though, and you'll save 320 calories and 48 grams of fat. Made from cultured nonfat milk thickened with vegetable gums, nonfat sour cream substitutes beautifully for its fatty counterpart in dips, spreads, and sauces.

All brands of nonfat sour cream can be substituted for the full-fat version in dips, dressings, and other cold dishes. However, a few brands will separate when added to hot sauces and gravies. For these recipes, use a brand like Land O Lakes No-Fat, Breakstone's Free, or Sealtest Free sour cream, all of which hold up well during cooking. Other nationally available brands include Guilt Free and Naturally Yours No Fat. Most stores also carry their own brand of nonfat sour cream.

Not ready to go totally fat-free with your sour cream yet? Many brands of reduced-fat and light sour cream are also available. These products contain one half to one third less fat than full-fat brands, and are a nice start for people who are just beginning to get the fat out of their diets.

Yogurt

Plain yogurt with 1 percent or less milkfat substitutes nicely for sour cream in cold dishes, dips, and dressings. This product also adds creamy richness and flavor to sauces, baked goods, and casseroles. Like some brands of nonfat sour cream, yogurt will curdle if added to hot sauces or gravies. To prevent this, let the yogurt warm to room temperature, and then stir in 2 tablespoons of unbleached flour or 1 tablespoon of cornstarch for each cup of yogurt to be used. The yogurt may then be added to the sauce without fear of separation.

Flavored yogurts make a nutritious, calcium-rich snack. Of course, these yogurts do come packaged with varying amounts of fat and sugar—as much as 9 teaspoons of sugar and $1\frac{1}{2}$ teaspoons of fat per cup. While it is a simple matter to avoid unwanted fat in yogurt—just select one of the many nonfat or 1-percent brands—it is harder to determine how much added sugar is in a given container. Why? The grams of sugar listed on the label include the naturally occurring milk sugar (lactose), plus any sugar present from added fruit, plus any added refined sugar. But if you keep in mind that one cup of plain yogurt contains about 16 grams of naturally occurring sugar, you can deduce that any sugar over this number has been added. For instance, if a cup of low-fat strawberry yogurt contains 46 grams of sugar, you can deduce that 30 of the grams come from added sugar (46 – 16 = 30). This is the equivalent of about $7\frac{1}{2}$ teaspoons of sugar (1 teaspoon of sugar = 4 grams). Some of the sugar is from the strawberries, but most is from a refined product.

To reduce your sugar intake, and therefore your calories, choose a plain unflavored yogurt, and then add your own fruit and just a couple of teaspoons of sugar or honey for sweetness. Or choose one of the many brands that are sweetened with aspartame, such as Dannon Light, Light n' Lively, or Weight Watchers Ultimate 90. These sugar-free brands contain 90 to 100 calories per cup—about half the calories of a sugar-sweetened yogurt. Realize, too, that yogurts come in both 6- and 8-ounce serving sizes, so the calories and sugar vary accordingly. And do be sure to select a brand that contains active yogurt cultures. Many brands display a seal on the label which indicates that the product meets National Yogurt Association standards for active cultures.

Yogurt Cheese

A good substitute for cream cheese in dips, spreads, and cheesecakes, yogurt cheese can be made at home with any brand of plain or flavored yogurt that does not contain gelatin. Simply place the yogurt in a funnel lined with cheesecloth or a coffee filter, and let it drain into a jar in the refrigerator for eight hours or overnight. When the yogurt is reduced by half, it is ready to use. The whey that collects in the jar may be used in bread and muffin recipes, in place of the listed liquid.

Nondairy Creamers and Whipped Toppings

Are nondairy coffee creamers and whipped toppings any better than the high-fat dairy products they are meant to replace? Sometimes. A glance at the ingredients list on most nondairy coffee creamers reveals them to be made of water; corn syrup; and partially hydrogenated vegetable oil, which contains cholesterol-raising trans-fatty acids. One tablespoon of these products contains about 20 calories and 1.5 grams of fat—about the same as that found in an equivalent amount of half-and-half. The bottom line is that neither should be used in large amounts. Instead, try one of the new fat-free nondairy coffee creamers. With about 10 calories and 2 grams of sugar per tablespoon, these products are a better choice than cream or half-and-half. For an even healthier choice, try evaporated skim milk or nonfat dry milk powder, both of which will add nutrients to your coffee as they lighten it.

As for nondairy whipped toppings, the light versions—like Cool Whip Lite—contain about 80 percent less fat than whipped heavy cream, and half the fat of regular nondairy whipped toppings. For a creamier taste and texture, try mixing two parts of Cool Whip Lite with one part of nonfat vanilla yogurt. The resulting product will not only have a taste and texture more like that of whipped cream, but also provide less fat and greater nutritional value.

Swiss Noodle Kugel

Yield: 6 servings

1. Cook the noodles al dente according to package directions. Drain well, and return the noodles to the pot.

2. Add the spinach, cottage cheese, Swiss cheese, and 2 tablespoons of the Parmesan topping to the noodles, and toss to mix well.

3. Coat a 2½-quart casserole dish with nonstick cooking spray, and spread the noodle mixture evenly in the dish. Combine the egg substitute, evaporated milk, and nutmeg in a small bowl, and pour the mixture over the noodles. Sprinkle the remaining 2 tablespoons of Parmesan over the top.

4. Cover the dish with aluminum foil, and bake at 350°F for 50 minutes. Remove the foil, and bake for 10 additional minutes, or until the top is lightly browned and a sharp knife inserted in the center of the dish comes out clean.

5. Remove the dish from the oven, and let sit for 10 minutes before serving.

6 ounces No Yolks cholesterol-free egg noodles

1 package (10 ounces) frozen chopped spinach, thawed and squeezed dry

1 cup Light n' Lively nonfat cottage cheese

1 cup shredded Jarlsberg Lite Swiss cheese

¼ cup Kraft Free nonfat grated Parmesan topping, divided

1 cup Egg Beaters egg substitute

¾ cup Carnation Lite evaporated skimmed milk

1 pinch ground nutmeg

NUTRITIONAL FACTS (PER 1¼-CUP SERVING)

Calories: 180	Fat: 2.8 g	Protein: 21.4 g
Cholesterol: 11 mg	Fiber: 1.8 g	Sodium: 371 mg

You Save: Calories: 210 Fat: 27.1 g

Spicy Vegetable Stew

Yield: *6 servings*

1 can (14½ ounces) Hunt's no salt added tomatoes, crushed

1 can (14½ ounces) Swanson vegetable broth

½ cup Hunt's no salt added tomato paste

1 medium yellow onion, chopped

1 medium green bell pepper, chopped

1 large sweet potato (about 12 ounces), peeled and diced

2½ cups fresh or frozen (unthawed) cauliflower florets

1 cup fresh or frozen (unthawed) cut green beans

1 can (1 pound) Bush's Best garbanzo beans, rinsed and drained

2 teaspoons crushed fresh garlic

1½ teaspoons ground paprika

½ teaspoon ground allspice

¼ teaspoon ground cinnamon

¼ cup golden raisins

1. Combine all of the ingredients except for the raisins in a 3-quart pot. Stir to mix well, and bring to a boil over high heat. Reduce the heat to low, cover, and simmer for 20 to 25 minutes, or until the vegetables are tender and the flavors are well blended.

2. Add the raisins to the pot, and simmer for 5 additional minutes, or until the raisins are plumped. Serve hot over whole wheat couscous, bulgur wheat, or brown rice if desired.

NUTRITIONAL FACTS (PER 1½-CUP SERVING)

Calories: 188	Fat: 2.1 g	Protein: 8 g
Cholesterol: 0 mg	Fiber: 7.2 g	Sodium: 448 mg

You Save: Calories: 80   Fat: 9 g

Eggplant Pastitsio

1. To make the filling, combine all of the filling ingredients in a 2-quart pot, and bring to a boil over high heat. Reduce the heat to low, cover, and simmer for about 30 minutes, or until the eggplant is soft and the mixture is thick. Remove the pot from the heat, and set aside.

2. While the filling is simmering, cook the macaroni al dente according to package directions. Drain well, and return the pasta to the pot. Add the Parmesan topping and egg substitute, stir to mix well, and set aside.

3. To make the sauce, combine the milk and evaporated milk in a 1-quart pot. Place the pot over medium heat, and cook, stirring constantly, until the mixture begins to boil. Add the Parmesan topping, and continue to cook and stir for another minute, or until the mixture thickens slightly. Reduce the heat to low.

4. Place the egg substitute in a small bowl. Stir ½ cup of the hot milk mixture into the egg substitute. Return the mixture to the pot, and cook, still stirring, for another minute or 2, or until the mixture thickens slightly. *Do not let the mixture boil.* Remove the pot from the heat, and set aside.

5. To assemble the dish, coat an 8-inch square casserole dish with nonstick cooking spray. Spread half of the macaroni mixture evenly over the bottom of the dish. Top with all of the filling, followed by the remaining macaroni mixture. Spoon the sauce evenly over the macaroni.

6. Bake at 350°F for about 30 minutes, or until the sauce layer is set and a sharp knife inserted in the center of the sauce layer comes out clean.

7. Remove the dish from the oven, and let sit for 5 minutes before cutting into squares and serving.

NUTRITIONAL FACTS (PER SERVING)

Calories: 219	Fat: 1.1 g	Protein: 16 g
Cholesterol: 7 mg	Fiber: 4.5 g	Sodium: 372 mg

You Save: Calories: 166 Fat: 21.8 g

Yield: 6 servings

MACARONI MIXTURE

6 ounces De Bole's whole wheat elbow macaroni or Mueller's elbow macaroni

⅓ cup Kraft Free nonfat grated Parmesan topping

3 tablespoons Healthy Choice egg substitute

FILLING

2 cups diced peeled eggplant (about 1 medium-small)

½ cup chopped onion

1 can (8 ounces) Hunt's no salt added tomato sauce

2 tablespoons Hunt's no salt added tomato paste

2 tablespoons Swanson vegetable broth

1½ teaspoons crushed fresh garlic

1 teaspoon dried oregano

¼ teaspoon ground cinnamon or allspice

¼ teaspoon ground black pepper

¼ teaspoon salt

SAUCE

1 cup skim milk

½ cup Pet evaporated skimmed milk

⅓ cup Kraft Free nonfat grated Parmesan topping

½ cup plus 2 tablespoons Healthy Choice egg substitute

Orzo and Vegetable Pie

Yield: *6 servings*

2 medium zucchini, halved
   lengthwise and sliced ¼ inch
   thick (about 2 cups)

1 cup sliced fresh mushrooms

1 cup diced plum tomatoes
   (about 3 medium)

1 teaspoon crushed fresh garlic

1 teaspoon dried Italian seasoning

2 tablespoons Kraft Free nonfat
   grated Parmesan topping

1 cup Sargento Light fancy
   shredded natural mozzarella
   cheese

CRUST

8 ounces Da Vinci orzo*

⅓ cup Kraft Free nonfat grated
   Parmesan topping

¼ cup Egg Beaters egg substitute

*A small pasta that resembles rice,
orzo can be found in most supermarkets.

1. To make the crust, cook the orzo al dente according to
package directions. Drain well, and return the pasta to the pot. Add
the Parmesan topping and egg substitute, and stir to mix well.

2. Coat a 9-inch deep dish pie pan with nonstick cooking spray,
and place the orzo mixture in the pan. Using the back of a spoon,
pat the mixture over the bottom and sides of the pan, forming an
even crust. Set aside.

3. Place the zucchini, mushrooms, tomatoes, garlic, and Italian
seasoning in a large nonstick skillet, and place the skillet over
medium heat. Cover and cook, stirring occasionally, for about 7
minutes, or until the zucchini is crisp-tender. Remove the skillet
from the heat, and toss in the Parmesan topping.

4. Spread the vegetable mixture evenly over the bottom of the
crust. Spread the mozzarella evenly over the vegetables, and bake
at 400°F for 20 minutes, or until the cheese is melted and nicely
browned.

5. Remove the dish from the oven, and let sit for 5 minutes before
cutting into wedges and serving.

NUTRITIONAL FACTS (PER SERVING)

Calories: 236	Fat: 2.8 g	Protein: 16 g
Cholesterol: 10 mg	Fiber: 2 g	Sodium: 237 mg

You Save: Calories: 110   Fat: 14.5 g

Fantastic Falafel

1. To make the dressing, combine all of the dressing ingredients in a blender or food processor, and process until smooth. Set aside.

2. Place the wheat germ in a shallow dish, and set aside.

3. Place all of the falafel mixture ingredients in the bowl of a food processor, and process until puréed, but still slightly chunky.

4. Coat a large baking sheet with nonstick cooking spray. Shape the falafel mixture into 12 (2-inch) patties. One at a time, lay the patties in the dish containing the wheat germ, and turn to coat both sides. Arrange the patties in a single layer on the prepared baking sheet.

5. Spray the tops of the patties lightly with the cooking spray, and bake at 400°F for 10 minutes. Turn the patties, and bake for 10 additional minutes, or until nicely browned.

6. To assemble the sandwiches, place 2 patties in each pita half. Add 3 slices of cucumber, 1 slice of tomato, and ¼ cup of sprouts. Drizzle with the dressing, and serve immediately.

NUTRITIONAL FACTS (PER SERVING)

Calories: 257	Fat: 5 g	Protein: 12 g
Cholesterol: 0 mg	Fiber: 7.3 g	Sodium: 331 mg

You Save: Calories: 198 Fat: 21.8 g

Yield: 6 servings

⅓ cup Kretschmer toasted wheat germ

PAM® Olive Oil No Stick Cooking Spray

3 Tofuyan whole wheat or oat bran pita pockets (2 ounces each), cut in half

18 thin slices cucumber

6 slices tomato

1½ cups alfalfa sprouts

FALAFEL MIXTURE

1 can (19 ounces) Progresso garbanzo beans, rinsed and drained

1 cup diced cooked sweet potato (about 1 medium)

4 scallions, chopped

¼ cup plus 2 tablespoons chopped fresh parsley

2 teaspoons crushed fresh garlic

1 teaspoon ground cumin

1 teaspoon ground coriander

½ teaspoon coarsely ground black pepper

DRESSING

¼ cup Dannon nonfat plain yogurt

2–3 tablespoons sesame tahini (sesame paste)

2 tablespoons Kimono seasoned rice vinegar

½ teaspoon crushed fresh garlic

¼ teaspoon ground ginger

Lentil Crunch Casserole

Yield: *6 servings*

¾ cup dried brown lentils, cleaned (page 130)

1¾ cups water

1⅔ cups Arrowhead Mills quick-cooking brown rice

1 can (14½ ounces) Swanson vegetable broth

1 cup coarsely chopped fresh mushrooms

⅔ cup chopped onion

⅔ cup thinly sliced celery

¼ cup chopped walnuts

½ teaspoon dried thyme

¼ cup plus 2 tablespoons Alpine Lace fat-free grated Parmesan cheese, divided

1. Combine the lentils and water in a 1½-quart pot, and bring to a boil over high heat. Reduce the heat to low, cover, and simmer for about 25 minutes, or until the lentils are tender. Remove the pot from the heat, drain off any excess water, and set aside.

2. Place the rice and broth in a 2½-quart pot, and bring to a boil over high heat. Reduce the heat to low, cover, and simmer for 12 minutes, or until the rice is tender and the liquid has been absorbed. Remove the pot from the heat, and let sit covered for 5 minutes.

3. Add the lentils, mushrooms, onion, celery, walnuts, thyme, and ¼ cup of the Parmesan to the rice. Toss to mix well.

4. Coat a 2-quart casserole dish with nonstick cooking spray, and spread the rice mixture evenly in the dish. Sprinkle with the remaining 2 tablespoons of Parmesan, cover with aluminum foil, and bake at 350°F for 30 minutes, or until the dish is heated through and the vegetables are crisp-tender. Serve hot.

NUTRITIONAL FACTS (PER SERVING)

Calories: 253	Fat: 4.4 g	Protein: 13 g
Cholesterol: 3 mg	Fiber: 5 g	Sodium: 408 mg

You Save: Calories: 86   Fat: 10.9 g

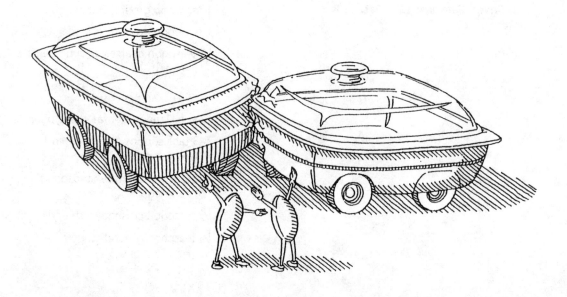

Black Bean Quesadillas

1. Place the beans, chili powder, and cumin in a medium-sized bowl, and mash with a fork until the mixture has the consistency of refried beans. Set aside.

2. Coat a large nonstick skillet with nonstick cooking spray, and preheat over medium-high heat. Add the garlic, red pepper, and onion, and stir-fry for about 3 minutes, or until the vegetables are crisp-tender. Remove the skillet from the heat, and set aside.

3. Arrange the tortillas on a flat surface, and spread a quarter of the bean mixture over the bottom half of each tortilla, extending the filling all the way to the edge. Layer a quarter of the red pepper mixture over the beans on each tortilla. Sprinkle $\frac{1}{4}$ cup of cheese over the vegetables. Fold the top half of each tortilla over the bottom half to enclose the filling.

4. Coat a large baking sheet with nonstick cooking spray. Arrange the quesadillas on the sheet, and spray the tops lightly with the cooking spray. Bake at 400°F for 4 minutes. Turn the quesadillas over, and bake for 5 additional minutes, or until the cheese is melted and the quesadillas are heated through.

5. Transfer the quesadillas to individual serving plates, and top each with 2 tablespoons of the sour cream, 2 tablespoons of the tomatoes, 1 tablespoon of the scallions, and a few olive slices. Serve hot.

Yield: 4 servings

1 can (15 ounces) Eden black beans, drained

2 teaspoons chili powder

$\frac{1}{4}$ teaspoon ground cumin

2 cloves garlic, crushed

1 small red bell pepper, cut into thin strips

1 small onion, cut into thin wedges

4 Buena Vida fat-free flour tortillas (8-inch rounds) or other fat-free tortillas

1 cup Healthy Choice fancy shredded fat-free pizza cheese

Mazola No Stick cooking spray

$\frac{1}{2}$ cup Naturally Yours nonfat sour cream

$\frac{1}{2}$ cup diced tomato

$\frac{1}{4}$ cup thinly sliced scallions

4 large pitted black olives, sliced

NUTRITIONAL FACTS (PER SERVING)		
Calories: 287	Fat: 1.4 g	Protein: 19 g
Cholesterol: 5 mg	Fiber: 7.1 g	Sodium: 600 mg

You Save: Calories: 215 Fat: 26.9 g

Bean Basics

If you really want to get the fat out of your diet, think beans. A hearty and satisfying alternative to meat, beans are fat-free and rich in protein, complex carbohydrates, B vitamins, iron, zinc, copper, and potassium. As for fiber, no food surpasses beans. Just a half cup of cooked beans provides 4 to 8 grams of fiber—up to four times the amount found in most other plant foods. Beans have also been found to lower cholesterol. As an added bonus, beans stabilize blood sugar levels, making you feel full and satisfied long after the meal is over—a definite benefit if you're watching your weight.

Some people avoid eating beans because of "bean bloat." What causes this problem? Complex sugars in beans, called oligosaccharides, sometimes form gas when broken down in the lower intestine. This side effect usually subsides when beans are made a regular part of the diet, and the body becomes more efficient at digesting them. The proper cleaning, soaking, and cooking of dried beans can also help prevent bean bloat. The following techniques will help you make beans a delicious and healthful part of your diet.

CLEANING

Because beans are a natural product, packages of dried beans sometimes contain shriveled or discolored beans, as well as small twigs and other items. Before cooking, sort through your beans and discard any discolored or blemished legumes. Rinse the beans well, cover them with water, and discard any that float to the top.

SOAKING

There are two methods used to soak beans in preparation for cooking. If you have time—if you intend to cook your dish the next day, for instance—you may want to use the long method, as this technique is best for reducing the gas-producing oligosaccharides. If dinner is just a couple of hours away, though, the quick method is your best bet. Keep in mind that not all beans must be soaked before cooking. Black-eyed peas, brown and red lentils, and split peas do not require soaking.

The Long Method

After cleaning the beans, place them in a large bowl or pot, and cover them with four times as much water. Soak the beans for at least four hours, and for as long as twelve hours. If soaking them for more than four, place the bowl or pot in the refrigerator. After soaking, discard the water and replace with fresh water before cooking.

The Quick Method

After cleaning the beans, place them in a large pot, and cover them with four times as much water. Bring the pot to a boil over high heat, and continue to boil for two minutes. Remove the pot from the heat, cover, and let stand for one hour. After soaking, discard the water and replace with fresh water before cooking.

COOKING

To cook beans for use in salads, casseroles, and other dishes that contain little or no liquid, clean and soak as described above, discard the soaking water, and replace with two cups of water for each cup of dried beans. When beans are to be cooked in soups or stews that include acidic ingredients—lemon juice, vinegar, or tomatoes, for instance—add these ingredients at the end of the cooking time. Acidic foods can toughen the beans' outer layer, slowing the rate at which the beans cook. You'll know that the beans are done when you can mash them easily with a fork. Keep in mind that old beans may take longer to cook. During long cooking times, periodically check the pot, and add more liquid if necessary.

The following table gives approximate cooking times for several different beans. Need a meal in a hurry? Lentils and split peas require no soaking and cook quickly. Lentils are the fastest cooking of all the legumes; they can be ready in less than thirty minutes. Split peas cook in less than an hour.

Cooking Times for Dried Beans & Legumes

Bean or Legume	Cooking Time
Black, garbanzo, great northern, kidney, navy, pinto, and white beans	$1\frac{1}{2}$–2 hours
Black-eyed peas*	1–$1\frac{1}{4}$ hours
Lentils, brown*	25–30 minutes
Lentils, red*	15–20 minutes
Lima beans, baby	45 minutes–$1\frac{1}{4}$ hours
Lima beans, large	1–$1\frac{1}{2}$ hours
Split peas*	45–50 minutes

*These beans do not require soaking.

Fiesta Bean Bake

1. Coat a large nonstick skillet with nonstick cooking spray, and preheat over medium-high heat. Add the cumin seeds, and stir-fry for about 1 minute, or until the seeds smell toasted and fragrant. Add the zucchini, onion, and red pepper, and stir-fry for about 2 minutes, or just until the vegetables are crisp-tender.

2. Remove the skillet from the heat, and toss in the rice and beans. Combine the cheeses in a medium-sized bowl, and toss to mix. Add 1 cup of the cheese to the rice mixture, and toss to mix well.

3. Coat a 2-quart casserole dish with nonstick cooking spray, and spread the rice mixture evenly in the dish. Sprinkle the remaining $\frac{1}{4}$ cup of cheese over the top, cover with aluminum foil, and bake at 350°F for 30 minutes, or until the casserole is heated through and the cheese is melted. Remove the foil, and bake for 5 additional minutes, or just until the cheese starts to brown. Serve hot.

Yield: 5 servings

1 teaspoon whole cumin seeds

1 medium zucchini, halved and sliced $\frac{1}{4}$ inch thick

$\frac{1}{2}$ cup chopped onion

$\frac{1}{4}$ cup finely chopped red bell pepper

4 cups cooked Mahatma brown rice

1 can (15 ounces) Garcia's pinto or black beans, rinsed and drained

$\frac{1}{2}$ cup plus 2 tablespoons Healthy Choice fancy shredded fat-free Cheddar cheese

$\frac{1}{2}$ cup plus 2 tablespoons shredded Kraft $\frac{1}{3}$ Less Fat Monterey Jack cheese

NUTRITIONAL FACTS (PER SERVING)

Calories: 319	Fat: 4.2 g	Protein: 17.2 g
Cholesterol: 10 mg	Fiber: 8 g	Sodium: 355 mg

You Save: Calories: 216 Fat: 21.8 g

Enchilada Pie

Yield: *6 servings*

1 can (14½ ounces) Hunt's no salt added tomatoes, crushed

2½ teaspoons chili powder

¾ cup Healthy Choice fancy shredded fat-free Cheddar cheese

¾ cup shredded Kraft ⅓ Less Fat Monterey Jack cheese

10 Tyson thin corn tortillas (6-inch rounds)

1 can (15 ounces) Garcia's black or pinto beans, rinsed and drained

1½ cups frozen (thawed) whole kernel corn

1 can (4 ounces) chopped green chilies, drained

½ cup plus 2 tablespoons Sealtest Free nonfat sour cream

1. Combine the tomatoes and chili powder in a small bowl, and set aside. Combine the cheeses in a small bowl, toss to mix, and set aside.

2. Spread ¼ cup of the tomato mixture over the bottom of a 10-inch pie pan. Line the bottom of the pan with 4 of the tortillas, overlapping them as needed to make them fit.

3. Spread half of the beans over the tortilla-lined pie pan. Top with half of the corn, half of the chilies, and ½ cup of the tomato mixture. Dot with half of the sour cream, and sprinkle with ½ cup of the cheese mixture. Repeat the layers, this time using only 3 tortillas. Top with the 3 remaining tortillas, and spread the remaining tomatoes over the top.

4. Coat a piece of aluminum foil with nonstick cooking spray, and cover the pan with the foil, coated side down. (This will prevent the tortillas from sticking to the foil.) Bake at 350°F for 35 minutes, or until the dish is heated through. Remove the foil, and sprinkle the remaining ½ cup of cheese over the top. Return the dish to the oven, and bake for 3 additional minutes, or until the cheese is melted.

5. Remove the dish from the oven, and let sit for 5 minutes before cutting into wedges and serving.

NUTRITIONAL FACTS (PER SERVING)

Calories: 258	Fat: 3.7 g	Protein: 16.3 g
Cholesterol: 11 mg	Fiber: 7.5 g	Sodium: 516 mg

You Save: Calories: 175 Fat: 22.6 g

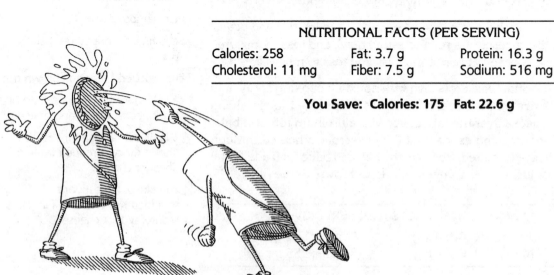

Top: Beef and Biscuit Bake (page 163), Center: Crispy Crust Sausage Pizza (page 152),
Bottom: Breast of Turkey Parmesan (page 150)

Top: Pork Tenderloins With Apple-Raisin Stuffing (page 161),
Center: Turkey Piccata (page 151), Bottom: Jiffy Jambalaya (page 156)

Top: Spaghetti With Scallops (page 169), Center: Garden Vegetable Linguine (page 176), Bottom: Penne With Sausage, Peppers, and Onions (page 181)

Top: Sicilian Baked Ziti (page 185), Center: Pasta Piselli (page 172),
Bottom: Slim Spaghetti Carbonara (page 171)

Curry in a Hurry

1. Combine all of the ingredients in a large skillet. Stir to mix well, and bring to a boil over high heat. Reduce the heat to low, cover, and simmer for 12 minutes, or until the rice is tender and the liquid has been absorbed.

2. Remove the skillet from the heat, and let sit covered for 5 minutes. Fluff with a fork, and serve hot.

Yield: *4 servings*

1 can (15 ounces) Joan of Arc red kidney beans, rinsed and drained

1½ cups Arrowhead Mills quick-cooking brown rice

¾ cup diced carrot

½ cup thinly sliced celery

½ cup chopped onion

1¾ cups water

2 teaspoons Vogue instant vege base, or 1 vegetable bouillon cube

2–3 teaspoons curry powder

NUTRITIONAL FACTS (PER SERVING)

Calories: 261	Fat: 3.6 g	Protein: 14.4 g
Cholesterol: 6 mg	Fiber: 7.5 g	Sodium: 430 mg

You Save: Calories: 109 Fat: 9.5 g

Spicy Spaghetti Squash

Yield: *4 servings*

8-inch spaghetti squash (about 4 pounds)

2 cups chopped tomato

1½ cups sliced fresh mushrooms

½ cup chopped onion

1 teaspoon crushed fresh garlic

1½ teaspoons dried oregano

½ teaspoon crushed red pepper

¼ cup Kraft Free nonfat grated Parmesan topping

1 cup Sargento Light fancy shredded natural mozzarella cheese

1. Cut the squash in half lengthwise, and remove the seeds. Coat a large baking sheet with nonstick cooking spray, and place the squash halves cut side down on the sheet. Bake at 375°F for 40 minutes, or until the squash is easily pierced with a sharp knife.

2. Remove the squash from the oven, and let it sit until cool enough to handle. Scoop out the pulp, and transfer it to a large bowl. Use a fork to separate the pulp into strands, and set aside.

3. Place the tomatoes, mushrooms, onion, garlic, and spices in a large skillet. Place over medium heat, cover, and cook, stirring occasionally, for 6 to 8 minutes, or until the vegetables are tender.

4. Spoon the tomato mixture over the squash, and toss gently to mix well. Add the Parmesan topping, and toss gently to mix.

5. Coat a 2-quart casserole dish with nonstick cooking spray, and spread the mixture evenly in the dish. Top with the mozzarella, and bake at 350°F for 35 minutes, or until the mixture is heated through and the cheese is melted. Serve hot.

NUTRITIONAL FACTS (PER SERVING)

Calories: 165	Fat: 3.7 g	Protein: 13.4 g
Cholesterol: 13 mg	Fiber: 3.5 g	Sodium: 274 mg

You Save: Calories: 129   Fat: 16.7 g

Go for the Grain

Just because a food is fat-free does not mean it is good for you. Fat-free products made from refined white flour and refined grains are practically devoid of fiber, and are not only pitifully poor in nutrients, but can actually deplete nutrient stores if eaten in excess. Whole grains and whole grain flours, on the other hand, contain vitamin E, vitamin B$_6$, folate, zinc, magnesium, chromium, potassium, and many other health-promoting nutrients that are lacking in refined grains. In addition, the fiber in whole grain products makes meals more satisfying. How? Fiber—like fat—provides a feeling of fullness and helps keep blood sugar levels stable. This, in turn, helps prevent hunger. Eating enough fiber is an essential part of any successful low-fat eating plan, as a diet of fat-free and low-fat refined foods is sure to leave you hungry.

Fortunately, once accustomed to the heartier taste and texture of whole grains, most people prefer them over refined grains, which are bland and tasteless in comparison. Following is a description of some grains and grain products used in the recipes in this book. Most of these products are readily available in grocery stores, while others may be found in health foods stores.

Barley. This grain has a light, nutty flavor, making it a great substitute for rice in pilafs, soups, casseroles, and other dishes. Hulled barley, like brown rice, cooks in about 50 minutes. Quick-cooking barley is also widely available. With all the fiber of hulled barley, this product, available from both Mother's and Quaker, cooks in about 12 minutes.

Bread flour. Made from high-gluten wheat flour, this product is made especially for use in yeast breads. Bread flour also contains dough conditioners, such as ascorbic acid (vitamin C), which make doughs rise better. You can find both Pillsbury's Best bread flour and Gold Medal Better for Bread flour in most grocery stores.

Brown rice. Brown rice is whole-kernel rice, meaning that all nutrients are intact. With a slightly chewy texture and a pleasant nutty flavor, brown rice makes excellent pilafs and stuffings.

Brown rice does take twice as long as white rice to cook. But if you place the rice in the cooking water and refrigerate it overnight, or for at least 8 hours, the grain will cook in just 20 to 25 minutes. Several brands of quick-cooking brown rice—including Arrowhead Mills, Minute Brand, and Uncle Ben's—are also widely available. These brands can be made in 10 to 12 minutes.

Brown rice flour. Brown rice flour is simply finely ground brown rice. It has a texture similar to that of cornmeal and adds a mildly sweet flavor to baked goods. Use it in cookies or waffles for a crisp and crunchy texture. Arrowhead Mills brown rice flour is available in many grocery and health foods stores.

Buckwheat. Buckwheat is technically not a grain, but the edible fruit seed of a plant that is closely related to rhubarb. Roasted buckwheat kernels, commonly known as kasha, are delicious in pilafs and hot breakfast cereals. Look for this product in your grocery store.

Buckwheat flour. Made from finely ground whole buckwheat kernels, buckwheat flour is delicious in pancakes, waffles, breads, and muffins. Arrowhead Mills buckwheat flour is available in many grocery and health foods stores.

Cornmeal. This grain adds a sweet flavor, a lovely golden color, and a crunchy texture to baked goods. Select whole grain (unbolted) cornmeal for the most nutrition. By contrast, bolted cornmeal is nearly whole grain, and degermed cornmeal is refined. Available from both Arrowhead Mills and Hodgson Mill, whole grain cornmeal can be found in many grocery and health foods stores.

Oat bran. Made of the outer part of the oat kernel, oat bran has a sweet, mild flavor and is a concentrated source of cholesterol-lowering soluble fiber. Oat bran also helps retain moisture in baked goods, making it a natural for fat-free and low-fat baking. Look for this product in the hot cereal section of your grocery store. The softer, more finely ground products, like Quaker and Mother's, can be substituted for up to a third of the flour in baked goods. Coarsely ground oat brans, like Hodgson Mill, add a pleasantly chewy texture to muffins and cookies. When using a coarsely ground product, soak it in some of the recipe's liquid for about 15 minutes before adding it to the recipe.

Oat flour. This mildly sweet flour is perfect for cakes, muffins, and other baked goods. Like oat bran, oat flour retains moisture in baked goods, reducing the need for fat. To add extra fiber and nutrients, substitute oat flour for up to a third of the refined wheat flour in your own recipes. Look for Arrowhead Mills oat flour in grocery and health foods stores, or make your own oat flour by grinding quick-cooking rolled oats in a blender.

Oats. Loaded with cholesterol-lowering soluble fiber, oats add a chewy texture and sweet flavor to muffins, quick breads, pancakes, cookies, and crumb toppings. They are also delicious in breakfast cereals and other dishes. The recipes in this book use quick-cooking rolled oats—the kind that cooks in one minute. Several national brands of quick-cooking oats are available, including Quaker, Mother's, and Minute Brand.

Unbleached flour. This is refined white flour that has not been subjected to a bleaching process. Unbleached white flour lacks significant amounts of nutrients compared with whole wheat flour, but does contain more vitamin E than bleached flour. Arrowhead Mills, Gold Medal, Hodgson Mill, and Pillsbury's Best all make unbleached flour.

White wheat flour. This is an excellent option for baking. Made from hard white wheat instead of the hard red wheat used to make regular whole wheat flour, white wheat flour contains all the fiber and nutrients of regular whole wheat flour, but is sweeter and lighter tasting than its red wheat counterpart. King Arthur white wheat flour is available in many grocery stores. Replace 1 cup of refined flour with 1 cup minus 1 tablespoon of white whole wheat flour.

Whole grain wheat. Available in many forms, this grain is perhaps easiest to use in the form of bulgur wheat. Cracked wheat that is precooked and dried, bulgur wheat can be prepared in a matter of minutes and can replace rice in any recipe. Look for it in grocery and health foods stores.

Whole wheat flour. Made of ground whole grain wheat kernels, whole wheat flour includes the grain's nutrient-rich bran and germ. Nutritionally speaking, whole wheat flour is far superior to refined flour. Sadly, many people grew up eating refined baked goods and find whole grain products too heavy for their taste. A good way to learn to enjoy whole grain flours is to use part whole wheat and part unbleached flour in recipes, and gradually increase the amount of whole wheat used over time. (Replace 1 cup of refined flour with 1 cup minus 2 tablespoons of whole wheat.) Most grocery stores stock Gold Medal, Pillsbury's Best, or Heckers whole wheat flour. If you find these brands too heavy for your taste, try either whole wheat pastry flour or white wheat flour.

Whole wheat pastry flour. When muffin, quick bread, cake, pastry, pancake, pie crust, and cookie recipes call for whole wheat flour, whole wheat pastry flour is an exceptional choice. The reason? Made from a finely ground, soft (low-protein) wheat, whole wheat pastry flour produces lighter, softer-textured baked goods than regular whole wheat flour does. Look for Arrowhead Mills whole wheat pastry flour in health foods stores and many grocery stores. Substitute whole wheat pastry flour for refined white flour on a one-for-one basis in recipes. Whole wheat pastry flour will also work nicely in some fat-free dessert breads, but for high-rising sandwich-type yeast breads, use regular whole wheat flour, which is higher in gluten, and will allow your yeast breads to rise better.

Three-Cheese Pizza

1. To make the crust, in a large bowl, combine ½ cup of the bread flour with all of the oat bran, yeast, sugar, and salt, and stir to mix well. Place the water in a small saucepan, and heat until very warm (125°F to 130°F). Add the water to the flour mixture, and stir for 1 minute. Stir in enough of the remaining flour, 2 tablespoons at a time, to form a stiff dough.

2. Sprinkle 2 tablespoons of the remaining flour over a flat surface, and turn the dough onto the surface. Knead the dough for 5 minutes, gradually adding enough of the remaining flour to form a smooth, satiny ball. Coat a large bowl with nonstick cooking spray, and place the dough in the bowl. Cover the bowl with a clean kitchen towel, and let rise in a warm place for about 35 minutes, or until doubled in size.

3. When the dough has risen, punch it down, shape it into a ball, and turn it onto a lightly floured surface. Using a rolling pin, roll the dough into a 12-inch circle. (For a thin crust, roll the dough into a 14-inch circle.) Coat a 12-inch (or 14-inch) pizza pan with nonstick cooking spray, and place the dough on the pan.

4. Spread the pasta sauce over the crust to within ½ inch of the edge. Sprinkle the sauce with first the Parmesan topping, then the mozzarella, and then the provolone. Sprinkle the oregano over the cheese.

5. Bake at 450°F for about 12 minutes, or until the cheese is melted and the crust is lightly browned. Cut into wedges and serve immediately.

Time-Saving Tip

To make the dough for Three-Cheese Pizza in a bread machine, place all of the dough ingredients except for ¼ cup of the bread flour in the machine's bread pan. (Do not heat the water.) Turn the machine to the "rise," "dough," "manual," or equivalent setting so that the machine will mix, knead, and let the dough rise once. Check the dough about 5 minutes after the machine has started. If the dough seems too sticky, add more of the remaining flour, a tablespoon at a time. When the dough is ready, remove it from the machine and proceed to shape, top, and bake it as directed in the recipe.

Yield: 8 slices

¾ cup Millina's Finest fat-free tomato and basil pasta sauce

1 tablespoon Kraft Free nonfat grated Parmesan topping

½ cup Healthy Choice fancy shredded fat-free mozzarella cheese

½ cup shredded Alpine Lace reduced-fat provolone cheese

½ teaspoon dried basil

CRUST

1½ cups Pillsbury's Best bread flour, divided

⅓ cup Quaker oat bran

1½ teaspoons Fleischmann's Rapid Rise yeast

1 teaspoon sugar

¼ teaspoon salt

½ cup plus 2 tablespoons water

NUTRITIONAL FACTS (PER SLICE)

Calories: 124	Fiber: 1.8 g
Chol: 5 mg	Protein: 8 g
Fat: 1.7 g	Sodium: 211 mg

You Save: Calories: 47 Fat: 5.8 g

Artichoke and Pepper Pizzas

Yield: *4 servings*

¾ cup Healthy Choice pasta sauce, any variety

2 tablespoons Kraft Free nonfat grated Parmesan topping

¾ cup Sargento Light fancy shredded natural mozzarella cheese

⅓ cup chopped frozen (thawed) or canned (drained) artichoke hearts

⅓ cup sliced fresh mushrooms or sliced black olives

⅓ cup diced roasted or fresh red bell pepper

½ teaspoon dried Italian seasoning

CRUST

1¼ cups Pillsbury's Best bread flour, divided

½ cup Pillsbury's Best whole wheat flour

1½ teaspoons Fleischmann's Rapid Rise yeast

1 teaspoon sugar

¼ teaspoon salt

½ cup plus 2 tablespoons water

NUTRITIONAL FACTS
(PER PIZZA)

Calories: 291	Fiber: 4.8 g
Chol: 9 mg	Protein: 15 g
Fat: 3 g	Sodium: 452 mg

You Save: Calories: 86 Fat: 11.8

1. To make the crust, in a large bowl, combine ½ cup of the bread flour with all of the whole wheat flour, yeast, sugar, and salt, and stir to mix well. Place the water in a small saucepan, and heat until very warm (125°F to 130°F). Add the water to the flour mixture, and stir for 1 minute. Stir in enough of the remaining bread flour, 2 tablespoons at a time, to form a stiff dough.

2. Sprinkle 2 tablespoons of the remaining bread flour over a flat surface, and turn the dough onto the surface. Knead the dough for 5 minutes, gradually adding enough of the remaining bread flour to form a smooth, satiny ball. Coat a large bowl with nonstick cooking spray, and place the dough in the bowl. Cover the bowl with a clean kitchen towel, and let rise in a warm place for about 35 minutes, or until doubled in size.

3. When the dough has risen, punch it down, shape it into a ball, and turn it onto a lightly floured surface. Divide the dough into 4 equal pieces, and shape each piece into a ball. Using a rolling pin, roll each ball into a 6½-inch circle. (For a thin crust, roll the dough into 8-inch circles.) Coat a large baking sheet with nonstick cooking spray, and place the crusts on the pan.

4. Spread 3 tablespoons of the pasta sauce over each crust to within ½ inch of the edge. Sprinkle first 1½ teaspoons of Parmesan topping and then 3 tablespoons of mozzarella over the sauce on each pizza. Next, divide the artichokes, mushrooms, and red peppers among the crusts. Sprinkle ⅛ teaspoon of Italian seasoning over each pizza.

5. Bake at 450°F for 10 minutes, or until the cheese is melted and lightly browned. Serve immediately.

Time-Saving Tips

Instead of making the crust for Artichoke and Pepper Pizzas from scratch, spread the sauce and toppings over four whole wheat or oat bran pita bread rounds, and bake as directed.

Like the dough for Three-Cheese Pizza, the Artichoke and Pepper Pizza dough may be mixed in a bread machine. See the Time-Saving Tip on page 137.

8. Hot and Hearty Entrées

"What's for dinner?" is a common question in any household. But if you have just adopted a low-fat lifestyle, you may be particularly baffled by this age-old question. Often, people who are trying to eat healthfully stick with the foods they know are safe—chicken, chicken, and more chicken. But while chicken makes a fine low-fat entrée, a steady diet of plain skinless chicken breasts can become old in a hurry.

What *can* you serve for dinner? These days, the possibilities are endless—and delicious. There are now several lean cuts of beef, including roasts, steaks, and even a ground beef with half the fat of most ground turkey. If pork is your pleasure, try pork tenderloin—a cut that fits beautifully into low-fat eating plans. You'll even find ultra-lean sausages that can perk up main dishes. And, of course, many types of seafood—as well as those low-fat favorites, chicken and turkey—are delicious in their own right, and can also be used to replace fatty meats in a variety of entrées. This chapter uses these lean cuts of meat, seafood, and poultry to create a wide range of main dishes that are tasty, satisfying, and nutritious, and have a minimum of fat and calories. Just as important, most of these hot and hearty entrées are simple enough to prepare any night of the week.

As you glance through the recipes in this chapter, you'll be amazed by your savings in fat and calories. How were these dishes made so much leaner than traditional versions of the same foods? First, fat was eliminated by using skinless poultry and the leanest cuts of beef and pork. Then the oil usually used for browning was replaced by nonstick skillets and nonstick cooking sprays. When making sauces, evaporated skimmed milk and nonfat sour cream replaced full-fat cream and sour cream. Finally, broth—not butter—was used to moisten savory stuffings, and nonfat buttermilk replaced the fat usually used to make biscuit toppings. Was flavor sacrificed along with the fat? Absolutely not! Herbs, spices, and condiments make these dishes as delicious as they are healthy.

To help you make the best choices when shopping for entrée ingredients, this chapter presents a Fat-Fighter's Guide to lean beef, pork, chicken, turkey, and more (page 140). You'll find that even bacon has its place in a low-fat diet—as long as you know what to look for! And for those days when time is in short supply, you'll find a Fat-Fighter's Guide to frozen entrées that provide all of the flavor, but just a fraction of the fat, of regular frozen dinners (page 165).

So the next time someone asks what you're making for dinner, feel free to promise them down-home Southern-Style Smothered Chicken, Crispy Crust Sausage Pizza, or even elegant Pork Tenderloins With Apple-Raisin Stuffing. Once you know the secrets of low-fat cooking, you'll find that all of your favorite entrées—and some great new ones, too—can be part of a low-fat diet.

FAT-FIGHTER'S GUIDE TO
Meat, Poultry, and Seafood

Because of the high fat and cholesterol contents of meats, many people have sharply reduced their consumption of meat, have limited themselves to white meat chicken or turkey, or have totally eliminated meat and poultry from their diets. Happily, whether you are a sworn meat eater, someone who only occasionally eats meat dishes, or a confirmed vegetarian, plenty of lean meats, lean poultry, and excellent meat substitutes are now available.

The most important point to remember when including meat in meals is to keep portions to a modest six ounces or less per day. For perspective, three ounces of meat is the size of a deck of cards. Here are some suggestions for choosing the leanest possible poultry and meat.

TURKEY

Although both chicken and turkey have less total fat and saturated fat than beef and pork, your very best bet when buying poultry is turkey. What's the difference between the fat and calorie contents of chicken and turkey? While 3 ounces of chicken breast without skin contain 139 calories and 3 grams of fat, the same amount of turkey breast without skin contains only 119 calories and 1 gram of fat.

Your best defense when preparing and eating poultry is removing the skin and any underlying visible fat. Doing just this eliminates over half the fat. Is there any advantage to removing the skin *before* cooking? A slight one. Poultry cooked without the skin has about 20 percent less fat than poultry whose skin is removed after cooking. This amounts to about 1.5 grams of fat saved by removing the skin from a chicken breast before cooking instead of after. Also, when the skin is removed after cooking, the seasoning is,

too. For this reason, the poultry recipes in this book all begin with skinless pieces.

All of the leanest cuts of turkey come from the breast, so that all have the same amount of fat and calories per serving. Below, you will learn about the cuts that you're likely to find at your local supermarket. Some brands to look for are Butterball, Cuddy Farms, Wampler-Longacre, Norbest, and Mr. Turkey.

Turkey Cutlets

Turkey cutlets, which are slices of fresh turkey breast, are usually about $\frac{1}{4}$-inch thick and weigh about 2 to 3 ounces each. These cutlets may be used as a delicious ultra-lean alternative to boneless chicken breast, pork tenderloin slices, or veal.

Turkey Medallions

Sliced from turkey tenderloins, medallions are about 1 inch thick and weigh about 2 to 3 ounces each. Turkey medallions can be substituted for pork or veal medallions.

Turkey Steaks

Cut from the turkey breast, these steaks are about $\frac{1}{2}$ to 1 inch in thickness. Turkey steaks may be baked, broiled, grilled, cut into stir-fry pieces or kabobs, or ground for burgers.

Turkey Tenderloins

Large sections of fresh turkey breast, tenderloins usually weigh about 8 ounces each. Tenderloins may be sliced into cutlets, cut into stir-fry or kabob pieces, ground for burgers, or grilled or roasted as is.

Whole Turkey Breasts

Perfect for people who love roast turkey but want only the breast meat, turkey breasts weigh 4 to 8 pounds each. These breasts may be roasted with or without stuffing.

Ground Turkey

Ground turkey is an excellent ingredient for use in meatballs, chili, burgers—in any dish that uses ground meat. When shopping for ground turkey, you'll find that different products have different percentages of fat. Butterball Extra Lean ground turkey is one of the leanest brands you will find. Approximately 97-percent lean, this product contains less than 1 gram of fat per ounce. Another option is to purchase your own fresh turkey meat and have the butcher grind it for you. Skinless dark meat will be about 95-percent lean, and skinless breast meat will be about 99-percent lean. In contrast, most brands that provide no nutrition information are made with added skin and fat. These products may contain up to 15 percent fat by weight, and are fattier than many kinds of ground beef. The moral is clear. Always check labels before making a purchase!

CHICKEN

Though not as low in fat as turkey, chicken is still lower in fat than most cuts of beef and pork, and therefore is a valuable ingredient in low-fat cooking. Beware, though: many cuts of chicken, if eaten with the skin on, contain more fat than some cuts of beef and pork. For the least fat, choose the chicken breast and always remove the skin. As the following table shows, there is a slight advantage to removing the skin *before* cooking.

Comparing Chicken Parts

Part (3-ounce cooked portion)	Calories	Fat
Breast, with skin	167	6.6 g
Breast, skin removed before cooking	125	1.4 g
Breast, skin removed after cooking	139	3.0 g
Leg, with skin	183	9.5 g
Leg, without skin	146	4.8 g
Thigh, with skin	210	13.2 g
Thigh, without skin	178	9.3 g
Wing, with skin	247	16.6 g
Wing, without skin	173	6.9 g

Where does ground chicken fit in? Like ground turkey, ground chicken often contains skin and fat. In fact, most brands contain at least 15 percent fat, so read the labels before you buy.

BEEF AND PORK

Although not as lean as turkey, beef and pork are both considerably leaner today than in decades past. Spurred by competition from the poultry industry, beef and pork producers have changed breeding and feeding practices to reduce the fat content of these products. In addition, butchers are now trimming away more of the fat from retail cuts of meat. The result? On average, grocery store cuts of beef are 27 percent leaner today than they were in the early 1980s, and retail cuts of pork are 43 percent leaner.

Of course, some cuts of beef and pork are leaner than others. Which are the smartest choices? The following table will guide you in selecting those cuts that are lowest in fat.

The Leanest Beef and Pork Cuts

Cut (3-ounce cooked portion)	Calories	Fat
Beef		
Eye of Round	143	4.2 g
Top Round	153	4.2 g
Round Tip	157	5.9 g
Top Sirloin	165	6.1 g
Pork		
Tenderloin	139	4.1 g
Ham (95% lean)	112	4.3 g
Boneless Sirloin Chops	164	5.7 g
Boneless Loin Roast	165	6.1 g
Boneless Loin Chops	173	6.6 g

While identifying the lowest-fat cuts of meat is an important first step in healthy cooking, be aware that even lean cuts have varying amounts of fat because of differences in *grades*. In general, the higher, and more expensive, grades of meat, like USDA Prime and Choice, have more fat due to a higher degree of *marbling*—internal fat that cannot be trimmed away. USDA Select meats have the least amount of marbling, and therefore the lowest amount of fat. How important are these differences? A USDA Choice piece of meat may have 15 to 20 percent more fat than a USDA Select cut, and USDA Prime may have even more fat. Clearly, the difference is significant. So when choosing beef and pork for your table, by all means check the package for grade. Then look for the least amount of marbling in the cut you have chosen, and let appearance be your final guide.

Ground Beef

No food adds more fat—and, most especially, saturated fat—to people's diets than ground beef. Just how fatty is ground beef? At its worst, it is almost 33 percent fat. And ground sirloin and round are not necessarily leaner. Terms like sirloin and round merely indicate the part of the animal from which the meat came, not the amount of fat it contains.

The only way to be sure of fat content is to buy meat whose label provides some nutrition information. However, if your only choices are unlabelled packages of ground beef, choose the type that is darkest in color. As the fat content goes up, the color of ground beef becomes paler.

To obtain the leanest ground beef possible, you can select a piece of top round and have the butcher trim and grind it for you. Ground beef made this way has about 132 calories and 4.9 grams of fat per 3-ounce cooked serving, and is about 95-percent lean. Most stores also carry prepackaged ground beef that is 93-percent lean. This is also an acceptable choice. In fact, you may be surprised to learn that 93-percent lean ground beef contains about *half* the fat of most ground turkey—which is about 85-percent lean—making the beef a better choice in this case. (Of course, 96- to 99-percent lean ground turkey is still the *best* choice.) The following table, which compares different grinds of beef, shows that as the percentage of fat decreases, so do the calorie and fat-gram counts.

Comparing Ground Beef

Grind (3-ounce cooked portion)	Calories	Fat
73% lean (27% fat by weight)	248	17.9 g
80% lean (20% fat by weight)	228	15.2 g
85% lean (15% fat by weight)	204	12.2 g
90% lean (10% fat by weight)	169	9.1 g
93% lean (7% fat by weight)	134	6.0 g
95% lean (5% fat by weight)	132	4.9 g

The nutrition information for the ground beef recipes in this book was calculated using 95-percent lean ground meat. When you use ground meat this lean, there is no fat to drain off. In fact, it may stick to the bottom of the pan during browning. If this happens, simply add a few tablespoons of water to the skillet.

LEAN PROCESSED MEATS

Because of our new fat-consciousness, low-fat bacon, ham, hot dogs, lunchmeats, and sausages are now available, with just a fraction of the fat of regular processed meats. Many of these low-fat products are used in the recipes in this book. Here are some examples.

Bacon

Turkey bacon, made with strips of light and dark turkey meat, looks and tastes much like pork bacon. But with 30 calories and 2 grams of fat per strip, turkey bacon has 50 percent less fat than crisp-cooked pork bacon, and shrinks much less during cooking. Besides being a leaner alternative to regular breakfast bacon, turkey bacon may be substituted for pork bacon in Southern-style vegetables, casseroles, and other dishes. Look for brands like Butterball, Louis Rich, and Mr. Turkey.

Canadian bacon, which has always been about 95-percent lean, is another useful ingredient to the low-fat cook. Use this flavorful product in breakfast casseroles and soups, and as a topping for pizzas.

Ham

Low-fat hams are made from either pork or turkey. These products contain as little as 0.5 gram of fat per ounce. Of course, all cured hams, including the leaner brands, are very high in sodium. However, used in moderation—to flavor bean soups or breakfast casseroles, for instance—these products can be incorporated into a healthy diet. Just avoid adding further salt to your recipes. Look for Hormel

Curemaster 96% fat-free ham, Butterball turkey ham, Hormel Light & Lean ham, and Boar's Head lean ham.

Hot Dogs

When most people think of lighter hot dogs, turkey franks immediately come to mind. True, turkey franks do contain 30 to 50 percent less fat than regular hot dogs, but most brands still contain about 8 grams—2 teaspoons—of fat each. Fortunately, some very low-fat and fat-free brands of hot dogs are now available. Oscar Mayer Free, Butterball Free, and Ball Park Free hot dogs are all good options. As the names imply, these dogs are fat-free, and therefore save you 16 grams of fat compared with full-fat franks. Healthy Choice hot dogs are another very low-fat option. As with all hot dogs, sodium is still a problem, so use these products in moderation.

Lunchmeats

Many brands of ultra-lean lunchmeats are now available, including Boar's Head, Healthy Choice, Butterball, Louis Rich, Mr. Turkey, Oscar Mayer Free, and others. Today's low-fat deli meats include everything from pastrami and corned beef to bologna, roast beef, turkey, and ham. These meats make ideal substitutes for fatty cold cuts in sandwiches and party platters, although, like all processed meats, they should be used in moderation due to their high sodium content.

Some processed meats are now labelled "fat-free." Since all meats naturally contain *some* fat, how can this be? The manufacturer first starts with a lean meat such as turkey breast, and then adds enough water to dilute the fat to a point where the product contains less than 0.5 gram of fat per serving. Fortunately, meats that are labelled 96- to 99-percent lean—and therefore contain 0.3 to 1 gram of fat per ounce—are also lean enough to be included in a low-fat diet.

Sausage

A variety of low-fat sausages made from turkey, or a combination of turkey, beef, and pork, are now available. These products contain a mere 30 to 40 calories and 0.75 to 3 grams of fat per ounce. Compare this with an ounce of full-fat pork sausage, which contains over 100 calories and almost 9 grams of fat, and you'll see what a boon these new healthier mixtures are. Beware, though: While labelled "light," some brands of sausage contain as much as 10 grams of fat per 2.5-ounce serving. This is half the amount of fat found in the same-size serving of regular pork sausage, but is still a hefty dose of fat for such a small portion of food.

When a recipe calls for smoked turkey sausage, try a brand like Healthy Choice, which has less than 1 gram of fat per ounce. Louis Rich and Butterball are other good reduced-fat brands. When buying bulk ground turkey breakfast sausage, try brands like Louis Rich, which contains 75 percent less fat than ground pork sausage. Many stores also make their own fresh turkey sausage, including turkey Italian sausage. When buying fresh sausage, always check the package labels and choose the leanest mixture available. Even better, make your own Turkey Breakfast Sausage (page 25) or Turkey Italian Sausage (page 182).

VEGETARIAN ALTERNATIVES

Nonmeat alternatives to ground meat, sausage, and other meat products are now widely available in grocery stores. One product you will find in the produce section of most stores is Marjon Tofu Crumbles. These precooked, mildly seasoned, texturized bits of tofu are a great substitute for all or part of the ground meat in chili, sloppy Joes, tacos, and other dishes. One ounce of tofu crum-

bles has 20 calories, 1.2 grams of fat, and no cholesterol.

To reduce the fat in your lean ground beef, turkey, or chicken, mix the ground meat with texturized vegetable protein (TVP). TVP, which is made from defatted soybean flour formed into small nuggets, is fat- and cholesterol-free, a good source of protein, and very economical. To mix TVP with ground meat, combine a half cup of TVP with 7 tablespoons of boiling water or broth. Let the mixture sit for about 5 minutes to rehydrate the TVP. Then combine it with 8 ounces of cooked ground meat, and you'll have the equivalent of one pound of ground meat. When used in recipes like chili or tacos, you won't even know it's there. If you choose to use TVP in burgers or meat loaf, rehydrate the nuggets before mixing them with the uncooked beef. Then form the beef into patties or loaves, and cook as desired.

Looking for a meatless burger? Try Green Giant Harvest Burgers, Wholesome & Hearty Gardenburgers, or Morningstar Farms Better'n Burgers, all of which can be found in the freezer case of many grocery stores. With just a fraction of the fat of their ground beef counterparts, these tasty burgers also provide some fiber.

Nonmeat breakfast alternatives are also available. Choose from Wholesome & Hearty Garden-Sausage, with only 1 gram of fat per ounce, Morningstar Farms Breakfast Strips, with about half the fat of pork bacon, and many others. (Again, these can be found in the freezer case.) Do read labels though. Just because a food is vegetarian, does not necessarily mean it is low in fat. In fact, some meat alternatives contain just as much fat as the meat they are meant to replace.

FISH AND OTHER SEAFOOD

Of the many kinds of fish and other seafood now available, some is almost fat-free, while some is moderately fatty. However, the oil in fish provides an essential kind of fat—known as omega-3 fatty acids—that most people's diets do not supply in sufficient quantities. The omega-3 fats in fish can help reduce blood cholesterol and triglycerides, lower blood pressure, and prevent the formation of deadly blood clots. This means that all kinds of fish, including the more oily ones like salmon, are considered healthful. In fact, eating just two meals of fish a week can help prevent heart disease.

Many commercial fish are now raised on "farms." Do these fish offer the same health benefits as fish caught in natural habitats? No. Farm-raised fish are fed grains instead of their natural diet of plankton and smaller fish. As a result, these fish contain as much or more fat than wild fish, but are much lower in the beneficial omega-3 fats.

What about the cholesterol content of shellfish? It may not be as high as you think it is. With the exception of shrimp and oysters, a 3-ounce serving of most shellfish has about 60 milligrams of cholesterol—well under the daily upper limit of 300 milligrams. The same-size serving of shrimp has about 166 milligrams of cholesterol, which is just over half the recommended daily limit. Oysters have about 90 milligrams of cholesterol. However, all seafood, including shellfish, is very low in saturated fat, which has a greater cholesterol-raising effect than does cholesterol. The following table, which compares several common fish and shellfish, should help you stay within your daily calorie, fat, and cholesterol budgets.

Comparing Seafood

Seafood (3-ounce cooked portion)	Calories	Fat	Cholesterol
Clams	126	1.7 g	57 mg
Crab, Alaskan King	82	1.3 g	45 mg
Flounder	99	1.3 g	58 mg
Grouper	100	1.1 g	40 mg
Haddock	95	0.8 g	63 mg
Halibut	119	2.5 g	35 mg
Lobster	83	0.5 g	61 mg
Mackerel, Spanish	134	5.4 g	62 mg
Mullet	127	4.1 g	54 mg
Mussels	147	3.8 g	48 mg
Oysters	117	4.2 g	89 mg
Pollock	96	1.0 g	82 mg
Salmon, Coho	157	6.4 g	42 mg
Scallops	113	3.3 g	34 mg
Shrimp	84	0.9 g	166 mg
Sole	99	1.3 g	58 mg
Swordfish	132	4.4 g	43 mg

Fish is highly perishable, so it is important to know how to select a high-quality product. First, make sure that the fish is firm and springy to the touch. Second, buy fish only if it has a clean seaweed odor, rather than a "fishy" smell. Third, when purchasing whole fish, choose those fish whose gills are bright red in color, and whose eyes are clear and bulging, not sunken or cloudy. Finally refrigerate fish as soon as you get it home, and be sure to cook it within forty-eight hours of purchase.

Chicken Breasts
With Sourdough Stuffing

Yield: 4 servings

4 skinless chicken breast halves
    with bone (about 6 ounces
    each)

Ground black pepper

STUFFING

5 slices Cobblestone Mill
    sourdough bread

¾ cup coarsely chopped fresh
    mushrooms

¼ cup finely chopped onion

¼ cup finely chopped celery
    (include leaves)

½ teaspoon poultry seasoning

¼ cup Campbell's Healthy
    Request chicken broth

¼ cup Scramblers egg substitute

1. Rinse the chicken with cool water, and pat it dry with paper towels. Lightly sprinkle both sides with the pepper, and set aside.

2. Place $2\frac{1}{2}$ of the bread slices in a blender or food processor, and process into coarse crumbs. Cut the remaining bread slices into ½-inch cubes.

3. Place the bread crumbs, bread cubes, mushrooms, onion, celery, and poultry seasoning in a medium-sized bowl, and toss to mix well. Combine the broth and egg substitute in a small bowl, and slowly add the liquid to the bread mixture, tossing gently until the stuffing is moistened and holds together. (Add a little more broth if necessary.)

4. Coat a 9-inch baking pan with nonstick cooking spray, and lay the chicken in the pan with the bone side up. Mound a quarter of the stuffing into the depression of the breast bone of each piece of chicken.

5. Cover the pan with aluminum foil, and bake at 350°F for 45 minutes. Remove the foil, and bake for 10 additional minutes, or until the chicken is tender, the juices run clear, and the stuffing is lightly browned. Serve hot.

NUTRITIONAL FACTS (PER SERVING)		
Calories: 233	Fat: 2.2 g	Protein: 32 g
Cholesterol: 65 mg	Fiber: 1.8 g	Sodium: 326 mg

You Save: Calories: 240 Fat: 24.8 g

Chicken Dijon

1. Rinse the chicken with cool water, and pat it dry with paper towels. Spread the garlic over the chicken, and sprinkle with the pepper.

2. Coat a large nonstick skillet with nonstick cooking spray, and preheat over medium-high heat. Place the chicken in the skillet, and cook for 2 minutes on each side, or until nicely browned.

3. Reduce the heat to low, and pour the broth into the bottom of the skillet. Arrange the mushrooms around the chicken, cover, and cook for 15 minutes, or until the chicken is tender and no longer pink inside.

4. Transfer the chicken to a warm serving platter. Remove the mushrooms from the skillet with a slotted spoon, and place on top of the chicken. Cover the platter to keep it warm.

5. Add the mustard and sugar to the liquid in the skillet, and whisk over low heat to mix well. Add the sour cream, and whisk until the sauce is smooth and heated through. Spoon the sauce over the chicken and mushrooms, and serve hot with wild rice, brown rice, or noodles if desired.

Yield: 4 servings

4 boneless skinless chicken breast halves (about 4 ounces each)

1½ teaspoons crushed fresh garlic

¼ teaspoon ground black pepper

⅓ cup Swanson Natural Goodness chicken broth

2 cups sliced fresh mushrooms

2 tablespoons Dijon mustard

1 teaspoon sugar

½ cup Land O Lakes no-fat sour cream

NUTRITIONAL FACTS (PER SERVING)		
Calories: 175	Fat: 2 g	Protein: 28.4 g
Cholesterol: 67 mg	Fiber: 0.6 g	Sodium: 335 mg

You Save: Calories: 180 Fat: 21.1 g

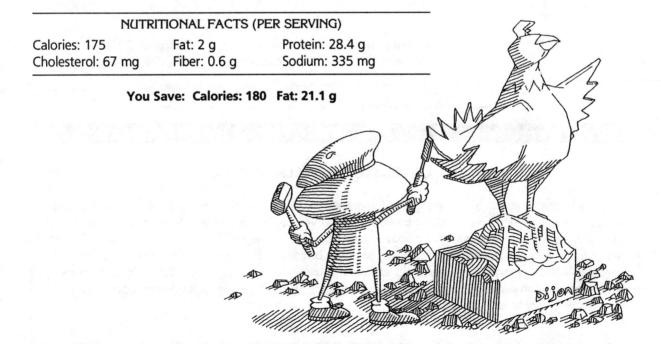

Southern-Style Smothered Chicken

Yield: *4 servings*

4 boneless skinless chicken breast halves (about 4 ounces each)

½ cup plus 2 tablespoons Gold Medal unbleached flour

½ teaspoon poultry seasoning

¼ teaspoon salt

¼ teaspoon ground black pepper

¼ cup Carnation Lite evaporated skimmed milk

¼ cup Egg Beaters egg substitute

1 cup Campbell's Healthy Request chicken broth

You Save: Cal: 191   Fat: 20.1 g

1. Rinse the chicken with cool water, and pat it dry with paper towels. Place the chicken on a flat surface, and use a meat mallet to pound each half to ¼-inch thickness.

2. Combine the flour, poultry seasoning, salt, and pepper in a shallow dish, and stir to mix well. Remove 2 tablespoons of the mixture, combine with the evaporated milk in a small jar with a tight-fitting lid, and shake to mix well. Set the milk mixture aside.

3. Place the egg substitute in a shallow dish. Dip the chicken pieces first in the egg substitute and then in the flour mixture, turning to coat both sides.

4. Coat a large nonstick skillet with nonstick cooking spray, and preheat over medium-high heat. Place the chicken in the skillet, and cook for 2 to 3 minutes on each side, or until nicely browned.

5. Pour the broth around the chicken. Reduce the heat to low, and stir the evaporated milk mixture into the broth. Cover the skillet, and simmer for about 10 minutes, scraping the bottom of the pan occasionally, until the chicken is tender and the gravy is thick. Serve hot with potatoes or rice if desired.

NUTRITIONAL FACTS (PER SERVING)

Calories: 180	Fat: 1.9 g	Protein: 29 g
Cholesterol: 67 mg	Fiber: 0.3 g	Sodium: 345 mg

FAT-FIGHTING TIP

Browning Without Fat

The traditional method of browning food requires oil, butter, or margarine. Indeed, some recipes require several tablespoons of oil for browning! However, as the recipes in this chapter show, all that extra oil is simply not necessary. To brown meat, chicken, or vegetables with virtually no added fat, spray a thin film of nonstick cooking spray over the bottom of a skillet. Then preheat the skillet over medium-high heat, and brown the food as usual. If the food starts to stick, add a few teaspoons of water, broth, sherry, or wine. If you use both a nonstick skillet *and* nonstick cooking spray, it should not be necessary to add any liquid at all.

Crusty Chicken Pot Pie

1. To make the filling, combine the soup and milk in a 2-quart pot, and stir to mix well. Place the pot over medium heat and cook, stirring frequently, until the mixture comes to a boil. Add the chicken or turkey and the vegetables, and heat until the mixture is warmed through.

2. Coat a 9-inch deep dish pie pan with nonstick cooking spray, and spread the warm chicken mixture evenly in the pan. Set aside.

3. To make the crust, combine the flour, oat bran, and baking powder in a medium-sized bowl, and stir to mix well. Using a pastry cutter or 2 knives, cut in the margarine until the mixture resembles coarse meal. Add enough of the buttermilk to form a stiff dough that leaves the sides of the bowl and forms a ball. Turn the dough onto a floured surface, and pat it into a 5-inch circle. Then, using a rolling pin, roll the dough into a 10-inch circle.

4. Using a sharp knife or a pizza wheel, cut the dough into $\frac{1}{2}$-inch-wide strips. Lay half of the crust strips over the filling, spacing them $\frac{1}{2}$ inch apart. Lay the remaining strips over the filling in the opposite direction to form a lattice top. Trim the edges to make the dough conform to the shape of the pan.

5. Bake at 375°F for 25 to 30 minutes, or until the filling is bubbly and the crust is lightly browned. Remove the dish from the oven, and let sit for 5 minutes before serving.

Yield: 5 servings

FILLING

1 can (10$\frac{3}{4}$ ounces) Campbell's Healthy Request condensed cream of celery soup, undiluted

$\frac{1}{2}$ cup skim milk

2 cups cooked diced chicken or turkey breast (about 10 ounces), or 3 cans (5 ounces each) Swanson premium chunk white chicken or turkey breast in water, drained

1 package (10 ounces) frozen (thawed) mixed vegetables, drained

CRUST

$\frac{3}{4}$ cup Gold Medal unbleached flour

$\frac{1}{4}$ cup plus 2 tablespoons Quaker oat bran

1$\frac{1}{2}$ teaspoons baking powder

2 tablespoons Promise Extra Light margarine, cut into pieces

$\frac{1}{3}$ cup nonfat buttermilk

NUTRITIONAL FACTS (PER SERVING)		
Calories: 244	Fat: 4.6 g	Protein: 24 g
Cholesterol: 46 mg	Fiber: 5 g	Sodium: 434 mg

You Save: Calories: 190   Fat: 19.4 g

Breast of Turkey Parmesan

Yield: *6 servings*

6 pieces Butterball fresh turkey breast cutlets or tenderloins (about 4 ounces each)

½ cup Healthy Choice egg substitute

½ cup Progresso Italian-style bread crumbs

¼ cup Pillsbury's Best unbleached flour

¼ cup plus 2 tablespoons Kraft Free nonfat grated Parmesan topping, divided

¾ cup Polly-O Free natural shredded nonfat mozzarella cheese

SAUCE

1 can (14½ ounces) Hunt's no salt added tomatoes, crushed

½ cup Hunt's no salt added tomato paste

¼ cup Campbell's Healthy Request chicken broth

½ cup finely chopped onion

1 teaspoon crushed fresh garlic

1½ teaspoons dried Italian seasoning

¼ teaspoon crushed red pepper

Turkey breast substitutes nicely for veal in this and many other recipes.

1. To make the sauce, combine all of the sauce ingredients in a 2-quart saucepan, and stir to mix well. Bring the mixture to a boil over high heat. Then reduce the heat to low, cover, and simmer for 20 minutes. Set aside to keep warm.

2. While the sauce is cooking, rinse the turkey with cool water, and pat it dry with paper towels. Place the turkey pieces on a flat surface, and use a meat mallet to pound each piece to ¼-inch thickness.

3. Place the egg substitute in a medium-sized shallow bowl. Combine the bread crumbs, flour, and ¼ cup of the Parmesan topping in another shallow bowl. Dip the turkey pieces first in the egg substitute, and then in the crumb mixture, turning to coat both sides.

4. Coat a 9-x-13-inch pan with nonstick cooking spray. Arrange the turkey pieces in a single layer on the pan, and bake at 400°F for 20 minutes, or until the turkey is lightly browned and no longer pink inside.

5. Pour the sauce over the turkey, and sprinkle first with the remaining 2 tablespoons of Parmesan, and then with the mozzarella. Bake at 400°F for 5 minutes, or until the cheese has melted. Serve with your choice of pasta.

NUTRITIONAL FACTS (PER SERVING)

Calories: 252	Fat: 1.7 g	Protein: 37 g
Cholesterol: 80 mg	Fiber: 2.1 g	Sodium: 524 mg

You Save: Calories: 174 Fat: 21.1 g

Time-Saving Tip

To reduce preparation time, make Breast of Turkey Parmesan with 3 cups of Ragu Light pasta sauce instead of the homemade sauce.

Turkey Piccata

1. Rinse the turkey with cool water, and pat it dry with paper towels. Place the turkey pieces on a flat surface, and use a meat mallet to pound each piece to $\frac{1}{4}$-inch thickness.

2. Place the egg substitute in a shallow dish. Combine the flour, tarragon, and pepper in another shallow dish. Dip the turkey pieces first in the egg substitute, and then in the flour mixture, turning to coat both sides.

3. Coat a large nonstick skillet with nonstick cooking spray, and preheat over medium heat. Place the turkey pieces in the pan, and cook for 2 to 3 minutes on each side, or until the turkey is golden brown and no longer pink inside. Transfer the turkey to a warm serving platter, and cover to keep warm.

4. Add the mushrooms to the skillet, and stir-fry for about 1 minute, or until the mushrooms begin to soften. (Add a little water if the skillet becomes too dry.) Add the broth, lemon juice, scallions, and garlic to the skillet. Cook, stirring occasionally, for 4 to 6 minutes, or just until the mushrooms are tender and the liquid is reduced by half.

5. Remove the skillet from the heat, and stir in the lemon rind and parsley. Spoon the sauce over the turkey and serve hot, accompanied by angel hair pasta if desired.

Yield: *4 servings*

8 pieces Butterball fresh turkey breast cutlets or tenderloins (about 2 ounces each)

$\frac{1}{3}$ cup Better'n Eggs egg substitute

$\frac{1}{2}$ cup Pillsbury's Best unbleached flour

$\frac{1}{2}$ teaspoon dried tarragon

$\frac{1}{4}$ teaspoon ground black pepper

$1\frac{1}{2}$ cups sliced fresh mushrooms

1 cup Swanson Natural Goodness chicken broth

1 tablespoon plus $1\frac{1}{2}$ teaspoons lemon juice

$\frac{1}{4}$ cup thinly sliced scallions

1 teaspoon crushed fresh garlic

1 tablespoon freshly grated lemon rind

2 tablespoons finely chopped fresh parsley

NUTRITIONAL FACTS (PER SERVING)		
Calories: 205	Fat: 1.7 g	Protein: 31 g
Cholesterol: 73 mg	Fiber: 2.2 g	Sodium: 354 mg

You Save: Calories: 121   Fat: 14.1 g

Crispy Crust Sausage Pizza

Yield: *8 slices*

CRUST

1½ cups Pillsbury's Best bread flour, divided

⅓ cup Quaker oat bran

1½ teaspoons Fleischmann's Rapid Rise yeast

1 teaspoon sugar

¼ teaspoon salt

½ cup plus 2 tablespoons water

TOPPINGS

¾ cup Ragú Light pasta sauce, any variety

1 cup Polly-O Free natural shredded nonfat mozzarella cheese

4 ounces Turkey Italian Sausage (page 182), cooked, crumbled, and drained

½ cup sliced fresh mushrooms

NUTRITIONAL FACTS (PER SLICE)

Calories: 130	Fiber: 1.7 g
Chol: 10 mg	Protein: 11 g
Fat: 0.9 g	Sodium: 281 mg

You Save: Cal: 88   Fat: 10.9 g

1. To make the crust, in a large bowl, combine ½ cup of the bread flour with all of the oat bran, yeast, sugar, and salt, and stir to mix well. Place the water in a small saucepan, and heat until very warm (125°F to 130°F). Add the water to the flour mixture, and stir for one minute. Stir in enough of the remaining flour, 2 tablespoons at a time, to form a stiff dough.

2. Sprinkle 2 tablespoons of the remaining flour over a flat surface, and turn the dough onto the surface. Knead the dough for 5 minutes, gradually adding enough of the remaining flour to form a smooth, satiny ball. Coat a large bowl with nonstick cooking spray, and place the dough in the bowl. Cover the bowl with a clean kitchen towel, and let rise in a warm place for about 35 minutes, or until doubled in size.

3. When the dough has risen, punch it down, shape it into a ball, and turn it onto a lightly floured surface. Using a rolling pin, roll the dough into a 14-inch circle. Coat a 14-inch pizza pan with nonstick cooking spray, and place the dough on the pan.

4. Spread the pasta sauce over the crust to within ½ inch of the edge. Sprinkle the cheese over the sauce, and top with the sausage and mushrooms.

5. Bake at 475°F for 10 minutes, or until the cheese is melted and the crust is lightly browned. Cut into wedges and serve immediately.

Time-Saving Tips

To make the dough for Crispy Crust Sausage Pizza in a bread machine, place all of the dough ingredients except for ¼ cup of the bread flour in the machine's bread pan. (Do not heat the water.) Turn the machine to the "rise," "dough," "manual," or equivalent setting so that the machine will mix, knead, and let the dough rise once. Check the dough about 5 minutes after the machine has started. If the dough seems too sticky, add more of the remaining flour, a tablespoon at a time. When the dough is ready, remove it from the machine and proceed to shape, top, and bake it as directed in the recipe.

As an alternative to making your crust from scratch, substitute one Pillsbury All Ready pizza crust for the homemade crust. (You'll find it in the refrigerated section of the grocery store.) Simply roll the dough out, lay it in the pan, and proceed with the recipe as directed.

Tempting Tuna Casserole

1. Cook the pasta al dente according to package directions. Drain well, return the pasta to the pot, and set aside.

2. In a medium-sized bowl, combine the mushroom soup, sour cream, and milk, and stir to mix well. Add the soup mixture to the pasta, and toss to mix well. Add the peas, and toss gently to mix. Add the tuna, and toss gently to mix.

3. Coat a 2-quart casserole dish with nonstick cooking spray, and spread the mixture evenly in the dish. Cover the dish with aluminum foil.

4. Bake at 375°F for 25 minutes, or until the dish is heated through. Remove the foil, spread the cheese over the top, and bake uncovered for 5 additional minutes, or until the cheese is melted. Serve hot.

Yield: *5 servings*

8 ounces Mueller's seashell pasta

1 can (10¾ ounces) Campbell's Healthy Request cream of mushroom soup, undiluted

½ cup Land O Lakes no-fat sour cream

3 tablespoons skim milk

¾ cup frozen (thawed) green peas

1 can (9 ounces) Bumble Bee solid white tuna in water, drained

½ cup Healthy Choice fancy shredded fat-free Cheddar cheese

NUTRITIONAL FACTS (PER 1¼-CUP SERVING)

Calories: 318	Fat: 2.3 g	Protein: 24 g
Cholesterol: 18 mg	Fiber: 2.5 g	Sodium: 538 mg

You Save: Calories: 114 Fat: 12.3 g

Fiesta Chili

Yield: *8 servings*

1 pound Butterball Extra Lean ground turkey or another brand of extra lean ground turkey

1 can (14½ ounces) Hunt's no salt added tomatoes

2 cans (8 ounces each) Hunt's no salt added tomato sauce

1 can (15 ounces) Joan of Arc red kidney beans or black beans, rinsed and drained

1 medium onion, chopped

2 tablespoons chili powder

1¼ teaspoons Maggi instant beef bouillon granules

½ teaspoon ground cumin

1½ cups fresh or frozen (thawed) whole kernel corn

1 can (4 ounces) chopped green chilies, drained

¾ cup Healthy Choice fancy shredded fat-free Cheddar cheese

1. Coat a 3-quart pot with nonstick cooking spray, and preheat over medium heat. Add the turkey, and cook, stirring to crumble, until the meat is no longer pink. (There will be no fat to drain off.)

2. Add the tomatoes, tomato sauce, beans, onions, chili powder, bouillon granules, and cumin to the pot, and bring the mixture to a boil. Reduce the heat to low, cover, and simmer for 20 minutes.

3. Add the corn and chilies to the pot. Cover and simmer for 5 minutes, or until the flavors are well blended. Serve hot, topping each serving with a rounded tablespoon of the cheese.

NUTRITIONAL FACTS (PER 1-CUP serving)

Calories: 182	Fat: 2 g	Protein: 21.6 g
Cholesterol: 37 mg	Fiber: 5.4 g	Sodium: 369 mg

You Save: Calories: 154   Fat: 15.9 g

Tex-Mex Chicken and Rice

1. Rinse the chicken with cool water, and pat it dry with paper towels. Cut the chicken into bite-sized pieces, and sprinkle with the salt.

2. Coat a large nonstick skillet with cooking spray, and preheat over medium-high heat. Add the chicken and garlic, and stir-fry for 5 minutes, or until the chicken is browned and no longer pink inside.

3. Add the remaining ingredients to the skillet. Stir to mix well, and bring to a boil. Reduce the heat to low, cover, and simmer for about 6 minutes, or until the rice is tender and the liquid is absorbed.

4. Remove from the heat, cover, and let stand for 5 minutes. Serve hot.

Yield: 5 servings

1 lb. boneless skinless chicken breasts

¼ teaspoon salt

1 teaspoon crushed fresh garlic

2 cups Minute Brand instant brown rice

1 can (1 pound) Joan of Arc red kidney beans, rinsed and drained

1¾ cups Health Valley no salt added chicken broth

½ cup Louise's salsa

⅓ cup finely chopped green bell pepper

⅓ cup finely chopped onion

1 tablespoon chili powder

NUTRITIONAL FACTS (PER 1½-CUP SERVING)

Calories: 359	Fat: 2.8 g	Protein: 32 g
Cholesterol: 53 mg	Fiber: 8 g	Sodium: 371 mg

You Save: Calories: 88   Fat: 9.5 g

Bueno Black Beans and Rice

1. Coat a large nonstick skillet with cooking spray, and preheat over medium-high heat. Add the sausage, onion, and green pepper, and sauté for 3 minutes, or until the sausage is browned.

2. Add the remaining ingredients, stir to mix well, and bring to a boil. Stir, reduce the heat to low, and cover. Simmer for 12 minutes, or until the rice is tender and the liquid is absorbed.

3. Remove from the heat, cover, and let stand for 5 minutes. Serve hot.

Yield: 5 servings

8 ounces Healthy Choice smoked turkey sausage, thinly sliced

½ cup chopped onion

½ cup chopped green bell pepper

2 cups Arrowhead Mills quick-cooking brown rice

1 can (15 ounces) Eden black beans, drained

1 bay leaf

½ teaspoon dried oregano

2¼ cups water or Health Valley no salt added chicken broth

NUTRITIONAL FACTS (PER 1¼-CUP SERVING)

Calories: 247	Fat: 2.4 g	Protein: 13.4 g
Cholesterol: 20 mg	Fiber: 6.2 g	Sodium: 474 mg

You Save: Calories: 132   Fat: 17.3 g

Jiffy Jambalaya

Yield: *6 servings*

¾ pound peeled and deveined raw shrimp

1 cup (about 5 ounces) thinly sliced Healthy Choice smoked turkey sausage

1 teaspoon crushed fresh garlic

2 cups Uncle Ben's instant brown rice

1¼ cups water or Health Valley no salt added chicken broth

1 can (8 ounces) Hunt's no salt added tomato sauce

1 can (1 pound) Bush's Best red kidney beans, rinsed and drained

½ cup thinly sliced celery

½ cup chopped green bell pepper

½ cup chopped onion

1 teaspoon Cajun seasoning

For variety, substitute bite-sized pieces of skinless chicken breast for the shrimp.

1. Rinse the shrimp with cool water, and pat them dry with paper towels. Coat a large skillet with nonstick cooking spray, and place over medium-high heat. Add the shrimp, sausage, and garlic, and stir-fry for about 4 minutes, or until the shrimp is no longer pink.

2. Add all of the remaining ingredients to the skillet, and bring the mixture to a boil. Stir, reduce the heat to low, and cover. Simmer for 6 to 8 minutes, or until the rice is tender and the liquid has been absorbed.

3. Remove the skillet from the heat, and let sit covered for 5 minutes before serving.

NUTRITIONAL FACTS (PER 1½-CUP SERVING)

Calories: 313	Fat: 2.9 g	Protein: 23 g
Cholesterol: 97 mg	Fiber: 6.9 g	Sodium: 480 mg

You Save: Calories: 170   Fat: 18.2 g

Grilled Teriyaki Fish

1. Combine all of the marinade ingredients in a small bowl, and stir to mix well. Set aside.

2. Rinse the fish steaks with cool water, and pat them dry with paper towels. Place the steaks in a shallow nonmetal container, and pour the marinade over the steaks, turning to coat all sides. Cover and refrigerate for several hours or overnight.

3. Spray the steaks lightly with the cooking spray, and grill over medium heat, covered, or under a broiler, for about 5 minutes on each side, or until the meat is easily flaked with a fork. Serve hot.

Yield: 6 servings

6 firm-fleshed fish steaks (5 ounces each), such as grouper, mahi mahi, swordfish, fresh tuna, or amberjack

I Can't Believe It's Not Butter! cooking spray

MARINADE

½ cup Dole unsweetened pineapple juice

2 tablespoons Kikkoman Lite soy sauce

2 tablespoons dry sherry

2 tablespoons dark brown sugar

1 scallion, finely minced

1 teaspoon crushed fresh garlic

1 teaspoon minced fresh ginger root, or ⅓ teaspoon ground ginger

1 teaspoon sesame oil

NUTRITIONAL FACTS (PER SERVING)

Calories: 149	Fat: 1.9 g	Protein: 28 g
Cholesterol: 53 mg	Fiber: 0 g	Sodium: 146 mg

You Save: Calories: 55 Fat: 6.1 g

Spicy Salsa Meat Loaf

Yield: *8 servings*

LOAF

1½ pounds 95% lean ground beef

¾ cup Quaker oat bran

½ cup Old El Paso thick and chunky salsa

½ cup finely chopped onion

¼ cup finely chopped green bell pepper

3 egg whites

¼ teaspoon ground black pepper

2 teaspoons chili powder

TOPPING

½ cup Hunt's no salt added tomato sauce

¼ cup Old El Paso thick and chunky salsa

"Lean" meat loaf pans are great for low-fat cooking. These pans have an inner liner with holes in it that allows the fat to drain into the bottom of the pan instead of being reabsorbed into the meat.

1. Combine the loaf ingredients in a large bowl, and mix well. Coat a 9-x-5-inch meat loaf pan with nonstick cooking spray, and press the mixture into the pan to form a loaf.

2. Bake at 350°F for 35 minutes. Combine the topping ingredients in a small bowl, and pour over the meat loaf. Bake for 30 additional minutes, or until the meat is no longer pink inside.

3. Remove the loaf from the oven, and let sit for 10 minutes before slicing and serving.

NUTRITIONAL FACTS (PER SERVING)

Calories: 158	Fat: 4.8 g	Protein: 22 g
Cholesterol: 56 mg	Fiber: 1.8 g	Sodium: 186 mg

You Save: Calories: 115   Fat: 12.8 g

Skillet Stroganoff

1. Place the meat in a large, deep skillet. Place the skillet over medium heat, and cook, stirring to crumble, until the meat is no longer pink. (If the meat is 95-percent lean, there will be no fat to drain.)

2. Add the mushrooms, onions, tomato paste, bouillon granules, pepper, and water to the skillet, and stir to mix well. Increase the heat to high, and bring the mixture to a boil.

3. Add the noodles to the skillet, and stir gently to mix. Reduce the heat to medium, cover, and simmer, stirring occasionally, for 8 to 10 minutes, or until the noodles are al dente and most of the liquid has been absorbed.

4. Reduce the heat to low, add the sour cream, and stir gently to mix well. Cook for 1 additional minute, or just until the sour cream is heated through. (Add a little more water or broth if the sauce seems too dry.) Serve hot.

Yield: 5 servings

¾ pound 95% lean ground beef

2 cups sliced fresh mushrooms

½ cup chopped onion

1 tablespoon plus 1½ teaspoons Hunt's no salt added tomato paste

2½ teaspoons Maggi instant beef bouillon granules

¼ teaspoon coarsely ground black pepper

2¼ cups water or Health Valley no salt added beef broth

6 ounces De Bole's whole wheat ribbon noodles or Hodgson Mill yolkless whole wheat pasta ribbons

¾ cup Land O Lakes no-fat sour cream

NUTRITIONAL FACTS (PER 1¼-CUP SERVING)		
Calories: 261	Fat: 4.2 g	Protein: 23 g
Cholesterol: 45 mg	Fiber: 4.5 g	Sodium: 462 mg

You Save: Calories: 142   Fat: 19.5 g

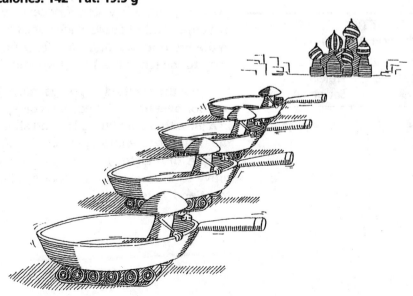

Pot Roast With Creamy Onion Gravy

Yield: *8 servings*

2½-pound top round roast or London Broil

½ teaspoon coarsely ground black pepper

1 envelope Lipton Recipe Secrets onion soup mix

1 cup water

1½ pounds potatoes (about 5 medium), scrubbed and quartered

1¼ pounds carrots (about 6 large), peeled and cut into 2-inch pieces

GRAVY

Roasted meat drippings

½ cup Carnation Lite evaporated skimmed milk

¼ cup Pillsbury's Best unbleached flour

NUTRITIONAL FACTS
(PER SERVING)

Calories: 308	Fiber: 4.2 g
Chol: 59 mg	Protein: 30 g
Fat: 5.3 g	Sodium: 414 mg

You Save: Cal: 163 Fat: 17.3 g

Top round roast—which is sometimes sold as London Broil—is one of the leanest cuts available, and can easily be substituted for pot roasts and briskets in any of your favorite recipes.

1. Trim the meat of any visible fat. Rinse the meat with cool water, and pat it dry with paper towels. Sprinkle the pepper over both sides.

2. Coat a large oven-proof skillet with nonstick cooking spray, and preheat over medium-high heat. Place the meat in the skillet, and brown for 2 to 3 minutes on each side. Remove the skillet from the heat.

3. Combine the onion soup mix and water in a small bowl, and pour the mixture over and around the meat. Cover tightly, and bake at 325°F for 1 hour and 30 minutes.

4. Remove the skillet from the oven and carefully remove the cover (steam will escape). Arrange the potatoes and carrots around the meat, cover, and return the skillet to the oven for 45 additional minutes, or until the meat and vegetables are tender. Transfer the meat and vegetables to a serving platter, and cover to keep warm.

5. To make the gravy, pour the meat drippings into a 2-cup measure, and add water, if necessary, to bring the volume up to 1½ cups. Add a couple of ice cubes to the broth, and let them float in the broth for about 1 minute. (Any fat present in the broth will cling to the ice cubes.) Remove and discard the ice cubes.

6. Pour the defatted drippings into a 1-quart saucepan, and bring to a boil over medium heat. Combine the evaporated milk and flour in a jar with a tight-fitting lid, and shake until smooth. Slowly pour the flour mixture into the boiling broth. Cook and stir for about 1 minute, or until the mixture is thickened and bubbly. Transfer the gravy to a warmed gravy boat or pitcher, and serve hot with the meat and vegetables.

Pork Tenderloins With Apple-Raisin Stuffing

1. To make the stuffing, place 3 of the bread slices in a blender or food processor, and process into coarse crumbs. Cut the remaining bread slices into ½-inch cubes.

2. Place the bread crumbs, bread cubes, apples, raisins, onion, celery, and rosemary in a large bowl, and toss to mix well. Combine the broth and egg substitute in a small bowl, and slowly add the liquid to the bread mixture, tossing gently until the stuffing is moistened and holds together. (Add a little more broth if necessary.) Set aside.

3. Combine all of the basting sauce ingredients in a small bowl, and stir to mix well. Set aside.

4. Trim the tenderloins of any visible fat and membranes. Rinse them with cool water, and pat dry with paper towels. Split each of the tenderloins lengthwise, cutting not quite all the way through, so that each tenderloin can be spread open like a book. Spread half of the stuffing mixture over half of each tenderloin, extending the stuffing all the way to the outer edges of the meat. Fold the facing half of the tenderloin over the stuffing-spread half, and use heavy string to tie the meat together at 2½-inch intervals.

5. Coat a 9-x-13-inch pan with nonstick cooking spray, and arrange the tenderloins in the pan, spacing them about 3 inches apart. Bake at 350°F for about 50 minutes, or until the meat is no longer pink inside, occasionally basting with the prepared sauce.

6. Remove the pan from the oven, cover loosely with foil, and let sit for 5 to 10 minutes before slicing ½-inch thick. Serve hot.

Yield: 8 servings

2 pork tenderloins, 1 pound each

STUFFING

6 slices Arnold Honey Wheatberry bread

¾ cup chopped peeled tart apples

¼ cup dark raisins

¼ cup finely chopped onion

¼ cup finely chopped celery (include leaves)

½ teaspoon dried rosemary

¼ cup plus 1 tablespoon Swanson Natural Goodness chicken broth

¼ cup Egg Beaters egg substitute

BASTING SAUCE

2 tablespoons frozen Seneca 100% apple juice concentrate, thawed

2 teaspoons Dijon mustard

½ teaspoon dried rosemary

NUTRITIONAL FACTS (PER SERVING)

Calories: 224	Fat: 5 g	Protein: 28.2 g
Cholesterol: 67 mg	Fiber: 2.9 g	Sodium: 214 mg

You Save: Calories: 115 Fat: 12.5 g

Savory Swiss Steak

Yield: *4 servings*

1-pound top round steak

$\frac{1}{3}$ cup Pillsbury's Best unbleached flour

$\frac{1}{2}$ teaspoon salt

$\frac{1}{4}$ teaspoon ground black pepper

1 can (14$\frac{1}{2}$ ounces) Del Monte no salt added stewed tomatoes, crushed

1. Trim the meat of any visible fat. Rinse the meat with cool water, and pat it dry with paper towels. Cut the meat into 4 pieces, and use a meat mallet to pound each piece to $\frac{1}{4}$-inch thickness.

2. Combine the flour, salt, and pepper in a shallow dish. Dip the meat in the flour mixture, turning to coat both sides.

3. Coat a large nonstick skillet with nonstick cooking spray, and preheat over medium-high heat. Place the meat in the skillet, and brown for 2 to 3 minutes on each side.

4. Pour the tomatoes over the meat, and reduce the heat to low. Cover and simmer for 45 minutes, or until the meat is very tender. Scrape the bottom of the pan occasionally, adding a little water if the skillet becomes too dry. Serve hot with noodles or brown rice if desired.

NUTRITIONAL FACTS (PER SERVING)

Calories: 213	Fat: 5.1 g	Protein: 26.7 g
Cholesterol: 59 mg	Fiber: 2 g	Sodium: 336 mg

You Save: Calories: 155   Fat: 16.5 g

FAT-FIGHTING TIP

Getting the Fat Out of Biscuit Toppings

Biscuit toppings add that down-home touch to casseroles and one-dish meals. Unfortunately they can also add a lot of fat. The good news is that it's a simple matter to reduce or even eliminate the fat in your biscuit toppings. Try replacing part or all of the oil in biscuit toppings with three-fourths as much nonfat buttermilk. (Replace shortening or butter with half as much buttermilk.) Mix the batter just until the dry ingredients are moistened, being careful not to overmix. If the mixture seems too dry, add a bit more buttermilk. For cobbler toppings, applesauce makes a great fat substitute. Drop the biscuits onto your casserole, bake as usual, and enjoy!

Beef and Biscuit Bake

1. Place the meat in a large oven-proof skillet. Place the skillet over medium heat, and cook, stirring to crumble, until the meat is no longer pink. (If the meat is 95% lean, there will be no fat to drain.) Add the onion, and cook for another minute or 2, or until the onion is crisp-tender.

2. Add 1½ cups of the broth and all of the corn, green beans, thyme or marjoram, bouillon granules, and pepper to the meat mixture. Bring to a boil over high heat, reduce the heat to low, and cover. Simmer for about 5 minutes, or until the vegetables are just tender.

3. Combine the remaining ½ cup of broth and the ¼ cup of flour in a jar with a tight-fitting lid, and shake until smooth. Stir the flour mixture into the meat mixture, and cook, stirring constantly, for about 2 minutes, or until the sauce has thickened. Remove the skillet from the heat, and set aside.

4. To make the topping, place the flour and baking powder in a medium-sized bowl, and stir to mix well. Add the buttermilk, and stir just until the dry ingredients are moistened, forming a moderately stiff batter. Drop heaping tablespoonfuls of batter onto the meat mixture to make 6 biscuits.

5. Bake at 400°F for about 15 minutes, or until the biscuits are lightly browned. Serve hot.

Yield: 6 servings

1 pound 95% lean ground beef

1 medium yellow onion, chopped

2 cups Health Valley no salt added beef broth, divided

1½ cups frozen (thawed) whole kernel corn

1½ cups frozen (thawed) cut green beans

½ teaspoon crushed dried thyme or marjoram

1¼ teaspoons Maggi instant beef bouillon granules

¼ teaspoon ground black pepper

¼ cup Gold Medal unbleached flour

BISCUIT TOPPING

1½ cups Gold Medal unbleached flour

2½ teaspoons baking powder

¾ cup nonfat buttermilk

NUTRITIONAL FACTS (PER SERVING)

Calories: 304	Fat: 4.5 g	Protein: 25 g
Cholesterol: 51 mg	Fiber: 3.6 g	Sodium: 414 mg

You Save: Calories: 170 Fat: 23.8 g

Jerk Pork Kabobs

Yield: *6 servings*

1½ pounds pork tenderloin

1 medium red bell pepper, cut into 6 wedges

6 Bird's Eye frozen sweet little ears corn on the cob, thawed and cut in half crosswise

1 medium green bell pepper, cut into 6 wedges

I Can't Believe It's Not Butter! cooking spray

MARINADE

1 medium yellow onion, finely chopped

¼ cup Dole unsweetened pineapple juice

1 tablespoon plus 1 teaspoon brown sugar

1 teaspoon ground allspice

1 teaspoon dried thyme

¼ teaspoon ground cinnamon

¼ teaspoon ground nutmeg

¼ teaspoon crushed red pepper

½ teaspoon coarsely ground black pepper

½ teaspoon salt

1. Combine all of the marinade ingredients in a small bowl, and stir to mix well. Set aside.

2. Rinse the meat with cool water, and pat it dry with paper towels. Cut the meat into 18 cubes, each about 1½ inches square. Place the meat and the marinade in a shallow nonmetal container, cover, and refrigerate for at least 8 hours or overnight.

3. To assemble the kabobs, thread 1 piece of meat onto a 12-inch skewer. Follow the meat with 1 wedge of red pepper, 1 piece of corn, 1 piece of meat, 1 piece of corn, 1 wedge of green pepper, and finally 1 piece of meat. Repeat to make 6 kabobs. Discard the remaining marinade.

4. Spray the kabobs lightly with the cooking spray, and grill over medium coals or under a broiler for about 10 minutes, turning every 3 minutes, until the meat is no longer pink inside and the vegetables are lightly browned. Serve hot.

NUTRITIONAL FACTS (PER SERVING)

Calories: 223	Fat: 4.7 g	Protein: 26.6 g
Cholesterol: 67 mg	Fiber: 3 g	Sodium: 140 mg

You Save: Calories: 73 Fat: 7.1 g

FAT-FIGHTER'S GUIDE TO
Frozen Dinners and Entrées

Today's busy lifestyles make frozen dinners a popular alternative to cooking. In the past, most brands of frozen dinners and entrées contained too much fat, too much salt, or too much of both to be a regular part of a prudent diet. Fortunately, this no longer holds true. Manufacturers have responded to consumer demand, and healthier options that are low in both fat and salt are now widely available.

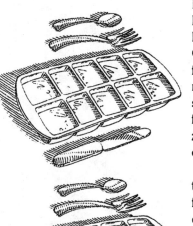

Healthy Choice was the first company to offer an entire line of low-fat dinners and entrées that were not loaded with sodium—and their popularity with consumers led to a revolution in the frozen food case. These days, alongside Healthy Choice frozen dinners and entrées, you will find several other brands of low-fat, reduced-sodium products. Tyson Healthy Portions is one such brand. Like Healthy Choice meals, all Tyson Healthy Portions get well under 30 percent of their calories from fat, and contain less than 600 milligrams of sodium. Many other brands—including Budget Gourmet Light and Healthy, Lean Cuisine, and Weight Watchers—offer some products that meet these same guidelines. How can you spot the best fat-fighting frozen dinners and entrées? Simply read the Nutrition Facts information. If your frozen meal contains less than 10 grams of fat and less than 600 milligrams of sodium, you will be able to stay within the bounds of your daily fat and sodium budgets.

One type of frozen entrée that is especially popular is the pizza. Happily, when made properly, pizza is not a junk food, but an excellent low-fat source of calcium, carbohydrates, and other nutrients. The freezer case of your local grocery store most likely has several brands of reduced-fat pizzas. Leading the low-fat pack are Stouffer's Lean Cuisine French Bread Pizza, Healthy Choice French Bread Pizza, Tombstone Light Vegetable Pizza, and Weight Watchers Deluxe Combo Pizza. These brands get from 16 to 26 percent of their calories from fat. As a basis of comparison, keep in mind that regular frozen pizzas—even vegetable pizzas—get close to *half* their fat from calories.

Many people complain that they still feel hungry after eating a frozen meal or entrée. If this is true of you, realize that an entire meal which supplies less than 300 calories won't stick with most people for more than a couple of hours—if, in fact, it satisfies them at all. Surprisingly, frozen meals tend to fall short in the vegetable department, with most providing less than a one-cup serving of this very important food group. For this reason, these dinners also often supply insufficient amounts of vitamins A and C, and dietary fiber. The solution? Add a salad—with nonfat dressing—or a piece of fruit to your meal. Unless your entrée is bread based, like pizza, also add a piece of whole grain bread. These additions will provide nutritional balance and keep you feeling full and satisfied until the next meal.

9. Perfect Pasta Dishes

Few foods can match the versatility and ease of preparation that pasta offers. This is great news for people who live the low-fat lifestyle, since pasta is practically fat-free. If calories are also a concern, you will be pleased to discover that one cup of cooked pasta provides a modest 200 calories, most of which come from energizing complex carbohydrates. And if you choose whole grain products, your pasta dish will also provide you with much-needed B vitamins, minerals, and dietary fiber, making it a real nutritional bargain.

But while pasta itself may be a fat-fighter's best friend, the same cannot always be said about the ingredients that top it. Cream-enriched sauces, gobs of fat-laden cheese, and greasy sausages are just some of the toppings that often change pasta from a low-fat delight to a high-fat nightmare. Take Spaghetti Carbonara, for instance. Made traditionally—with bacon, cream, egg yolks, and cheese—even a moderate portion of this dish delivers a whopping 600 calories and 40 grams of fat!

The good news is that with the many excellent low-fat and fat-free products now available, it is possible to transform all of your favorite pasta dishes into light and healthful meals. Can high-fat ingredients like cream and full-fat cheeses be eliminated without sacrificing flavor? Absolutely. This chapter will show you how.

The recipes that follow combine pasta with nonfat cheeses, skim milk, ultra-lean meats and poultry, seafood, vegetables, herbs and spices, and other wholesome ingredients. The result is a dazzling selection of pasta creations that are every bit as tempting as their full-fat counterparts. And, as a bonus, most of these dishes can be prepared in less than thirty minutes—a real boon to the busy cook.

To help you make the best possible ingredient choices, this chapter includes a Fat-Fighter's Guide that provides simple guidelines for selecting the most nutritious pastas available (page 168). For those days when time is in short supply, the guide also steers you towards low-fat prepared sauces. And informative Fat-Fighting Tips help you slim down your own favorite pasta recipes, allowing them to take an important place in your low-fat menu.

So if you've been afraid that adopting a healthy lifestyle means giving up your favorite pasta dish, put your fears aside. From cheese-filled manicotti, to spicy Cajun shrimp and fettuccine, to pesto-topped pasta primavera, to a fabulously low-fat spaghetti carbonara, you'll find that pasta is the perfect answer whenever you want a great-tasting, quick-cooking low-fat meal.

FAT-FIGHTER'S GUIDE TO
Pastas and Sauces

Pasta makes a great quick meal—especially if you use a bottled sauce. And these days, there are several low-fat and fat-free brands from which to choose. As a rule, marinara (tomato based) sauces are much lower in fat than creamy white sauces. Ragu Light and Healthy Choice each feature an entire line of fat-free tomato pasta sauces that have only about 50 calories per half-cup serving. Compare this with brands made with oil, which can contain 6 or more grams of fat and 120 calories for the same size serving, and your savings are clear. If you want a meat sauce, it is best to start with a fat-free marinara sauce. Then add your own 95-percent lean ground beef or turkey Italian sausage.

What about sodium? Many bottled marinara sauces—including the fat-free brands—contain close to 400 milligrams per half-cup serving, which is a sizable amount considering the suggested daily limit of 2,400 milligrams. However, several brands of low- and no-fat pasta sauces contain only 200 to 300 milligrams of sodium per serving. Among these are Millina's Finest Fat Free, Garden Valley Naturals Fat Free, and Mama Rizzo's Low Fat. For a no-salt-added low-fat sauce, try Eden Organic No Salt Added pasta sauce, or Enrico's All Natural No Salt Added sauces.

On those days when you have slightly more time—and a few minutes is all you'll need!—it's easy to make a sauce that's practically sodium- and fat-free. Start with canned unsalted tomatoes like Eden No Salt Added tomatoes, Hunt's No Salt Added tomatoes, Del Monte No Salt Added stewed tomatoes, or Cento crushed tomatoes. Progresso Recipe Ready crushed tomatoes with added purée contains about half the sodium of most other brands, giving you a good start on a reduced-sodium sauce. Then add your own seasonings for a truly homemade taste. You can

even afford to add some nonfat cheese or turkey Italian sausage and still remain well within your sodium budget.

As for the pasta itself, except for egg pastas, most are practically fat- and sodium-free. Keep in mind, though, that pastas are usually made from refined durum wheat flour, which, like other refined flours, lacks many of the nutrients found in whole grains. A better choice is a whole wheat pasta. Some manufacturers, including De Bole's, Eden Foods, Hodgson Mill, Westbrae Natural, and Pritikin, offer some delicious whole wheat pastas. Now widely available, these pastas will add extra fiber and nutrients to your meal. What about Jerusalem artichoke pastas? A combination of durum wheat flour and Jerusalem artichoke flour, these products have a pleasant, slightly sweet flavor and smooth texture. Unless these pastas are made with whole grain durum wheat, however, they are no more nutritious than other refined pastas. For a nutritious artichoke-based pasta, look for De Bole's whole grain and Jerusalem artichoke products.

If you're looking for a real change of pace, you may wish to sample pastas made from other whole grains, like brown rice, quinoa, spelt, and kamut. Kamut is a strain of durum whole wheat that is particularly well suited for making pasta. Compared with regular whole wheat pastas, kamut pasta has a more delicate, buttery flavor and a smoother texture. Look for brands like Eden, Cleopatra, and Mrs. Leeper's. Or try spinach or other vegetable pastas. Most brands do start out with refined durum wheat flour, but the addition of vegetables to the dough can significantly boost the level of nutrients like vitamin A.

Although most egg noodles have no place in a low-fat diet, there are exceptions to even this rule. Products like Mueller's Yolk Free noodles and

No Yolks noodles contain the cholesterol-free egg whites only, making them great additions to a healthful meal.

So the next time you need a delicious dinner in a hurry—or you're just in the mood for a satisfying plate of comfort food—boil up some pasta, and enjoy the pleasures of light and healthy eating.

Spaghetti With Scallops and Tomato Cream Sauce

1. To make the sauce, place the tomatoes and broth in a small saucepan, and bring to a boil over medium heat. Reduce the heat to low, cover, and simmer for 2 minutes, or until the tomatoes are plumped. Remove the pot from the heat, and set aside to cool slightly. (Do not drain.)

2. Combine the evaporated milk, Parmesan topping, oregano, and pepper in a small bowl, and stir to mix well. Add the evaporated milk mixture to the tomato mixture, stir to mix well, and set aside.

3. Cook the pasta al dente according to package directions. Drain well, return the pasta to the pot, and cover to keep warm.

4. While the pasta is cooking, rinse the scallops with cool water, and pat them dry with paper towels. Set aside.

5. Coat a large nonstick skillet with nonstick cooking spray, and place the skillet over medium-high heat. Add the garlic, and stir-fry for 30 seconds, or until the garlic is browned. Add the scallops, and stir-fry for about 4 minutes, or until the scallops turn opaque and are thoroughly cooked.

6. Reduce the heat under the skillet to medium-low. Add the pasta to the skillet, and pour the sauce over the pasta. Toss gently over low heat for about 2 minutes, or until the sauce thickens slightly. Add the scallions, and toss to mix well. Remove the skillet from the heat, and serve hot.

Yield: *4 servings*

8 ounces Ronzoni thin spaghetti or Hodgson Mill whole wheat thin spaghetti

¾ pound large raw scallops

1½ teaspoons crushed fresh garlic

¼ cup thinly sliced scallions

SAUCE

½ cup chopped sun-dried tomatoes (not packed in oil)

¾ cup Campbell's Healthy Request chicken broth

1¼ cups Pet evaporated skimmed milk

¼ cup Kraft Free nonfat grated Parmesan topping

1 teaspoon dried oregano, or 1 tablespoon fresh

¼ teaspoon ground black pepper

NUTRITIONAL FACTS (PER 1⅔-CUP SERVING)

Calories: 376	Fat: 1.7 g	Protein: 31 g
Cholesterol: 34 mg	Fiber: 1.5 g	Sodium: 421 mg

You Save: Calories: 260 Fat: 36 g

Ragin' Cajun Pasta

Yield: *6 servings*

12 ounces Shiloh Farms kamut fettuccine pasta or Mueller's fettuccine pasta

½ pound peeled and deveined raw shrimp

2 teaspoons crushed fresh garlic

4 ounces Healthy Choice smoked turkey sausage, thinly sliced

½ cup chopped onion

½ cup chopped green bell pepper

1 can (14½ ounces) Del Monte no salt added stewed tomatoes, crushed

1½ teaspoons Cajun seasoning (or more to taste)

1. Cook the pasta al dente according to package directions. Drain well, return the pasta to the pot, and cover to keep warm.

2. While the pasta is cooking, rinse the shrimp with cool water, and pat them dry with paper towels.

3. Coat a large nonstick skillet with olive oil cooking spray, and place over medium-high heat. Add the shrimp, garlic, and sausage, and stir-fry for 4 minutes, or until the shrimp and sausage are nicely browned.

4. Add the onions and peppers to the shrimp mixture, and stir to combine. Reduce the heat to low, and add the tomatoes, including their juice, and the Cajun seasoning. Cover and simmer for 10 minutes, or until the onions and peppers are tender.

5. Add the pasta to the sauce, and toss gently to mix well. Serve hot.

NUTRITIONAL FACTS (PER 1⅔-CUP SERVING)

Calories: 299	Fat: 2 g	Protein: 18.5 g
Cholesterol: 66 mg	Fiber: 6.8 g	Sodium: 320 mg

You Save: Calories: 127   Fat: 16.2 g

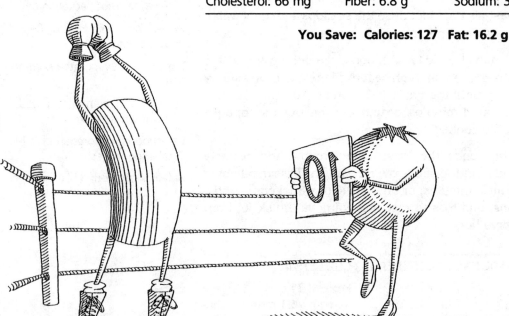

Slim Spaghetti Carbonara

Yield: 4 servings

1. Cook the pasta al dente according to package directions. Drain well, return the pasta to the pot, and cover to keep warm.

2. Combine the evaporated milk, egg substitute, Parmesan topping, and pepper in a small bowl. Stir to mix well, and set aside.

3. Coat a large nonstick skillet with butter-flavored cooking spray, and place the skillet over medium-high heat. Add the garlic, and stir-fry for 30 seconds, or until the garlic is lightly browned.

4. Reduce the heat under the skillet to medium-low, and add the spaghetti. Slowly pour the milk mixture over the spaghetti, and toss gently for a minute or 2, or until the sauce thickens slightly. Add a little more evaporated milk if the sauce seems too dry.

5. Add the bacon, scallions, and parsley to the skillet mixture, and toss to mix well. Remove the skillet from the heat, and serve hot.

8 ounces Creamette thin spaghetti

1¼ cups Carnation Lite evaporated skimmed milk

¼ cup Egg Beaters egg substitute

⅓ cup Kraft Free nonfat grated Parmesan topping

¼ teaspoon coarsely ground black pepper

1½ teaspoons crushed fresh garlic

4 slices Louis Rich turkey bacon, cooked, drained, and crumbled

¼ cup thinly sliced scallions

2 tablespoons finely chopped fresh parsley

NUTRITIONAL FACTS (PER 1⅓-CUP SERVING)

Calories: 339	Fat: 3.5 g	Protein: 20 g
Cholesterol: 16 mg	Fiber: 1.6 g	Sodium: 428 mg

You Save: Calories: 300 Fat: 36.8 g

FAT-FIGHTING TIP

Creamy Sauces Without the Cream

Cream is a key ingredient in many deliciously rich pasta dishes. But with 821 calories and 88 grams of fat per cup, this is one ingredient you should learn to live without. Does this mean giving up creamy, satisfying sauces? Fortunately, no. Evaporated skimmed milk substitutes beautifully for the cream in pasta sauce recipes. And it eliminates over 600 calories and all 88 grams of fat for every cup you use in place of cream. As a bonus, this ingredient adds extra calcium and potassium to your dishes, making them not just creamy, but also nutritious.

Pasta Piselli

Yield: *4 servings*

8 ounces Ronzoni thin spaghetti

¾ cup frozen (thawed) green peas

1 cup plus 2 tablespoons Pet evaporated skimmed milk

3 tablespoons Better'n Eggs egg substitute

3 tablespoons Kraft Free nonfat grated Parmesan topping

1 teaspoon crushed fresh garlic

1 cup sliced fresh mushrooms

5 ounces Hormel Light & Lean ham, diced (about 1 cup)

1. Cook the pasta until almost al dente according to package directions. Two minutes before the pasta is done, add the peas to the pot, and cook until the peas are tender and the pasta is al dente. Drain well, return the pasta and peas to the pot, and cover to keep warm.

2. Combine the evaporated milk, egg substitute, and Parmesan topping in a small bowl. Stir to mix well, and set aside.

3. Coat a large nonstick skillet with nonstick cooking spray, and place the skillet over medium-high heat. Add the garlic, mushrooms, and ham, and stir-fry for about 4 minutes, or until the mushrooms are tender and the ham is nicely browned.

4. Reduce the heat under the skillet to medium-low, and add the pasta to the skillet mixture. Slowly pour the evaporated milk mixture over the pasta, and toss gently for a minute or 2, or until the sauce thickens slightly. Add a little more evaporated milk if the sauce seems too dry. Remove the skillet from the heat, and serve hot.

NUTRITIONAL FACTS (PER 1⅔-CUP SERVING)

Calories: 354	Fat: 2.2 g	Protein: 25 g
Cholesterol: 22 mg	Fiber: 3.2 g	Sodium: 533 mg

You Save: Calories: 238   Fat: 31.4 g

FAT-FIGHTING TIP

An Egg Yolk Alternative

Egg yolks add richness and thickness to a variety of pasta sauces. The bad news is that one egg yolk contains about 5 grams of fat and two-thirds of your daily cholesterol allowance. By substituting a tablespoon of fat-free egg substitute for each egg yolk called for in a recipe, you can continue to enjoy thick, rich-tasting sauces—without the fat and cholesterol.

Seashells With Spicy Tomato-Shrimp Sauce

1. Cook the pasta al dente according to package directions. Drain well, return the pasta to the pot, and cover to keep warm.

2. While the pasta is cooking, rinse the shrimp with cool water, and pat them dry with paper towels. Set aside.

3. Coat a large skillet with olive oil cooking spray, and place the skillet over medium-high heat. Add the onion, celery, and garlic, and stir-fry for 1 to 2 minutes, or until the vegetables are crisp-tender.

4. Add the tomatoes, tomato paste, Italian seasoning, crushed red pepper, and salt to the skillet mixture, and stir to mix. Reduce the heat to medium, cover, and cook, stirring occasionally, for about 5 minutes, or until the tomatoes are soft.

5. Add the shrimp to the skillet mixture, and stir to mix. Cover and cook for 5 minutes, or until the shrimp turn pink.

6. Reduce the heat under the skillet to low, add the pasta to the skillet, and toss to mix well. Serve hot, topping each serving with a rounded tablespoon of the Parmesan topping.

Yield: *6 servings*

12 ounces Mueller's seashell pasta or De Bole's whole wheat seashell pasta

1 pound peeled and deveined raw shrimp

½ cup chopped onion

½ cup thinly sliced celery

1 tablespoon crushed fresh garlic

1½ pounds fresh tomatoes (about 3 medium), chopped

⅓ cup Hunt's Italian-style tomato paste

1 tablespoon dried Italian seasoning

½ teaspoon crushed red pepper

¼ teaspoon salt

½ cup Kraft Free nonfat grated Parmesan topping

NUTRITIONAL FACTS (PER 1⅔-CUP SERVING)

Calories: 363	Fat: 2.7 g	Protein: 28 g
Cholesterol: 119 mg	Fiber: 3.4 g	Sodium: 395 mg

You Save: Calories: 123 Fat: 15.4 g

Spaghetti With Garlic, Chicken, and Sun-Dried Tomatoes

Yield: *4 servings*

$\frac{1}{4}$ cup diced sun-dried tomatoes (not packed in oil)

1 cup Campbell's Healthy Request chicken broth, divided

1 teaspoon cornstarch

$\frac{1}{8}$ teaspoon ground white pepper

8 ounces Creamette thin spaghetti or De Bole's whole wheat angel hair pasta

$\frac{3}{4}$ pound boneless skinless chicken breasts

$\frac{1}{4}$ teaspoon salt

1 tablespoon crushed fresh garlic

$\frac{1}{4}$ cup plus 2 tablespoons sliced scallions

$\frac{1}{4}$ cup Kraft Free nonfat grated Parmesan topping

1. Place the tomatoes and $\frac{1}{4}$ cup of the broth in a small saucepan, and bring to a boil over medium heat. Reduce the heat to low, cover, and simmer for about 2 minutes, or until the tomatoes are plumped and the liquid is absorbed. Remove the pot from the heat, and cover to keep warm.

2. Place the remaining $\frac{3}{4}$ cup of broth in a small dish. Add the cornstarch and pepper, and stir to mix well. Set aside.

3. Cook the pasta al dente according to package directions. Drain well, return the pasta to the pot, and cover to keep warm.

4. While the pasta is cooking, rinse the chicken with cool water, and pat it dry with paper towels. Cut the chicken into bite-sized pieces, sprinkle with the salt, and set aside.

5. Coat a large skillet with olive oil cooking spray, and place over medium-high heat. Add the garlic and chicken, and stir-fry for about 4 minutes, or until the chicken is nicely browned.

6. Reduce the heat under the skillet to medium, and add the tomatoes and pasta to the skillet mixture. Stir the cornstarch mixture, and pour over the pasta. Toss gently for a minute or 2, or until the sauce thickens slightly.

7. Add the scallions to the pasta mixture, and toss to mix well. Remove the skillet from the heat, and serve hot, topping each serving with a tablespoon of the Parmesan topping.

NUTRITIONAL FACTS (PER 1$\frac{2}{3}$-CUP SERVING)		
Calories: 346	Fat: 2.1 g	Protein: 31 g
Cholesterol: 52 mg	Fiber: 2 g	Sodium: 482 mg

You Save: Calories: 174   Fat: 20.8 g

Pasta Pesto Primavera

1. Cook the pasta until almost al dente according to package directions. Add the vegetables to the pot, and cook for another minute, or until the vegetables are crisp-tender and the pasta is al dente. Drain well, return the pasta and vegetables to the pot, and cover to keep warm.

2. While the pasta is cooking, place all of the pesto ingredients in a blender or food processor, and process until smooth.

3. Pour the pesto over the pasta and vegetables, and toss to mix well. Add the Parmesan topping, and toss to mix. Serve hot.

NUTRITIONAL FACTS (PER 1⅔-CUP SERVING)

Calories: 318	Fat: 4.6 g	Protein: 16 g
Cholesterol: 8 mg	Fiber: 3.7 g	Sodium: 323 mg

You Save: Calories: 269 Fat: 31.8 g

Yield: 4 servings

8 ounces Mueller's thin spaghetti

¾ cup thinly sliced cauliflower florets

¾ cup yellow squash, halved and sliced ¼ inch thick

¾ cup red bell pepper, cut into thin strips

¾ cup sliced fresh mushrooms

½ cup plus 2 tablespoons Kraft Free nonfat grated Parmesan topping

PESTO SAUCE

¾ cup tightly packed fresh basil

¾ cup tightly packed fresh spinach

½ cup Campbell's Healthy Request chicken broth

1 tablespoon plus 1 teaspoon Pompeian extra virgin olive oil

3–4 cloves garlic, peeled

2 teaspoons lemon juice

¼ teaspoon ground white pepper

¼ cup chopped walnuts or pine nuts (optional)

Garden Vegetable Linguine

Yield: *4 servings*

¼ cup diced sun-dried tomatoes
(not packed in oil)

1 cup plus 2 tablespoons
Swanson vegetable broth,
divided

8 ounces Creamette linguine
pasta or Contadina spinach
fettuccine

2 teaspoons crushed fresh garlic

1½ cups broccoli florets

2 medium-small yellow squash,
halved lengthwise and sliced
(about 1 cup)

1 cup sliced fresh mushrooms

½ cup diagonally sliced carrots

1 tablespoon finely chopped fresh
oregano, or 1 teaspoon dried

¼ cup chopped toasted pecans
(optional) (page 191)

1 teaspoon cornstarch

¼ cup Kraft Free nonfat grated
Parmesan topping

1. Place the tomatoes and ¼ cup of the broth in a small sauce-pan, and bring to a boil over medium heat. Reduce the heat to low, cover, and simmer for about 2 minutes, or until the tomatoes are plumped and the broth is absorbed. Remove the pot from the heat, and cover to keep warm.

2. Cook the pasta al dente according to package directions. Drain well, return the pasta to the pot, and cover to keep warm.

3. While the pasta is cooking, coat a large nonstick skillet with nonstick cooking spray, and place the skillet over medium-high heat. Add the garlic, and stir-fry for about 30 seconds, or until the garlic is browned. Add the vegetables, oregano, and ¼ cup of the remaining broth. Cover, and cook for 1 to 2 minutes, or until the vegetables are crisp-tender.

4. Reduce the heat under the skillet to medium-low, and add the pasta, the plumped tomatoes, and, if desired, the pecans to the skillet mixture. Stir the cornstarch into the remaining ½ cup plus 2 tablespoons of broth, and pour over the pasta and vegetables. Toss gently for about 1 minute, or until the sauce thickens slightly. Add a little more broth if the mixture seems too dry.

5. Remove the skillet from the heat, and toss in the Parmesan topping. Serve hot.

NUTRITIONAL FACTS (PER 1¾-CUP SERVING)

Calories: 274	Fat: 1.5 g	Protein: 12.5 g
Cholesterol: 3 mg	Fiber: 3.8 g	Sodium: 467 mg

You Save: Calories: 125 Fat: 15.4 g

Linguine With Creamy Clam Sauce

1. Cook the pasta al dente according to package directions. Drain well, return the pasta to the pot, and cover to keep warm.

2. While the pasta is cooking, drain the clams, reserving the juice. Set aside.

3. Place the evaporated milk in a small bowl. Stir in the Parmesan topping and pepper, and set aside.

4. Coat a large nonstick skillet with olive oil nonstick cooking spray, and place the skillet over medium-high heat. Add the garlic, and stir-fry for about 30 seconds, or until the garlic is browned.

5. Reduce the heat under the skillet to medium, and add the pasta, clams, and $\frac{1}{4}$ cup of the reserved clam juice to the skillet. Toss gently to mix well.

6. Stir the evaporated milk mixture. Pour the mixture over the pasta, and toss gently for a minute or 2, or until the mixture thickens slightly. Add a little more evaporated skimmed milk if the mixture seems too dry.

7. Remove the skillet from the heat, and add the scallions and parsley to the pasta mixture. Toss to mix well, and serve hot.

Yield: *4 servings*

8 ounces Mueller's linguine pasta

2 cans (6$\frac{1}{2}$ ounces each) Gorton's chopped clams, undrained

1 cup Pet evaporated skimmed milk

$\frac{1}{3}$ cup Kraft Free nonfat grated Parmesan topping

$\frac{1}{8}$ teaspoon ground white pepper

2 teaspoons crushed fresh garlic

$\frac{1}{4}$ cup finely chopped fresh scallions

$\frac{1}{4}$ cup finely chopped fresh parsley

NUTRITIONAL FACTS (PER 1$\frac{1}{3}$-CUP SERVING)		
Calories: 371	Fat: 2.2 g	Protein: 30 g
Cholesterol: 43 mg	Fiber: 1.7 g	Sodium: 270 mg

You Save: Calories: 183 Fat: 25 g

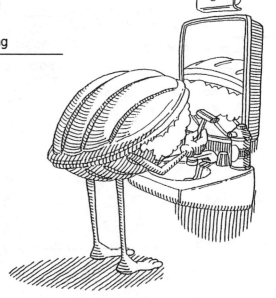

Chinese Chicken and Noodles

Yield: *4 servings*

8 ounces De Bole's linguine or fettuccine pasta

¾ pound boneless skinless chicken breasts

1½ teaspoons crushed fresh garlic

1½ teaspoons freshly grated ginger root, or ½ teaspoon ground ginger

1 small red bell pepper, cut into thin strips

1 cup sliced fresh mushrooms

2 cups packed chopped bok choy or napa cabbage

SAUCE

½ cup Swanson Natural Goodness chicken broth

¼ cup Kimono seasoned rice vinegar

2 tablespoons La Choy Lite soy sauce

1½ teaspoons sesame oil

2 teaspoons cornstarch

2 teaspoons dark brown sugar

½ teaspoon crushed red pepper (optional)

1. Cook the pasta al dente according to package directions. Drain well, return the pasta to the pot, and cover to keep warm.

2. While the pasta is cooking, combine the sauce ingredients in a small dish. Stir to mix well, and set aside.

3. Rinse the chicken with cool water, and pat it dry with paper towels. Cut the chicken into bite-sized pieces.

4. Coat a large nonstick skillet with nonstick cooking spray, and preheat over medium-high heat. Add the garlic, ginger, and chicken, and stir-fry for about 4 minutes, or until the chicken is nicely browned and no longer pink inside.

5. Add the peppers and mushrooms to the skillet mixture, and stir-fry for 1 to 2 minutes, or until the vegetables are almost crisp-tender. Add the bok choy or cabbage, and stir-fry for another minute, or until the bok choy starts to wilt and the vegetables are crisp-tender. (Add a tablespoon of water or broth if the skillet becomes too dry.)

6. Reduce the heat under the skillet to medium, and add the pasta to the skillet. Stir the sauce, and pour it over the skillet mixture. Gently toss the mixture together for a minute or 2, or until the sauce thickens. Serve hot.

NUTRITIONAL FACTS (PER 1⅔-CUP SERVING)

Calories: 357	Fat: 3.8 g	Protein: 29 g
Cholesterol: 49 mg	Fiber: 2.3 g	Sodium: 503 mg

You Save: Calories: 108   Fat: 12.2 g

Rigatoni Cannellini

1. Cook the pasta al dente according to package directions. Drain well, return the pasta to the pot, and cover to keep warm.

2. While the pasta is cooking, place the tomatoes, beans, scallions, garlic, pepper, and olives in a large deep skillet. Place the skillet over medium heat, cover, and cook for about 5 minutes, or until the mixture is heated through and the tomatoes just begin to soften.

3. Add the pasta to the skillet mixture, and toss to mix well.

4. Remove the skillet from the heat, add the Parmesan topping and basil, and toss to mix. Add the diced mozzarella, toss to mix, and serve hot.

Yield: *6 servings*

12 ounces Ronzoni rigatoni pasta

1 pound fresh plum tomatoes (about 8 medium), cut into ¾-inch pieces

1 can (15 ounces) La Russa cannellini beans, rinsed and drained

½ cup sliced scallions

2 teaspoons crushed fresh garlic

½ teaspoon crushed red pepper

8 colossal pitted black olives, sliced

¼ cup Kraft Free nonfat grated Parmesan topping

¼ cup finely chopped fresh basil

1 cup diced Polly-O Free natural nonfat mozzarella cheese

NUTRITIONAL FACTS (PER 1¾-CUP SERVING)

Calories: 344	Fat: 2.1 g	Protein: 19.5 g
Cholesterol: 4 mg	Fiber: 6.1 g	Sodium: 368 mg

You Save: Calories: 110   Fat: 14.3 g

Nutty Noodles

Yield: *4 servings*

½ pound turkey breast tenderloin
  or pork tenderloin

8 ounces Creamette angel hair
  pasta or bean threads*

1½ teaspoons crushed fresh garlic

1½ teaspoons minced fresh
  ginger root, or ½ teaspoon
  ground ginger

¾ cup thinly sliced celery

¾ cup thinly sliced scallions

¾ cup matchstick-sized pieces of
  red bell pepper

2 cups packed chopped fresh
  spinach

3 tablespoons chopped Planters
  reduced-fat honey-roasted
  peanuts

SAUCE

½ cup plus 1 tablespoon Health
  Valley no salt added chicken
  broth

3 tablespoons Kimono seasoned
  rice vinegar

2 tablespoons Kikkoman Lite soy
  sauce

1 tablespoon plus 1 teaspoon
  Smucker's natural creamy
  peanut butter

1 tablespoon dark brown sugar

2 teaspoons cornstarch

½ teaspoon crushed red pepper
  (optional)

*Translucent noodle-like threads
made from mung beans, bean
threads can be found in many grocery
and health foods stores.

1. Combine all of the sauce ingredients in a blender, and process until smooth. Set aside.

2. Rinse the turkey or pork with cool water, and pat it dry with paper towels. Cut the meat into bite-sized pieces, and set aside.

3. Cook the pasta or bean threads al dente according to package directions. Drain well, return to the pot, and cover to keep warm.

4. While the pasta is cooking, coat a large nonstick skillet with nonstick cooking spray, and preheat over medium-high heat. Add the garlic, ginger, and turkey or pork, and stir-fry for about 4 minutes, or until the meat is nicely browned and no longer pink inside.

5. Add the celery, scallions, and red pepper to the skillet mixture, and stir-fry for about 2 minutes, or until the vegetables are crisp-tender. Add the spinach and peanuts to the skillet, and stir-fry for another 30 seconds, or just until the spinach starts to wilt.

6. Reduce the heat under the skillet to medium, and add the pasta to the skillet mixture. Stir the sauce, and pour it over the skillet mixture. Gently toss the mixture together for a minute or 2, or until the ingredients are mixed and the sauce is slightly thickened. Serve hot.

NUTRITIONAL FACTS (PER 1⅔-CUP SERVING)

Calories: 376	Fat: 5.4 g	Protein: 27 g
Cholesterol: 42 mg	Fiber: 3.7 g	Sodium: 416 mg

You Save: Calories: 149   Fat: 15 g

Top: Raspberry Ripple Cheesecake (page 202), Center: Cinnamon Apple Crisp (page 205),
Bottom: Cherry Cobbler Cake (page 193)

Top Left: Black Forest Cake (page 199), Top Right: Luscious Lemon Trifle (page 208),
Bottom: Very Strawberry Pie (page 203)

Penne With Sausage, Peppers, and Onions

1. Cook the pasta al dente according to package directions. Drain well, return the pasta to the pot, and cover to keep warm.

2. While the pasta is cooking, coat a large nonstick skillet with nonstick cooking spray, and preheat over medium heat. Add the sausage to the skillet, and cook, stirring to crumble, until the meat is no longer pink.

3. Add all of the remaining ingredients to the skillet, and stir to mix. Cover and cook over medium heat, stirring occasionally, for 7 to 10 minutes, or until the vegetables are tender and the flavors are well blended.

4. Pour the skillet mixture over the pasta, and toss to mix well. Serve hot.

Yield: 5 servings

8 ounces Bella penne or ziti pasta

¾ pound Turkey Italian Sausage (page 182)

1 can (14½ ounces) Hunt's no salt added tomatoes, crushed

1 medium yellow onion, cut into thin wedges

1 medium green bell pepper, cut into strips

1 medium red bell pepper, cut into strips

3 tablespoons Contadina tomato paste

1 teaspoon dried Italian seasoning

NUTRITIONAL FACTS (PER 1¾-CUP SERVING)

Calories: 284	Fat: 2.8 g	Protein: 23 g
Cholesterol: 43 mg	Fiber: 3.3 g	Sodium: 295 mg

You Save: Calories: 186   Fat: 21 g

Making Your Own Italian Sausage

Italian sausage is used to add richness and a distinctive flavor to a variety of pasta creations, and to many other dishes as well. Fortunately, it's easy to make a sausage mixture that is just as flavorful as a traditional one, but contains a fraction of the fat and calories. Stir Turkey Italian Sausage into sauces or use it to top your favorite pizza, and enjoy an authentic taste of Italy.

Turkey Italian Sausage

Yield: *1 pound*

1 pound Butterball Extra Lean ground turkey or another brand of extra lean ground turkey

2 teaspoons crushed fresh garlic

2 teaspoons ground paprika

1½ teaspoons whole fennel seeds

1 teaspoon dried Italian seasoning

¼ teaspoon crushed red pepper

½ teaspoon salt

1. Combine all of the ingredients in a medium-sized bowl, and mix thoroughly. Cover and refrigerate for several hours to allow the flavors to blend.

2. To precook for use in recipes, coat a large skillet with nonstick cooking spray, and preheat over medium heat. Add the sausage, and cook, stirring to crumble, until the meat is no longer pink. Use as directed in your recipe.

NUTRITIONAL FACTS (PER 2-OUNCE COOKED SERVING)

Calories: 66	Fat: 1.5 g	Protein: 13.2 g
Cholesterol: 35 mg	Fiber: 0 g	Sodium: 231 mg

You Save: Calories: 117   Fat: 13.1 g

Baked Rigatoni With Sausage, Tomatoes, and Cheese

1. Cook the pasta al dente according to package directions. Drain well, return the pasta to the pot, and cover to keep warm.

2. While the pasta is cooking, coat a large nonstick skillet with nonstick cooking spray, and preheat over medium heat. Add the sausage, and cook, stirring to crumble, until the meat is no longer pink.

3. Add the tomatoes, onion, oregano, and pepper to the skillet mixture, and bring to a boil over medium-high heat. Reduce the heat to low, cover, and cook, stirring occasionally, for 10 minutes, or until the onions are tender and the flavors are blended.

4. Pour the tomato mixture over the pasta, and toss to mix well. Add the Parmesan topping, and toss to mix well.

5. Coat a 9-x-13-inch baking pan with nonstick cooking spray, and spread the mixture evenly in the dish. Sprinkle first the mozzarella and then the provolone over the top. Cover the dish with aluminum foil, and bake at 350°F for 25 minutes. Uncover, and bake for 10 additional minutes, or until the cheese is lightly browned. Serve hot.

Yield: 8 servings

12 ounces DeCecco rigatoni pasta

1 pound Turkey Italian Sausage (page 182)

1 can (28 ounces) Cento crushed tomatoes

½ cup chopped onion

1 teaspoon dried oregano

½ teaspoon crushed red pepper (optional)

¼ cup Kraft Free nonfat grated Parmesan topping

1 cup Healthy Choice fancy shredded fat-free mozzarella cheese

½ cup shredded Alpine Lace reduced-fat provolone cheese

NUTRITIONAL FACTS (PER 1⅔-CUP SERVING)

Calories: 333 Fat: 3.5 g Protein: 29 g
Cholesterol: 43 mg Fiber: 4.3 g Sodium: 299 mg

You Save: Calories: 146 Fat: 20 g

Spinach Manicotti Alfredo

Yield: *6 servings*

12 Ronzoni manicotti tubes (about 8 ounces)

1 cup Polly-O Free natural shredded nonfat mozzarella cheese

FILLING

15 ounces Maggio nonfat ricotta cheese

1 cup Sealtest Free nonfat cottage cheese

1 cup Polly-O Free natural shredded nonfat mozzarella cheese

1 package (10 ounces) frozen chopped spinach, thawed and squeezed dry

1/4 cup plus 2 tablespoons Scramblers egg substitute

1/4 cup Kraft Free nonfat grated Parmesan topping

SAUCE

1/2 cup Pet evaporated skimmed milk

2 tablespoons cornstarch

1/8 teaspoon ground white pepper

2 1/2 cups skim milk

1/2 cup Kraft Free nonfat grated Parmesan topping

1. Cook the manicotti al dente according to package directions. Drain well, and set aside.

2. To make the filling, combine all of the filling ingredients in a large bowl, and stir to mix well.

3. Coat a 9-x-13-inch baking pan with nonstick cooking spray. Using a small spoon, stuff the filling mixture into the tubes, and arrange the tubes in the prepared pan, leaving a 1/4-inch space between them. Set aside.

4. To make the sauce, combine the evaporated milk, cornstarch, and pepper in a small bowl, and stir to mix well. Set aside.

5. Place the skim milk in a 2-quart pot over medium heat. Cook and stir for about 5 minutes, or until the milk starts to boil. Stir the cornstarch mixture, and whisk it into the hot milk. Cook and stir for another minute or 2, or until the mixture thickens slightly.

6. Reduce the heat to low, and slowly whisk the Parmesan topping into the sauce. Cook and stir for another minute or 2, or until the mixture thickens a bit more.

7. Pour the sauce evenly over the manicotti, and sprinkle the cup of mozzarella over the top. Bake at 350°F for about 40 minutes, or until hot and bubbly. Remove the dish from the oven, and let stand for 10 minutes before serving.

NUTRITIONAL FACTS (PER SERVING)

Calories: 363	Fat: 0.9 g	Protein: 42 g
Cholesterol: 26 mg	Fiber: 0.8 g	Sodium: 698 mg

You Save: Calories: 292   Fat: 41.1 g

Sicilian Baked Ziti

1. To make the sauce, combine all of the sauce ingredients except for the roasted peppers in a 3-quart pot, and bring to a boil over medium-high heat. Reduce the heat to low, cover, and simmer for 25 minutes, or until the vegetables are tender. Add the peppers, and simmer for 5 additional minutes. Remove the pot from the heat, and set 1½ cups of the sauce aside in a medium-sized bowl.

2. Cook the ziti al dente according to package directions. Drain the pasta, and return it to the pot. Add the sauce (except for the reserved sauce) and the Parmesan topping, and toss to mix.

3. Coat a 9-x-13-inch baking pan with nonstick cooking spray, and spread the ziti mixture evenly in the pan. Top first with the reserved sauce, and then with the mozzarella.

4. Cover the pan with aluminum foil, and bake at 350°F for 25 minutes. Remove the foil, and bake for 15 additional minutes, or until the cheese is bubbly and lightly browned. Serve hot.

NUTRITIONAL FACTS (PER 1⅔-CUP SERVING)

Calories: 299	Fat: 3.8 g	Protein: 18 g
Cholesterol: 12 mg	Fiber: 4 g	Sodium: 469 mg

You Save: Calories: 114 Fat: 13.8 g

Yield: *8 servings*

12 ounces De Bole's ziti pasta

¼ cup plus 2 tablespoons Kraft Free nonfat grated Parmesan topping

2 cups Sargento Light fancy shredded natural mozzarella cheese

SAUCE

1 can (28 ounces) Progresso Recipe Ready crushed tomatoes with added purée

2 cups diced peeled eggplant (about 1 medium-small)

2 cups sliced fresh mushrooms

1 medium onion, chopped

1½ teaspoons crushed fresh garlic

2 teaspoons dried Italian seasoning

½ teaspoon crushed red pepper

1 jar (12 ounces) La Russa roasted red peppers, drained and coarsely chopped

10. Deceptively Decadent Desserts

For some of us, a meal just isn't complete without a taste of something sweet. And while a tempting selection of fat-free and low-fat baked goods is now available in supermarkets, you can get a great deal of pleasure and satisfaction from making and serving your own no- or low-fat cakes, fruit pies, cookies, and brownies. Anyway, there's nothing quite as appealing as the smell of baking cookies or the sight of a bubbling cobbler!

While you may be aware that the oil and butter in desserts pose a danger to your health, you may not know that cutting down on fats goes a long way toward cutting down on calories. Surprisingly, fat contributes far more calories to most desserts than sugar does. Consider the ingredients that might be used to make a carrot cake, for instance. A cake whose batter includes $1\frac{1}{2}$ cups of sugar gets 1,080 calories and no fat from the sugar. Stir in $1\frac{1}{2}$ cups of oil, though, and you've added almost 3,000 calories and 327 grams of fat! And don't forget about the icing. Made with cream cheese and margarine, the usual carrot cake topping adds close to 80 grams of fat.

All this talk about fat does not mean that you should forget about reducing sugar consumption. One of the pitfalls of many commercial fat-free desserts is that when fat is removed, extra sugar is added. For this very reason, some fat-free cookies, cakes, and other dessert items contain just as many calories as do their high-fat counterparts.

The recipes in this chapter will prove to you that reducing the fat in your baked goods does not have to mean adding extra sugar. Indeed, many of the fat substitutes used in these recipes—applesauce, fruit juices, and puréed fruits, for instance—can actually *reduce* the need for sugar. An extra dash of cinnamon, nutmeg, or vanilla, as well as the inclusion of healthful ingredients like whole wheat pastry flour and oat bran, can also enable you to reduce the amount of sweeteners without compromising taste.

To help you make wise selections during your next visit to the grocery store, this chapter includes three informative Fat-Fighter's Guides. The guide on page 188 introduces reduced-fat products such as light butter, as well as a variety of fat substitutes—products that can either reduce or totally replace the fats in your baked goods. For those days when you have little time to spare, the guide on page 207 steers you toward some of the best low-fat baking mixes. And for those days when you're too busy to even *think* about baking, the guide on page 211 highlights some of the best ready-to-eat low-fat baked goods and frozen treats.

Of course, when all is said and done, if a dessert does not taste good, your family won't eat it, no matter how low the fat. You'll be delighted to discover that the low- and no-fat treats presented in this chapter are truly great tasting. They are so moist and luscious, in fact, that no one but you will ever guess just how wholesome they are.

FAT-FIGHTER'S GUIDE TO
Fats, Oils, and Fat Substitutes

They're in everything from cakes, muffins, and cookies, to casseroles, vegetables, and main dishes. You can eat them without even knowing they're there, and they can bust your fat budget for the entire day. What are they? Fats and oils—including butter, margarine, and other solid shortenings, and vegetable oil. The good news is that there are many reduced-fat and fat-free alternatives to these products, as well as strategies that can reduce the amount of fat needed when you do wish to use a little oil in your cooking or baking. Let's see how you can make use of some fat-saving alternatives.

REDUCED-FAT MARGARINE AND LIGHT BUTTER

These products, which are made with less fat and more water, contain 33 to 80 percent less fat than full-fat versions. If you are used to spreading foods with butter or margarine, you can easily reduce your dietary fat simply by switching to a reduced-fat brand, and using it sparingly.

Products like Land O Lakes Light butter, Land O Lakes Country Morning Blend Light, I Can't Believe It's Not Butter! Light, Promise Extra Light, and Mazola Light contain about half the fat of full-fat spreads. To cut fat by more than half, try a brand like Fleischmann's Lower Fat, Promise Ultra 65% Less Fat, Weight Watchers Light, or Smart Beat. To eliminate fat completely, choose a fat-free product like I Can't Believe It's Not Butter! spray, Fleischmann's nonfat squeeze margarine, and Promise Ultra Fat Free.

Just how great are your savings when you switch to a lower-fat product? Each tablespoon of nonfat margarine that you substitute for full-fat margarine saves you 11 grams of fat and about 95 calories. The savings with reduced-fat prod-

ucts are less, of course, and depend on the brand used.

You may be surprised to find that you can also cook with reduced-fat margarines—and with light butter, too! Crisp cookies and light and tender cakes, biscuits, muffins, and other goodies can easily be prepared with half the fat by substituting reduced-fat margarine or butter for the full-fat products, and by making simple adjustments in the recipe. (For details on using these products in your baked goods, see the Fat-Fighting Tip on page 194.)

VEGETABLE OILS

Liquid vegetable oils have long been promoted as being "heart healthy." The reason? These oils are low in artery-clogging saturated fat, and contain no cholesterol. Unfortunately, many people also assume that these products are low in total fat and calories, and therefore may be used liberally. Not so. The fact is that all oils are pure fat. Just one tablespoon of *any* oil has 13.6 grams of fat and 120 calories. Vegetable oils do provide the essential fats that are needed for good health, but a couple of teaspoons of polyunsaturated vegetable oil—such as safflower, sunflower, corn, or soy—or a couple of tablespoons of nuts or seeds can supply enough essential fat for an entire day.

Which vegetable oils are best? Those that are low in saturated fats and rich in monounsaturated fats—like olive and canola oil—are the oils of choice these days. However, if you keep your use of all fats and oils to a minimum, any liquid vegetable oil, depending on your taste and cooking preferences, is fine. Some vegetable oils, though, are more useful to the low-fat cook than others. Here are a few oils you might consider buying on your next trip to the grocery store.

Canola oil

This has become one of the oils of choice in recent years. Low in saturated fats and rich in monounsaturated fats, canola oil also contains a fair amount of linolenic acid, an essential omega-3 type fat—similar to the fat found in fish oils—that most people do not eat in sufficient quantities. Canola oil has a very mild, bland taste, so it is a good all-purpose oil for cooking and baking when you want no interfering flavors. Like all oils, this product should be used sparingly to keep calories under control.

Extra Virgin Olive Oil

Unlike most vegetable oils, which are very bland, olive oil adds its own delicious flavor to foods. Extra virgin olive oil is the least processed and most flavorful type of olive oil. And a little bit goes a long way, making this product a good choice for use in low-fat recipes. What about "light" olive oil? In this case, light refers to flavor, which is mild and bland compared with that of extra virgin oils. This means that you have to use more oil for the same amount of flavor—not a good bargain.

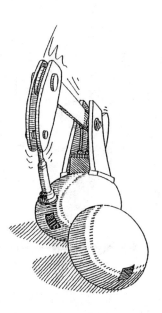

Macadamia Nut Oil

Like olive and canola oils, macadamia nut oil is low in saturated fats and rich in monounsaturated fats. And like canola oil, macadamia nut oil contains a fair amount of linolenic acid. An excellent all-purpose oil for cooking and baking, this product adds a delicate nutty flavor to foods.

Sesame Oil

Like olive oil, sesame oil can enhance the flavors of foods. And because it is so flavorful, a little bit goes a long way. Used in small amounts, this ingredient will add a distinctive taste to foods without blowing your fat budget.

Unrefined Vegetable Oils

Most of the vegetable oils sold in grocery stores today have been highly processed and refined, greatly extending their shelf life. Unfortunately, processing also depletes oils of much of their natural nutty flavor and aroma—and of close to half of their vitamin E content. Most people grew up on these comparatively bland, tasteless refined oils, and have never even seen an unprocessed vegetable oil. They don't know what they're missing.

Many stores stock at least one brand of unrefined oil, such as the widely available Spectrum unrefined corn oil. This amber-colored, buttery tasting oil is excellent for baking. And because it is so flavorful, a small amount is all you'll need in your low-fat baked goods. Unrefined walnut oil is another excellent choice for baking and cooking. This oil contains a fair amount of linolenic acid, and adds a delicate nutty flavor to foods. Most brands of walnut oil have been only minimally processed.

Once opened, unrefined oils can turn rancid quickly. For this reason, you should purchase small bottles—a pint or less—and store the oil in the refrigerator.

NONSTICK VEGETABLE OIL COOKING SPRAY

Available unflavored and in butter and olive oil flavors, these products are pure fat. The advantage to using them is that the amount that comes out during a one-second spray is so small that it adds an insignificant amount of fat to a recipe. Nonstick cooking sprays are very useful to the low-fat cook to promote the browning of foods and to prevent foods from sticking to pots and pans. Look for products like PAM® Butter Flavor No Stick Cooking Spray, PAM® Olive Oil No Stick Cooking Spray, Mazola No Stick cooking spray, and Wesson No Stick cooking spray. When a recipe directs you to both grease and flour a pan, use Baker's Joy spray, which combines oil and flour in one handy product.

FAT SUBSTITUTES FOR BAKING

Almost any moist ingredient can replace part or all of the fat in cakes, muffins, quick breads, and other baked goods. The recipes in this book use a variety of fat substitutes, including applesauce, puréed fruits, fruit juice concentrate, nonfat yogurt, nonfat buttermilk, and skim milk. These products are readily available in grocery stores. Two additional substitutes— Prune Butter and Prune Purée—not only can be found on grocery store shelves, but can easily be made at home using the following directions.

Prune Butter

This sweet, nutritious, fiber-rich fat substitute works beautifully in brownies and other chocolate treats, and in spice cakes. And most grocery stores stock at least one type of Prune Butter in the jam and jelly section. Look for Levkar Prune Butter or Solo Prune Plum Filling.

If you would prefer to use a homemade product, you'll find that it's easy to whip up your own Prune Butter. To make 1 cup, combine 8 ounces (about $1\frac{1}{3}$ cups) of pitted prunes with 6 tablespoons of water in a food processor, and process into a smooth paste. Prune Butter keeps beautifully for up to three weeks when refrigerated in an airtight container.

Prune Purée

Like Prune Butter, Prune Purée works well in a variety of baked goods. When you don't have time to whip up your own Prune Purée, look for WonderSlim fat substitute. A nutritious product, it can be found in many health foods and grocery stores.

Like Prune Butter, Prune Purée is a snap to make at home. For $1\frac{1}{2}$ cups of Prune Purée, combine 3 ounces (about $\frac{1}{2}$ cup) of pitted prunes, 1 cup of water, and 2 teaspoons of lecithin granules* in a blender or food processor, and process until smooth. Store Prune Purée in the refrigerator for up to three weeks.

*Lecithin, a nutritious by-product of soybean-oil refining, is sold in health foods stores as a food supplement. Because lecithin improves the texture of baked goods, commercial bakers often add small amounts of this product to fat-free and low-fat cakes, cookies, breads, and muffins.

Light and Luscious Strawberry Cake

1. Combine the sliced strawberries and sugar in a medium-sized bowl. Using a potato masher or fork, mash the berries slightly. Cover the mixture, and refrigerate for at least 2 hours to let the juices develop.

2. When ready to assemble the cake, place the Cool Whip Lite in a medium-sized bowl. Pour off any liquid that has risen to the top of the yogurt, and stir the yogurt. Gently fold the yogurt into the whipped topping, and set aside.

3. Place the cake on a cutting board, and use a bread knife to cut the cake into 3 layers. Using a fork, pierce the bottom layer at $\frac{1}{2}$-inch intervals.

4. Transfer the bottom cake layer to a serving platter, and top with half of the mashed strawberry mixture, including half of the juice. Spread $\frac{3}{4}$ cup of the Cool Whip mixture over the berries. Repeat with the second layer. Top with the third cake layer, and spread the remaining Cool Whip mixture over the top and sides of the cake. Sprinkle the almonds over the top of the cake if desired.

5. Chill the cake for at least 2 hours before slicing and serving.

Yield: 12 servings

3 cups sliced fresh strawberries

2 tablespoons sugar

2½ cups Cool Whip Lite

8 ounces Dannon low-fat vanilla yogurt

1 angel food cake (1 pound)

3 tablespoons toasted sliced almonds (optional) (below)

NUTRITIONAL FACTS
(PER SERVING)

Calories: 165	Fiber: 1.5 g
Chol: 0 mg	Protein: 3.5 g
Fat: 2.4 g	Sodium: 305 mg

You Save: Calories: 87 Fat: 11 g

FAT-FIGHTING TIP

Getting the Most Out of Nuts

Nuts add crunch, great taste, and essential nutrients to all kinds of baked goods. Unfortunately, nuts also add fat. But you can halve the fat—without halving the taste—simply by toasting nuts before adding them to your recipe. Toasting intensifies the flavor of nuts so much that you can often cut the amount used in half. Simply arrange the nuts in a single layer on a baking sheet, and bake at 350°F for about 10 minutes, or until lightly browned with a toasted, nutty smell. (For sliced almonds or chopped nuts, bake for only 6 to 8 minutes.) To save time, toast a large batch and store leftovers in an airtight container in the refrigerator for several weeks, or keep them in the freezer for several months.

Boston Cream Cake

Yield: *12 servings*

1 box Betty Crocker Super Moist
   Light yellow cake mix

½ cup plus 1 tablespoon Egg
   Beaters egg substitute

1⅓ cups water

Baker's Joy nonstick cooking spray

FILLING

1 package (4-serving size) Royal
   instant vanilla pudding mix
   (sugar-free or regular)

2 cups skim milk

GLAZE

1½ cups confectioner's sugar

2 tablespoons Hershey's Dutch
   Processed European Style cocoa
   powder

2 tablespoons plus 2 teaspoons
   skim milk

NUTRITIONAL FACTS
(PER SERVING)

Calories: 253	Fiber: 0.7 g
Chol: 1 mg	Protein: 4.3 g
Fat: 2.7 g	Sodium: 364 mg

You Save: Calories: 171 Fat: 18 g

1. In a large bowl, combine the cake mix, egg substitute, and water. Using an electric mixer, beat at low speed for 30 seconds. Then beat at medium speed for 2 additional minutes.

2. Coat two 9-inch round cake pans with the cooking spray. (If using a spray other than Baker's Joy, lightly flour the pans after spraying.) Divide the batter between the pans, and bake at 350°F for 25 to 30 minutes, or just until the tops spring back when lightly touched. Cool the cakes in the pans for 15 minutes. Then invert onto wire racks, and cool completely.

3. While the cakes are baking, place the pudding mix and milk in a medium-sized bowl. Mix with an electric mixer or wire whisk for 2 minutes, or until well blended. Cover and refrigerate until ready to assemble the cake.

4. When the cakes have cooled, use a serrated knife or a piece of strong thread to slice each cake in half lengthwise so that you have 4 layers. Place 1 cake layer upside-down on a serving platter, and spread a third of the pudding over the cake, extending the pudding to within ½ inch of the edge. Repeat this procedure with 2 more layers. Finally, place the remaining layer right side up over the last layer of filling.

5. To make the glaze, combine all of the glaze ingredients in a small bowl, and stir to make a thick glaze. If using a microwave oven, place the glaze in the microwave and heat at high power for 30 seconds, or until runny. If using a conventional stove top, transfer the glaze to a small saucepan and, stirring constantly, place over medium heat for 30 seconds, or until runny.

6. Spread the glaze over the top of the cake, allowing some of the glaze to drip down the sides. Chill the cake for at least 2 hours before slicing and serving.

Cherry Cobbler Cake

For variety, substitute other flavors of pie filling for the cherry pie filling.

1. In a large bowl, combine the cake mix, yogurt, and egg substitute. Beat by hand or with an electric mixer just until well mixed.

2. Coat a 9-x-13-inch baking pan with nonstick cooking spray, and spread the batter evenly in the pan. Spoon the pie filling back and forth over the batter in an "S" pattern. (The filling will sink into the batter as the cake bakes.)

3. Bake at 350°F for about 40 minutes, or until the top is golden brown and a wooden toothpick inserted in the center of the cake comes out clean. (Find a spot that is free of filling.)

4. Cool the cake to room temperature before cutting into squares and serving.

Yield: *12 servings*

1 box Betty Crocker Super Moist butter recipe yellow cake mix

¾ cup Dannon nonfat plain yogurt

½ cup Egg Beaters egg substitute

1 can (1 pound, 4 ounces) Lucky Leaf Lite cherry pie filling

NUTRITIONAL FACTS
(PER SERVING)

Calories: 223	Fiber: 1 g
Chol: 0 mg	Protein: 2.8 g
Fat: 2.1 g	Sodium: 265 mg

You Save: Calories: 69 Fat: 8.7 g

FAT-FIGHTING TIP

Baking With Reduced-Fat Margarine and Light Butter

Contrary to popular belief, you *can* bake with reduced-fat margarine and light butter. These products make it possible to reduce fat by more than half, and still enjoy light, tender, buttery-tasting cakes; crisp cookies; flaky pie crusts; and other goodies that are not easily made fat-free.

Because reduced-fat margarine and butter are diluted with water, they cannot be substituted for their full-fat counterparts on a one-for-one basis. To compensate for the extra water, substitute three-fourths of the light product for the full-fat butter or margarine. For instance, if a cake recipe calls for 1 cup of butter, use ¾ cup of light butter. Be sure to use a brand that contains 5 to 6 grams of fat and 50 calories per tablespoon. (Full-fat brands contain 11 grams of fat and 100 calories per tablespoon.) Brands with less fat than this generally do not work well in baking.

Be careful not to overbake your reduced-fat creations, as they can become dry. Bake cakes and quick breads at 325°F to 350°F, muffins at 350°F, and biscuits and scones at 375°F to 400°F, and check the product for doneness a few minutes before the end of the usual baking time. Bake cookies at 325°F until golden brown. Then enjoy!

Orange-Poppy Seed Pound Cake

Yield: *16 servings*

½ cup (1 stick) Land O Lakes light butter, softened to room temperature

1½ cups sugar

¼ cup plus 2 tablespoons Better'n Eggs egg substitute

2 tablespoons frozen (thawed) orange juice concentrate

2⅓ cups Pillsbury's Best unbleached flour

⅔ cup Quaker oat bran

½ teaspoon baking soda

2 tablespoons poppy seeds

1 teaspoon dried grated orange rind

8 ounces Stonyfield Farm nonfat vanilla yogurt

GLAZE

½ cup confectioner's sugar

1 tablespoon frozen (thawed) orange juice concentrate

1. Combine the butter and sugar in the bowl of an electric mixer, and beat until smooth. Beat in first the egg substitute, and then the juice concentrate.

2. In a medium-sized bowl, combine the flour, oat bran, baking soda, poppy seeds, and orange rind, and stir to mix well. Add half of the flour mixture and half of the yogurt to the butter mixture, and beat just until well mixed. Add the remaining flour mixture and yogurt, and again beat until well mixed.

3. Coat a 12-cup bundt pan with nonstick cooking spray, and spread the batter evenly in the pan. Bake at 350°F for 35 to 40 minutes, or just until a wooden toothpick inserted in the center of the cake comes out clean. Cool the cake in the pan for 20 minutes. Then invert onto a wire rack, and cool to room temperature.

4. To make the glaze, combine the glaze ingredients in a small bowl, and stir until smooth. Transfer the cake to a serving platter, and drizzle the glaze over the cake. Let sit for at least 15 minutes before slicing and serving.

NUTRITIONAL FACTS (PER SERVING)

Calories: 208	Fat: 3.7 g	Protein: 3.9 g
Cholesterol: 10 mg	Fiber: 1.4 g	Sodium: 54 mg

You Save: Calories: 135 Fat: 12.1 g

Carrot Spice Cake

1. Combine the flour, sugar, baking soda, and spices in a medium-sized bowl, and stir to mix well. Add the applesauce and egg substitute, and stir just until the dry ingredients are moistened. Stir in the carrots, raisins, and, if desired, the pecans.

2. Coat a 9-inch round cake pan with nonstick cooking spray. Spread the batter evenly in the pan, and bake at 325°F for 30 to 35 minutes, or just until the top springs back when lightly touched, and a wooden toothpick inserted in the center of the cake comes out clean. Cool the cake to room temperature in the pan.

3. To make the frosting, combine the cream cheese, sugar, and vanilla extract in the bowl of a food processor, and process until smooth. Transfer the mixture to a medium-sized bowl, and gently fold in the Cool Whip Lite.

4. Remove the cake from the pan, and transfer to a serving platter. Spread the frosting over the top and sides of the cooled cake, and serve immediately, or refrigerate until needed.

Yield: 10 servings

1⅓ cups Pillsbury's Best unbleached flour

¾ cup sugar

1¼ teaspoons baking soda

1 teaspoon ground cinnamon

½ teaspoon ground nutmeg

¼ teaspoon ground cloves

⅔ cup Mott's natural applesauce

¼ cup plus 2 tablespoons Better'n Eggs egg substitute

1½ cups grated carrots

¼ cup dark raisins

¼ cup chopped pecans (optional)

CREAM CHEESE FROSTING

1 block (8 ounces) Philadelphia Free nonfat cream cheese, softened to room temperature

1 tablespoon plus 1½ teaspoons sugar

½ teaspoon vanilla extract

¾ cup Cool Whip Lite

NUTRITIONAL FACTS (PER SERVING)

Calories: 184	Fat: 0.8 g	Protein: 6 g
Cholesterol: 1 mg	Fiber: 1.4 g	Sodium: 287 mg

You Save: Calories: 197   Fat: 23.3 g

FAT-FIGHTING TIP

Using Fat-Free Cream Cheese in Frostings and Fillings

If you've ever tried to defat a cream cheese frosting recipe by substituting fat-free cream cheese for the full-fat product, you probably ended up with a runny, watery mess. Why? Fat-free cream cheese has a higher water content than full-fat cream cheese. When more than a couple of tablespoons of sugar are added to the fat-free product, water is released from the cheese, resulting in a runny glaze.

The solution? Use a low-sugar frosting, like the one that tops the Carrot Spice Cake. As another option, make the frosting with Neufchatel—a reduced-fat cheese. Or beat in a tablespoon or two of instant vanilla pudding mix. This will thicken the mixture to the desired consistency.

FAT-FIGHTING TIP

Trimming the Fat From Carrot Cakes

Carrot cakes are among the highest-fat desserts you can make. Just one piece can contain 25 grams of fat! Fortunately, it is easy to eliminate virtually all of the fat from your favorite carrot cake recipe. All you need do is replace the oil with three-fourths as much applesauce or fruit juice (try orange, apple, or pineapple). WonderSlim fat substitute, which can be found in health foods stores, and homemade Prune Purée (page 190) may also be used. Mix up the batter, and add a bit more substitute if it seems too dry.

To keep your fat-free carrot cake moist, reduce the oven temperature by 25°F, and check the cake for doneness a few minutes before the end of the usual baking time. Remove the cake from the oven just as soon as a toothpick inserted in the center comes out clean.

By substituting applesauce or another fat substitute for the oil in your recipe, you will cut fat so dramatically that you will be able to add a few nuts or a little coconut to the batter without blowing your fat budget. Fruitful fat substitutes will also enhance the flavor of your cake, allowing you to reduce the sugar by as much as 25 percent.

Cherry Cheese Kugel

Yield: *8 servings*

4 ounces Mueller's medium or wide no-yolk egg noodles

1 block (8 ounces) Healthy Choice fat-free cream cheese, softened to room temperature

½ cup sugar

1 cup Light 'n Lively nonfat cottage cheese

1 cup Egg Beaters egg substitute

1 teaspoon vanilla extract

1½ cups fresh or frozen (unthawed) pitted cherries, halved

TOPPING

1 tablespoon plus 1½ teaspoons sugar

1 tablespoon plus 1½ teaspoons finely ground almonds

1. Cook the noodles al dente according to package directions. Drain, rinse with cool water, and drain again. Set aside.

2. Combine the cream cheese and sugar in a large bowl, and stir to mix. Add the cottage cheese, egg substitute, and vanilla, and stir to mix well. Gently stir in first the noodles, and then cherries.

3. Coat a 1½-quart casserole dish with nonstick cooking spray, and spread the mixture evenly in the dish. Combine the sugar and almonds in a small dish, and sprinkle over the noodle mixture.

4. Bake at 350F for 1 hour, or until bubbly around the edges and lightly browned on top. Allow to cool for 30 minutes before serving warm or at room temperature. Refrigerate any leftovers.

NUTRITIONAL FACTS (PER SERVING)

Calories: 189	Fat: 1.2 g	Protein: 12 g
Cholesterol: 3 mg	Fiber: 1 g	Sodium: 176 mg

You Save: Calories: 133   Fat: 16.1 g

Trimming the Fat From Made-From-Mix Baked Goods

It's easier than you think to reduce the fat in made-from-mix baked goods by using a variety of readily available ingredients to replace the added oil or butter, and by substituting egg whites or egg substitute for the added whole eggs. Baked products made this way are not only lower in fat, but also higher in nutrients.

The steps outlined below will guide you in slimming down your favorite made-from-mix cakes, muffins, quick breads, brownies, and cookies. Bear in mind that most of the fat substitutes mentioned—including WonderSlim fat substitute—can be purchased in grocery and health foods stores. Prune Butter and Prune Purée can be either made at home or purchased as ready-made products. (See page 190 for details.)

CAKE MIXES

To reduce the fat in your favorite made-from-mix cake by more than 60 percent:

❑ First, choose the fat substitute that will give you the result you're looking for. For instance, use applesauce when you want very little flavor change. Use WonderSlim fat substitute, Prune Purée, or applesauce in chocolate cakes and spice cakes. For a change of pace, use mashed bananas or puréed raspberries in chocolate

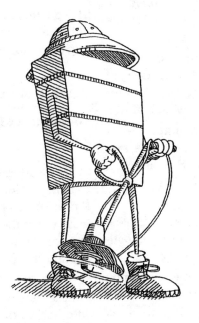

cakes, mashed bananas or puréed apricots in spice cakes, puréed apricots or peaches in yellow cakes, and puréed strawberries in white cakes. For even more flavor, try substituting applesauce or fruit purée on a one-for-one basis for up to half the water called for.

❑ If the directions call for oil, replace the oil with three-fourths as much of the chosen fat substitute. For instance, if the directions call for $\frac{1}{3}$ cup of oil, substitute $\frac{1}{4}$ cup of fat substitute.

❑ If the directions call for butter, margarine, or another solid shortening, replace these products with half as much fat substitute. For instance, if the directions call for $\frac{1}{2}$ cup of butter, substitute $\frac{1}{4}$ cup of fat substitute.

❑ To eliminate even more fat and cholesterol, substitute 3 tablespoons of fat-free egg substitute or egg white for each whole egg called for in the recipe.

❑ To maintain moistness, check the cake for doneness a few minutes before the end of the usual baking time.

MUFFIN AND QUICK BREAD MIXES

To reduce the fat in your favorite made-from-mix muffins or quick breads by 50 to 100 percent:

❑ First, choose the fat substitute that will give you the result you're looking for. Use applesauce when you want very little flavor change—in blueberry or poppy seed muffin mixes, for instance. For a change of pace, make banana-blueberry muffins by substituting mashed bananas for the fat. Use applesauce, mashed bananas, puréed fruit, WonderSlim fat substitute, or Prune Purée in bran muffin and oatmeal muffin mixes. Use mashed bananas, puréed apricots, or applesauce in gingerbread and spice muffin mixes. For extra flavor, substitute applesauce or puréed fruit on a one-for-one basis for up to half of the water called for.

❑ If the directions call for oil, replace the oil with three-fourths as much of the chosen fat substitute. For instance, if the directions call for $\frac{1}{3}$ cup of oil, substitute $\frac{1}{4}$ cup of fat substitute.

❑ If the directions call for butter, margarine, or another solid shortening, replace these fats with half as much fat substitute. For instance, if the directions call for $\frac{1}{2}$ cup of butter, substitute $\frac{1}{4}$ cup of fat substitute.

❑ To eliminate even more fat and cholesterol, substitute 3 tablespoons of egg substitute or egg white for each whole egg.

❑ To maintain moistness, bake low-fat muffins and quick breads at 350°F, and check the muffins or loaf for doneness a few minutes before the end of the usual baking time.

BROWNIE MIXES

To reduce the fat in your favorite made-from-mix brownies by more than 75 percent:

❑ First, choose the fat substitute that will give you the result you're looking for. Use applesauce, WonderSlim fat substitute, or Prune Purée when you want little flavor change. For a change of pace, use mashed bananas or puréed raspberries. For extra flavor, substitute

applesauce or fruit purée on a one-for-one basis for all of the water in the recipe.

❑ If the directions call for oil, replace the oil with three-fourths as much of your chosen fat substitute. For instance, if the directions call for $\frac{1}{2}$ cup of oil, substitute $\frac{1}{4}$ cup plus 2 tablespoons of fat substitute.

❑ To maintain moistness, reduce the oven temperature by 25°F, and check the brownies for doneness a few minutes before the end of the usual baking time.

❑ To eliminate even more fat and cholesterol, substitute 3 tablespoons of egg substitute or egg white for each whole egg.

COOKIE MIXES

To trim made-from-mix cookies of at least half their fat:

❑ If the recipe directions call for oil, replace this ingredient with three-fourths as much Prune Purée or WonderSlim fat substitute. For instance, if the directions call for $\frac{1}{2}$ cup of oil, replace it with $\frac{1}{4}$ cup plus 2 tablespoons of fat substitute.

❑ If the directions call for butter, margarine, or another solid shortening, replace these fats with half as much Prune Purée or WonderSlim fat substitute.

❑ Replace each whole egg with 2 tablespoons of Prune Purée or WonderSlim fat substitute, or with 2 tablespoons of water.

❑ Spray the cookie sheet with nonstick cooking spray (even if the directions say to use an ungreased sheet), and flatten the cookie dough slightly with the tip of a spoon before baking to facilitate spreading.

❑ Bake the cookies for the directed amount of time and at the recommended oven temperature, or until golden brown.

Black Forest Cake

1. In a large bowl, combine the cake mix, egg substitute, and water. Using an electric mixer, beat at low speed for 30 seconds. Then beat at medium speed for 2 additional minutes.

2. Coat two 9-inch round cake pans with the cooking spray. (If using a spray other than Baker's Joy, lightly flour the pans after spraying.) Divide the batter between the pans, and bake at 350°F for 25 to 30 minutes, or just until the tops spring back when lightly touched. Cool the cakes in the pans for 15 minutes. Then invert onto wire racks, and cool completely.

3. Place 1 cake layer upside-down on a serving platter, and spread the cherry filling over the cake, extending the filling all the way to the edges. Top with the other cake layer, placing it right side up. (Some of the filling will drip down the sides of the cake.)

4. To make the glaze, combine all of the glaze ingredients in a small bowl, and stir to mix well. Spread the glaze over the top of the cake, allowing some of the glaze to drip down the sides. If desired, sprinkle the almonds over the top of the cake.

5. Chill the cake for at least 2 hours before slicing and serving.

Yield: *12 servings*

1 box Betty Crocker Super Moist Light devil's food cake mix

½ cup plus 1 tablespoon Better'n Eggs egg substitute

1⅓ cups water

Baker's Joy nonstick cooking spray

2 tablespoons sliced almonds (optional)

FILLING

1 can (20 ounces) Comstock Light cherry pie filling or Thank You More Fruit Light cherry pie filling

GLAZE

1¼ cups confectioner's sugar

1 tablespoon skim milk

½ teaspoon almond extract

NUTRITIONAL FACTS (PER SERVING)		
Calories: 255	Fat: 2.5 g	Protein: 1.6 g
Cholesterol: 0 mg	Fiber: 0.3 g	Sodium: 342 mg

You Save: Calories: 178 Fat: 15.3 g

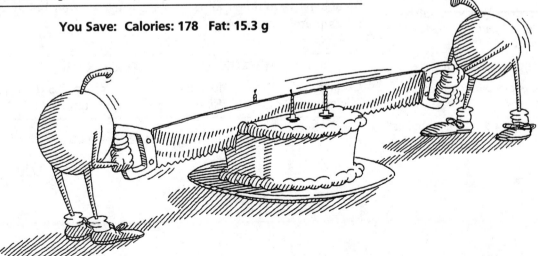

Fabulous Fudge Cake

Yield: *16 servings*

1¼ cups Hodgson Mill unbleached flour

1 cup sugar

½ cup Hershey's Dutch Processed European Style cocoa powder

2 teaspoons baking powder

1 teaspoon baking soda

½ cup Levkar Prune Butter, Solo Prune Plum Filling, or Prune Butter (page 190)

½ cup skim milk

¼ cup Healthy Choice egg substitute

1½ teaspoons vanilla extract

1½ cups finely shredded unpeeled zucchini (about 2 medium)

⅓ cup chopped walnuts

⅓ cup semi-sweet chocolate chips

GLAZE

1½ cups confectioner's sugar

2 tablespoons Hershey's Dutch Processed European Style cocoa powder

1 teaspoon vanilla extract

2 tablespoons plus 2 teaspoons skim milk

⅓ cup chopped walnuts (optional)

1. Combine the flour, sugar, cocoa, baking powder, and baking soda in a large bowl, and stir to mix well.

2. Combine the Prune Butter, milk, egg substitute, and vanilla extract in a blender, and process until smoooth. Add the Prune Butter mixture and the zucchini to the flour mixture, and stir just until the dry ingredients are moistened. Fold in the walnuts and chocolate chips.

3. Coat a 9-x-13-inch baking pan with nonstick cooking spray, and spread the batter evenly in the pan. Bake at 350°F for 23 to 25 minutes, or just until the top springs back when lightly touched and a wooden toothpick inserted in the center of the cake comes out coated with fudgy crumbs. Cool the cake to room temperature in the pan.

4. To make the glaze, combine the confectioner's sugar, cocoa, and vanilla extract in a medium-sized bowl. Stir in enough of the milk to make a thick glaze. Stir in the walnuts if desired.

5. If using a microwave oven, place the glaze in the microwave and heat at high power for 35 seconds, or until runny. If using a conventional stove top, transfer the glaze to a small saucepan and, stirring constantly, place over medium heat for 30 seconds, or until runny.

6. Drizzle the glaze back and forth over the cake. Let the cake sit for at least 15 minutes, allowing the glaze to harden, before cutting into squares and serving.

NUTRITIONAL FACTS (PER SERVING)		
Calories: 185	Fat: 3.1 g	Protein: 3.5 g
Cholesterol: 0 mg	Fiber: 2.6 g	Sodium: 137 mg

You Save: Calories: 172 Fat: 14.5 g

Chocolate Flavor With a Fraction of the Fat

For rich chocolate flavor with minimal fat, substitute cocoa powder for high-fat baking chocolate. Simply use 3 tablespoons of cocoa powder plus 2 teaspoons of water or another liquid to replace each ounce of baking chocolate in cakes, brownies, puddings, and other goodies. You'll save 111 calories and 13.5 grams of fat for each ounce of baking chocolate you replace!

For the deepest, darkest, richest cocoa flavor, use Dutch processed cocoa in your chocolate treats. Dutching, a process that neutralizes the natural acidity in cocoa, results in a darker, sweeter, more mellow-flavored cocoa. Look for a brand like Hershey's Dutch Processed European Style cocoa. Like regular cocoa, this product has only half a gram of fat per tablespoon—although some brands do contain more fat. Dutched cocoa can be substituted for regular cocoa in any recipe, and since it has a smoother, sweeter flavor, you may find that you can reduce the sugar in your recipe by up to 25 percent.

Here's another fat-fighting chocolate tip. Replace the butter, margarine, or shortening in chocolate cakes, cookies, and brownies with homemade or store-bought Prune Butter (page 190). Sweet, nutritious, and fat-free, Prune Butter adds moistness to baked goods and enhances the flavor of chocolate. You will never miss the fat!

Magnificent Mexican Brownies

1. Place the brownie mix, coffee granules, and cinnamon in a medium bowl, and stir to mix well. Add the applesauce and egg substitute, and stir until well blended. Fold in the pecans if desired.

2. Coat a 9-x-13-inch baking pan with nonstick cooking spray, and spread the mixture evenly in the pan. Bake at 325°F for about 24 minutes, or until the edges are firm and the center is almost set. Be careful not to overbake. Cool to room temperature.

3. To make the glaze, combine all of the glaze ingredients in a small bowl, and stir to mix well. Drizzle the glaze back and forth over the cooled brownies. Let sit for at least 15 minutes before cutting into 2-x-3-inch bars and serving.

Yield: 18 servings

1 box Betty Crocker traditional chewy fudge brownie mix

2 teaspoons instant coffee granules

¼ teaspoon ground cinnamon

½ cup plus 2 tablespoons Mott's natural applesauce

¼ cup plus 2 tablespoons Better'n Eggs egg substitute

⅓ cup chopped pecans (optional)

GLAZE

½ cup confectioner's sugar

1 tablespoon cocoa powder

½ teaspoon instant coffee granules

1 pinch ground cinnamon

1 tablespoon skim milk

NUTRITIONAL FACTS (PER SERVING)		
Calories: 154	Fat: 2 g	Protein: 1.5 g
Cholesterol: 0 mg	Fiber: 1.2 g	Sodium: 143 mg

You Save: Calories: 78   Fat: 7.8 g

Raspberry Ripple Cheesecake

Yield: *10 servings*

CRUST

5½ large (2½-x-5-inch) Honey Maid reduced-fat chocolate graham crackers

2 tablespoons sugar

1 tablespoon plus 1½ teaspoons Land O Lakes light butter, softened to room temperature

RASPBERRY RIPPLE

3 tablespoons sugar

1 tablespoon cornstarch

2 tablespoons Welch's 100% white grape juice

1¼ cups fresh or frozen (unthawed) raspberries

FILLING

2 blocks (8 ounces each) Philadelphia Free nonfat cream cheese, softened to room temperature

15 ounces Sorrento nonfat ricotta cheese

¾ cup sugar

½ cup Egg Beaters egg substitute

¼ cup plus 2 tablespoons unbleached flour

2 teaspoons vanilla extract

NUTRITIONAL FACTS
(PER SERVING)

Calories: 229	Fiber: 0.9 g
Chol: 12 mg	Protein: 15 g
Fat: 1.8 g	Sodium: 339 mg

1. To make the crust, break the crackers into pieces, and place in the bowl of a food processor or blender. Process into fine crumbs. Measure the crumbs. There should be ¾ cup. (Adjust the amount if necessary.)

2. Return the crumbs to the food processor or blender, add the sugar, and process for a few seconds to mix. Add the butter, and process until the mixture is moist and crumbly.

3. Coat a 9-inch springform pan with nonstick cooking spray, and use the back of a spoon to press the mixture against the bottom and ½ inch up the sides of the pan, forming an even crust. (Periodically dip the spoon in sugar, if necessary, to prevent sticking.) Bake at 350°F for 8 minutes, or until the edges feel firm and dry. Set aside to cool.

4. To make the raspberry ripple, combine the sugar and cornstarch in a 1-quart pot, and stir to mix well. Add the juice, and stir to mix well. Place the pot over medium heat, and cook, stirring constantly, until the mixture begins to boil. Add the raspberries, and cook, stirring frequently, for about 4 minutes, or until the mixture is thick and bubbly, and the raspberries break up. Remove the pot from the heat, and set aside to cool to room temperature.

5. To make the filling, place the cream cheese, ricotta, and sugar in a food processor or blender, and process until well mixed. Add the egg substitute, flour, and vanilla extract, and process until smooth.

6. Spread half of the cheesecake batter evenly over the crust. Spoon the raspberry mixture randomly over the plain batter, and top with the remaining batter. Draw a knife through the batter in an "S" pattern to produce a marbled effect.

7. Bake at 325°F for 1 hour, or until the center is set. Turn the oven off, and allow the cake to cool in the oven with the door ajar for 30 minutes.

8. Chill the cake for at least 8 hours. Remove the collar of the pan just before slicing and serving.

You Save: Calories: 295 Fat: 36.8 g

Creamy Cheesecakes Without the Fat

Cheesecakes are definitely one of the most delicious desserts there are. Unfortunately, they are also very high in fat. Just one slice of cheesecake can contain a whopping 500 calories and 40 grams of fat! Even worse, most of this fat is the saturated, artery-clogging type. But don't fear. Creamy, delicious, ultra-light cheesecakes can now be made using nonfat cream cheese.

To defat your favorite cheesecake recipe, substitute a block-style nonfat cream cheese, like Philadelphia Free, for the full-fat cream cheese on a one-for-one basis. For a lighter taste and texture, substitute nonfat ricotta for half of the full-fat cream cheese. Both of these nonfat cheeses contain more water than full-fat products, so you will need to add a tablespoon of flour to the batter for each 8-ounce block of nonfat cream cheese or cup of ricotta used. This should produce a firm, nicely-textured cake that is rich and creamy, yet remarkably low in calories and fat.

Very Strawberry Pie

Yield: 8 servings

CRUST

1 cup Post Grape-Nuts cereal

¼ cup finely ground pecans

2 tablespoons light brown sugar

3 tablespoons Scramblers egg substitute

FILLING

4 cups halved strawberries

GLAZE

¼ cup plus 2 tablespoons sugar

¼ cup cornstarch

½ cup frozen (thawed) cran-strawberry juice concentrate, or another strawberry juice concentrate blend

1 cup water

1½ teaspoons unflavored gelatin

1. To make the crust, combine the cereal, nuts, and brown sugar in a small bowl, and stir to mix well. Stir in the egg substitute.

2. Coat a 9-inch pie pan with nonstick cooking spray, and use the back of a spoon to press the crust mixture across the bottom and sides of the pan to form an even crust. Bake at 350°F for 12 to 14 minutes, or until the edges are lightly browned. Set aside to cool.

3. To make the glaze, place the sugar and cornstarch in a 1-quart pot, and mix well. Stir in the juice concentrate and water, and bring to boil over medium heat, stirring constantly with a whisk. Reduce the heat to low, and cook and stir for 1 minute, or until the mixture is thickened and bubbly. Remove from the heat, sprinkle gelatin over the top, and whisk to mix. Set aside for 20 minutes.

4. Place the berries in a large bowl. Stir the glaze, and pour over the berries, tossing gently to coat.

5. Spread the strawberry mixture over the prepared crust, and chill for several hours, or until the glaze is set. Serve cold.

NUTRITIONAL FACTS (PER SERVING)

Calories: 189	Fat: 2.4 g	Protein: 2.8 g
Cholesterol: 0 mg	Fiber: 2.7 g	Sodium: 107 mg

You Save: Cal.: 133 Fat: 11.1 g

Very Blackberry Cobbler

Yield: *9 servings*

For variety, substitute blueberries for the blackberries.

FILLING

6 cups fresh or frozen (partially thawed) blackberries

3 tablespoons cornstarch

¼ cup plus 2 tablespoons sugar

½ teaspoon dried grated orange rind

TOPPING

1⅓ cups Pioneer Low-Fat Baking Mix

¼ cup sugar

½ cup plus 2 tablespoons skim milk

1 quart Crowley nonfat frozen vanilla yogurt (optional)

1. Combine the berries, cornstarch, sugar, and orange rind in a large bowl, and stir to mix well. Set aside for 20 minutes to allow the juices to develop.

2. Coat a 2-quart casserole dish with nonstick cooking spray, and spread the berries evenly in the dish. Cover the dish with aluminum foil, and bake at 375°F for 30 to 40 minutes, or until the mixture is hot and bubbly.

3. To make the topping, combine the baking mix and sugar in a medium-sized bowl, and stir to mix well. Add just enough of the milk to form a moderately stiff batter, stirring just until the dry ingredients are moistened. Drop heaping tablespoonfuls of the batter onto the berry mixture to make 9 biscuits.

4. Bake uncovered at 375°F for 18 to 20 minutes, or until the topping is lightly browned. Cool at room temperature for 10 minutes, and serve warm, topping each serving with a scoop of the frozen yogurt if desired.

NUTRITIONAL FACTS (PER SERVING)		
Calories: 208	Fat: 0.7 g	Protein: 3 g
Cholesterol: 0 mg	Fiber: 4.5 g	Sodium: 307 mg

You Save: Calories: 132   Fat: 11.3 g

Cinnamon Apple Crisp

1. To make the topping, place the cereal, flour, sugar, and cinnamon in a small bowl, and stir to mix well. Add the juice concentrate, and stir until the mixture is moist and crumbly. Set aside.

2. To make the filling, combine the sugar, cornstarch, cinnamon, and apple juice in a 3-quart pot, and stir to mix well. Place the pot over medium-low heat, and bring to a boil, stirring constantly. Cook and stir for another minute, or until the mixture is thick and bubbly. Add the sliced apples and raisins, and stir just until the fruit is coated with the glaze. Remove the pot from the heat.

3. Coat a 9-inch deep dish pie pan with nonstick cooking spray. Spread the filling evenly in the pan, and sprinkle the topping over the filling. Bake at 375°F for 40 minutes, or until the filling is bubbly around the edges and the topping is golden brown. (If the top starts to brown too quickly, loosely cover it with aluminum foil during the last 15 minutes of baking.)

4. Cool at room temperature for at least 10 minutes, and serve warm, topping each serving with a scoop of the ice cream if desired.

Yield: 6 servings

FILLING

2 tablespoons sugar

1 tablespoon plus 1½ teaspoons cornstarch

½ teaspoon ground cinnamon

½ cup Tree Top 100% apple juice

6 cups sliced peeled apples (6 to 8 medium)

¼ cup dark raisins

TOPPING

⅓ cup Post Grape-Nuts cereal

¼ cup Gold Medal whole wheat flour

¼ cup light brown sugar

½ teaspoon ground cinnamon

1 tablespoon plus 1 teaspoon frozen (thawed) Tree Top 100% apple juice concentrate

3 cups Healthy Choice premium low-fat vanilla ice cream (optional)

NUTRITIONAL FACTS (PER SERVING)

Calories: 188	Fat: 0.5 g	Protein: 1.8 g
Cholesterol: 0 mg	Fiber: 3.6 g	Sodium: 48 mg

You Save: Calories: 134 Fat: 14.5 g

Tiramisu Treats

Yield: *4 servings*

4 slices (¾ inch each) Entenmann's fat-free golden loaf cake

BERRY MIXTURE

1½ cups fresh or frozen (thawed) strawberries or raspberries

1 tablespoon sugar

RICOTTA MIXTURE

1¼ cups Sorrento nonfat ricotta cheese

2 tablespoons plus 2 teaspoons sugar

¾ teaspoon vanilla extract

LIQUEUR MIXTURE

2 tablespoons plus 2 teaspoons coffee liqueur

1 teaspoon Hershey's Dutch Processed European Style cocoa powder

TOPPING

¼ cup plus 2 tablespoons Cool Whip Lite

¼ teaspoon Hershey's Dutch Processed European Style cocoa powder

1. To make the berry mixture, place the berries and sugar in a small bowl. Using a potato masher or fork, mash the berries and sugar together. Set aside.

2. To make the ricotta mixture, combine the ricotta, sugar, and vanilla extract in the bowl of a food processor or blender, and process at medium speed for 1 minute, or until smooth. Set aside.

3. To make the liqueur mixture, combine the liqueur and cocoa in a small bowl, and stir to mix well. Set aside.

4. To assemble the desserts, crumble a half slice of the cake into the bottom of each of four 10-ounce balloon wine glasses. Top the cake with 1½ tablespoons of the berry mixture, 2½ tablespoons of the ricotta mixture, and 1 teaspoon of the liqueur mixture. Repeat the layers, and top each dessert with 1½ tablespoons of the whipped topping and a sprinkling of cocoa. Serve immediately, or cover and refrigerate until ready to serve.

NUTRITIONAL FACTS (PER SERVING)		
Calories: 203	Fat: 1.1 g	Protein: 12.3 g
Cholesterol: 12 mg	Fiber: 1.2 g	Sodium: 302 mg

You Save: Calories: 302   Fat: 34.4 g

FAT-FIGHTER'S GUIDE TO
Baking Mixes

Of all the Nutrition Facts labels, the labels on boxes of cake, brownie, cookie, muffin, and quick bread mixes are the most confusing and misleading. The reason? Calories are provided both for the mix alone and for the mix prepared according to package directions. People often look only at the information for the mix, and disregard the Nutrition Facts for the prepared product—which includes the oil and eggs you add during mixing. Even worse, total fat grams are given only for the mix alone—not for the prepared product. For the prepared product, fat is expressed as a percentage of the Daily Value, a recommended daily amount based on a diet of 2,000 calories. This means that you can't readily see the dramatic rise in fat grams that occurs when the dry mix is combined with the necessary oil and eggs. Just how much fat gets added to your mix? Most cake mixes contain 2.5 to 5 grams of fat per serving in the mix alone. One third cup of oil and 3 eggs add another 7 grams of fat per serving—and that's before you ice or frost the cake.

But sometimes you can have your made-from-mix cake, muffins, brownies, and cookies, and eat them too. Lower-fat mixes for all of these products are available. Pillsbury Lovin' Lite brownie mixes, Betty Crocker Super Moist Light cake mixes, Betty Crocker low-fat brownie and fat-free muffin mixes, and Krusteaz low-fat cookie and fat-free muffin mixes are some examples. Products made from these mixes have just a fraction of the fat of those made from regular mixes.

However, you can just as easily take your favorite baking mix and make it lower in fat by replacing the oil or butter with an ingredient like applesauce, mashed bananas, or puréed fruit. Regular mixes prepared with fat substitutes often have even less fat than products made with light mixes. (See the inset on page 197 for details.)

Bear in mind that even if you use a light mix or prepare a regular mix with fat substitutes, most of these products are high in sugar, refined flour, artificial ingredients, and calories. So while the finished product may be low in fat or even fat-free, it should have only a limited place in your diet. The exceptions to this rule are products made with whole grain mixes, like those by Arrowhead Mills. These mixes contain only whole grains, are low in sugar, and are free of artificial flavors, artificial colors, and other additives.

Luscious Lemon Trifle

Yield: *12 servings*

CAKE MIXTURE

2 packages (4-serving size) Jell-O instant lemon pudding mix

4 cups skim milk

1 large angel food cake (1¼ pounds)

BERRY MIXTURE

2 cups fresh or frozen (thawed) raspberries

2 tablespoons sugar

TOPPING MIXTURE

2 cups Cool Whip Lite

½ cup Dannon low-fat vanilla yogurt

1. To make the pudding, place the pudding mix and milk in a large bowl, and beat with an electric mixer or wire whisk for 2 minutes, or until well blended. Chill for at least 1 hour.

2. To make the berry mixture, place the berries and sugar in a medium-sized bowl. Using a potato masher or fork, mash the berries and sugar together. Set aside.

3. To make the topping, place the whipped topping in a medium-sized bowl, and gently fold in the yogurt. Set aside.

4. Cut the angel food cake into 1½-inch cubes, and place the cubes in a large bowl. Add 3 cups of the chilled pudding, and toss gently to coat. (Reserve the remainder of the pudding for another use.)

5. To assemble the trifle, spread half of the cake mixture evenly in the bottom of a 3-quart trifle bowl or other decorative glass bowl. Drizzle half of the berry mixture over the cake. Repeat the cake and berry layers. Spread the topping over the trifle, swirling with a knife.

6. Cover and refrigerate for at least 2 hours before serving.

NUTRITIONAL FACTS (PER SERVING)

Calories: 235	Fat: 2.1 g	Protein: 5.5 g
Cholesterol: 2 mg	Fiber: 1.5 g	Sodium: 479 mg

You Save: Calories: 93 Fat: 13.3 g

Soft and Chewy Ginger Cookies

1. Combine the flours, sugar, baking soda, orange rind, cinnamon, and ginger in a medium-sized bowl, and stir to mix well.

2. Combine the Prune Butter, molasses, and egg substitute in a small bowl, and stir to mix well. Add the Prune Butter mixture to the flour mixture, and stir to mix well. (The mixture will seem dry at first, but will form a stiff dough as you keep stirring.)

3. Coat a baking sheet with nonstick cooking spray. Roll the dough into 1-inch balls, and place $1\frac{1}{2}$ inches apart on the sheet. (If the dough is too sticky to handle, place it in the freezer for a few minutes.) Using the bottom of a glass dipped in sugar, flatten the cookies to $\frac{3}{8}$-inch thickness. Alternatively, press a pecan or walnut half into the center of each cookie to flatten.

4. Bake at 325°F for about 12 minutes, or until golden brown. Cool the cookies on the pan for 1 minute. Then transfer the cookies to wire racks, and cool completely. Serve immediately, or transfer to an airtight container and arrange in single layers separated by sheets of waxed paper.

Yield: *36 cookies*

1 cup Arrowhead Mills whole wheat pastry flour

1 cup Pillsbury's Best unbleached flour

½ cup plus 2 tablespoons sugar

1 teaspoon baking soda

1 teaspoon dried grated orange rind

¾ teaspoon ground cinnamon

¾ teaspoon ground ginger

¼ cup plus 2 tablespoons Levkar Prune Butter, Solo Prune Plum Filling, or Prune Butter (page 190)

¼ cup plus 2 tablespoons molasses

2 tablespoons Egg Beaters egg substitute

36 pecan or walnut halves (optional)

NUTRITIONAL FACTS (PER COOKIE)

Calories: 52	Fat: 0.1 g	Protein: 1 g
Cholesterol: 0 mg	Fiber: 0.7 g	Sodium: 38 mg

You Save: Calories: 20 Fat: 3 g

Mocha Macadamia Biscotti

Yield: *24 biscotti*

¾ cup plus 2 tablespoons
    Pillsbury's Best unbleached flour

¾ cup Arrowhead Mills whole
    wheat pastry flour

⅔ cup sugar

¼ cup plus 2 tablespoons
    Hershey's Dutch Processed
    European Style cocoa powder

2 teaspoons baking powder

1 teaspoon instant coffee granules

¼ cup Promise Extra Light
    margarine, cut into pieces

¼ cup toasted chopped
    macadamia nuts (page 191)

¼ cup milk chocolate chips
    (optional)

¼ cup plus 2 tablespoons
    Scramblers egg substitute

1½ teaspoons vanilla extract

1. Combine the flours, sugar, cocoa, baking powder, and coffee granules in a large bowl, and stir to mix well. Using a pastry cutter or 2 knives, cut in the margarine until the mixture resembles coarse meal. Stir in the nuts and, if desired, the chocolate chips. Add the egg substitute and vanilla extract, and stir just until the mixture holds together.

2. Turn the dough onto a lightly floured surface, and shape into two 9-x-2-inch logs. Coat a baking sheet with nonstick cooking spray, and place the logs on the sheet, leaving 4 inches of space between them to allow for spreading. Bake at 350°F for about 25 minutes, or until lightly browned.

3. Cool the logs at room temperature for 10 minutes. Then use a serrated knife to slice the logs diagonally into ½-inch-thick slices.

4. Return the slices to the baking sheet, and arrange them in a single layer, cut side down. Bake at 300°F for 10 minutes. Turn the slices, and bake for about 8 additional minutes, or until dry and crisp.

5. Transfer the biscotti to wire racks, and cool completely. Serve immediately or store in an airtight container.

NUTRITIONAL FACTS (PER BISCOTTI)

Calories: 74	Fat: 2 g	Protein: 1.7 g
Cholesterol: 0 mg	Fiber: 1.1 g	Sodium: 45 mg

You Save: Calories: 37   Fat: 4.1 g

FAT-FIGHTER'S GUIDE TO
Sweet Treats

The past few years have brought a multitude of fat-free and low-fat ways to satisfy a sweet tooth. Cookies, brownies, cakes, pies, pastries, and ice cream are all now being made with little or no fat. Unfortunately, as many weight-conscious people have discovered, many of these products, while lower in fat, fall short of what you might wish them to be both nutritionally and as a means of controlling weight. A glance at the Nutrition Facts label on many no- and low-fat baked goods and frozen desserts reveals that when fat is removed, sugar is often added. The result? The fat content of the product is lower, but, very often, the calorie count has not been greatly changed.

Are reduced-fat sweets an improvement over their high-fat counterparts? You bet. But nutritional powerhouses they are not. In fact, many of these products are made from nutrient-poor refined grains and with an abundance of sugar and artificial ingredients. For this reason, when choosing any sweets, let not only your fat budget, but also your sugar budget (about 50 grams a day) and calorie budget be your guide. With these guidelines in mind, let's take a look at some of the no- and low-fat products that can make your snack and dessert times a little bit sweeter.

COOKIES AND BROWNIES

An amazing array of fat-free and low-fat cookies are now available at your local grocery store. Your best bets are cookies that are lower on both the sugar end and the fat end. Examples are Frookie Fat Free, Health Valley, Jammers, Keebler low-fat graham crackers, Honey Maid reduced-fat chocolate graham crackers, Keebler reduced-fat vanilla wafers, Midel 100% whole wheat honey grahams, Murray's low-fat gingersnaps, Nabisco Newtons, SnackWell's cinnamon grahams, SnackWell's oatmeal raisin, Sunshine golden fruit biscuits, and most brands of animal crackers. Besides being fat-free, Health Valley and Jammers cookies are made with whole grain flours.

As for fat-free brownies, most brands deliver 4 to 5 teaspoons of sugar (16 to 20 grams) apiece. Still, the fat-free versions are a better option than those made with fat. Famous Amos, Greenfield, Pepperidge Farm, Jammers, SnackWell's, and many other companies offer these nonfat treats.

GRANOLA BARS

In years past, granola bars were little more than candy bars in disguise, with unhealthy amounts of fat and sugar wrapped around otherwise healthful oats and other grains. These days, many brands of granola bars have really lightened up, making them a far better snack choice than most cookies. Select brands like Fibar Low Fat, Health Valley, Kellogg's Low Fat, Kudos Low Fat, Quaker Low Fat, and Nature Valley Low Fat. But don't think you're filling up with fiber when you eat a granola bar. With the exception of Health Valley and Fibar granola bars, most contain only 1 gram of fiber. Still, these products do contain more whole grains than most cookies, and tend to be lower in sugar, too.

CAKES, PIES, AND PASTRIES

In this category, Entenmann's has developed an extensive line of fat-free and low-fat cakes, Danish pastries, pies, and other goodies. Hostess also offers some fat-free and low-fat baked goods. Like all sweets, though, these should be considered an occasional indulgence.

Perhaps the best cake choice of all has been around for years—angel food cake. This sweet treat has always been fat-free. Topped with fresh fruit, it makes a light, elegant, and comparatively low-sugar dessert.

FROZEN DESSERTS

Unlike most cookies, cakes, and other sugary treats, frozen dairy desserts do provide some nutritional value. One cup of most brands of low- and no-fat frozen yogurt or ice cream supplies 20 to 30 percent of the Daily Value for calcium. And, of course, these brands save you an astounding amount of fat over full-fat premium products, which can contain about 40 grams per cup!

Look for brands with no more than 3 grams of fat per 1-cup serving. Good choices include Ben & Jerry's no-fat frozen yogurt, Borden Fat Free ice cream, Breyers Fat Free ice cream and frozen yogurt, Colombo Nonfat frozen yogurt, Crowley Nonfat frozen yogurt, Haagen Daz Low-Fat frozen yogurt bars, Healthy Choice Premium Low Fat ice cream, Edy's Fat Free frozen yogurt, Sealtest Free ice cream, and Stonyfield Farm Nonfat frozen yogurt. When perusing the frozen foods case, note that most ice creams list their serving size as $\frac{1}{2}$ cup, but most people eat a full cup.

Other frozen treats to look for include sorbets and ices, most of which have always been fat-free; Dole Fruit Juice and Fruit 'n' Juice bars; Welch's fruit juice bars; and fat-free fudgsicles.

Mocha Mousse Pie

1. To make the crust, break the crackers into pieces, and place in a food processor or blender. Process into fine crumbs. Measure the crumbs. There should be $1\frac{1}{4}$ cups. (Adjust the amount if necessary.)

2. Return the crumbs to the food processor or blender, add the sugar, and process for a few seconds to mix well. Add the egg substitute, and process until the mixture is moist and crumbly.

3. Coat a 9-inch pie pan with nonstick cooking spray, and use the back of a spoon to press the mixture against the sides and bottom of the pan, forming an even crust. (Periodically dip the spoon in sugar, if necessary, to prevent sticking.) Bake at 350°F for 10 to 12 minutes, or until the edges feel firm and dry. Set aside to cool.

4. To make the filling, place the evaporated milk in a 1-quart pot. Sprinkle the gelatin over the milk, and let sit for 2 minutes to allow the gelatin to soften. After 2 minutes, place the pot over low heat, and cook and stir for about 2 minutes, or until the gelatin is completely dissolved. (Do not let the mixture boil.) Remove the pot from the heat, transfer the mixture to a medium-sized mixing bowl, and set aside to cool to room temperature.

5. While the gelatin mixture is cooling, combine the ricotta, sugar, liqueur, cocoa, and vanilla extract in a food processor or blender, and process until smooth. Set aside.

6. When the gelatin mixture has reached room temperature, beat at high speed with an electric mixer for 2 to 3 minutes, or until the mixture has the consistency of whipped cream. Add the ricotta mixture to the gelatin mixture, and beat just until well mixed. Fold in the whipped topping.

7. Spoon the mixture into the pie shell, and chill for several hours, or until firm. When ready to serve, top each wedge with a tablespoon of Cool Whip Lite and a sprinkling of cocoa powder, and serve immediately.

Yield: *8 servings*

CRUST

9 large ($2\frac{1}{2}$-x-5-inch) Honey Maid reduced fat chocolate graham crackers

2 tablespoons sugar

2 tablespoons Egg Beaters egg substitute

FILLING

$\frac{1}{4}$ cup plus 2 tablespoons Carnation Lite evaporated skimmed milk

1 envelope ($\frac{1}{4}$ ounce) unflavored gelatin

15 ounces Polly-O Free nonfat ricotta cheese

$\frac{1}{4}$ cup plus 2 tablespoons sugar

3 tablespoons coffee liqueur

$\frac{1}{4}$ cup Hershey's Dutch Processed European Style cocoa powder

1 teaspoon vanilla extract

1 cup Cool Whip Lite

TOPPING

$\frac{1}{2}$ cup Cool Whip Lite

Hershey's Dutch Processed European Style cocoa powder

NUTRITIONAL FACTS
(PER SERVING)

Calories: 212	Fiber: 1.2 g
Chol: 2 mg	Protein: 11 g
Fat: 3 g	Sodium: 197 mg

You Save: Cal: 155 Fat: 22 g

Index

Other Fat-Free Cookbooks From Avery

Secrets of Fat-Free Baking

*Make delicious baked goods at home
and still reduce the fat in your family's diet.*
Sandra Woodruff, RD

Who can resist moist and delicious homemade cookies, breads, cakes, and muffins, especially if they are fat-free and incredibly simple to make? *Secrets of Fat-Free Baking* features a variety of baked goods, from Strawberry Streusal Muffins to Peach Pizzaz Pie to Colossal Chocolate Chippers to Fresh Apple Cake. And every treat is totally fat-free or greatly reduced in fat. Experienced bakers and novices alike will be surprised by the number of creative and healthful ways in which you can replace fat in baked goods, and still enjoy spectacular results.

   Secrets of Fat-Free Baking presents over 130 scrumptious recipes that use fat substitutes such as fruit purées and juices, fruit juice concentrate, applesauce, honey, maple syrup, nonfat yogurt and buttermilk, and mashed sweet potatoes, squash, and pumpkin. You will learn how to replace refined flours with healthy whole-grain flours, how to replace high-fat dairy products with nonfat yogurt and buttermilk, how to whip up fat-free frostings and icings, and much more. In addition, each taste-tempting recipe includes a helpful nutritional analysis. **$13.95**

Fat-Free Holiday Recipes

*Finally, a cookbook of holiday foods
that are both delicious and healthy!*
Sandra Woodruff, RD

You will be the life of the party with this guide to healthful entertaining! Holidays are known for their lavish feasts, overflowing with sweet treats and more fat than you can imagine. If you worry about putting on extra pounds each holiday season, *Fat-Free Holiday Recipes* is the answer to your prayers. Here are over 200 easy-to-make recipes that are either very low in fat or fat-free, so you won't have to give up your favorite party foods anymore. Featured are a large selection of hors d'oeuvres and finger foods, complete dinner-party menus, and a taste-tempting section on holiday baking.

   In addition to cutting down on fat, these recipes are simple to prepare and feature ingredients that are readily available. Each recipe contains a complete nutritional analysis to help you plan for the most nutritious and delicious holiday ever. Every menu even includes strategies for preparing foods in advance! **$13.95**

Secrets of Fat-Free Cooking

Over 150 Fat-Free and Low-Fat Recipes from Breakfast to Dinner—Appetizers to Desserts

Low-fat cooking is sweeping the nation, and why not? Along with limiting sugar and salt, we now know that reducing fat-intake has a tremendously positive impact on health. While a flood of low-fat cookbooks is now available, many of these books reduce fat and calories by using artificial fat substitutes and sweeteners, and often rely on many highly refined processed foods. *Secrets of Fat-Free Cooking* is a very different kind of cookbook. It was designed to help you create low- and no-fat dishes that are easy to make, taste delicious, and are also high in nutrition. Here are over 150 kitchen-tested recipes that will absolutely delight your family and friends.

Secrets of Fat-Free Cooking begins by guiding you through the basics of nutrition. It tells you about the nonfat and low-fat ingredients that will help you reduce fat without reducing taste. Following are ten spectacular chapters filled with exciting and imaginative dishes. Recipes are designed to be used for breakfast, lunch, and dinner, or for those special occasions—family get-togethers, cocktail parties, and buffets. Also included are a wide range of soups, salads, breads, hors d'oeuvres, and desserts. In *Secrets of Fat-Free Cooking*, you will find the secrets to making Golden French Toast, Fresh Corn Chowder, Pot Roast With Sour Cream Gravy, Hearty Oven Fries, Cranapple Acorn Squash, Refreshing Fruit Pie, and more—most with less than one gram of fat per serving, and all totally delicious.

Perhaps best of all, *Secrets of Fat-Free Cooking* shows you how to eliminate the fat in your own recipes so that you and your family can enjoy new versions of family favorites. Dozens of helpful tips throughout the book help insure great results each and every time you cook. So preheat the oven and hold on to your spatula—*Secrets of Fat-Free Cooking* is just about to prove that there is taste after fat! **$13.95**

Available at Your Local Bookseller.
For a Complete Catalog of Our Other Healthy Cookbooks,
Call Us at 1–800–548–5757.